# 1993

## POCKET GUIDE TO THE

# WINES

## OF AUSTRALIA
### AND
## NEW ZEALAND

## JAMES HALLIDAY

HarperCollins*Publishers*

This edition published in December 1992 by
HarperCollins*Publishers*
London

Copyright © James Halliday 1991, 1992

First published in Australia by
CollinsAngus&Robertson Publishers Pty Limited 1992

A CIP catalogue record for this book is available
from the British Library.

ISBN 0 00 412825 7

Printed in Hong Kong

# CONTENTS

# HOW TO USE THIS GUIDE

In an endeavour to keep this guide as compact as possible, a number of abbreviations and symbols have been used. A full list of those abbreviations and symbols is provided on page 8. Hopefully, you will quickly become used to the symbols and will not need to constantly cross-refer to them. I will now walk you through the information for each entry in the order in which it occurs in the entry.

---

**COLDSTREAM HILLS** NR Est 1985 NFR/CD/ML/UK
(Whiclar & Gordon) $10–22 R YARR V
Lot 6, Maddens Lane, Coldstream, Vic 3770 (059) 64 9388
fax (059) 649 389
**OPEN** W'ends 10–5 **PRODUCTION** 20 000 cases
**WINEMAKERS** James Halliday and Philip Dowell
**PRINCIPAL WINES** Steels Range (second label) Chard, Pinot; varietal range Chard, Fumé, Pinot, Cab Sauv, Cab Merl; Reserve range Chard, Pinot, Merl.
**BEST VINTAGES** W '86, '88, '90, '91, R '87, '88, '90, '91
**SUMMARY** The author's own winery, and therefore not rated; however, from 231 entries in 29 shows, Coldstream Hills has won 33 trophies, 63 gold medals, 45 silver medals and 67 bronze medals in Australian wine shows, with a medal success rate of over 75%, twice the national average.

---

## WINERY NAME                                    COLDSTREAM HILLS

This may seem straightforward, but is not necessarily so. Wherever possible, I have used the name which appears most prominently on the label, and have not made reference to an associated trading name. Likewise, the label frequently abbreviates the winery name (dropping off such words as 'Wines', 'Estate', 'Pty Ltd', and so on), and I have used that abbreviated name.

---

## RATINGS                                                          NR

### QUALITY
A  Very good to outstanding
B  Good
C  Adequate commercial wine
D  Variable or poor
NR Not rated

### PRICE
A  Very well priced
B  Fairly priced
C  Borderline value
D  Over-priced for quality

eg a B–A rating indicates good wines which are very well priced.

Two letters linked in a rating (eg CA) means one of two things: either that there is some real variation in the quality or value from wine to wine (within the terms of reference of each), or simply that the average falls somewhere between the levels ascribed to each single letter rating. To try to avoid this ambiguity would have led to an impossibly complex rating scheme, and at the end of the day one has to accept the ratings as subjective and arbitrary, and as an imprecise guide at best.

In the manner of wine shows — notwithstanding that the real difference between a gold and a silver medal can be one-third of a point (out of 20), with gold, silver or bronze medals commonly given at different shows to the same wine — all of the attention will be given to the gold medals, in other words, the A–A ratings. But I urge you to realise there is only the finest distinction between a BA–A rating (or an A–AB rating) and an A–A rating — and so on down the scale. And please remember, too, that a B–B rating indicates the winery is producing good wines offered at a fair price.

In the case of the major producers, I have had to take a flexible approach in relation to the quality ratings; had I not done so, none of the medium to large-sized companies could have achieved an A rating simply because they have such a wide range of products. What the A rating means in this circumstance is that across the board, the wines (relative to their station in life) are very good to outstanding.

Finally, quality ratings are like vintage ratings in any event. They represent a gut-feel at a given point of time. They will not be valid for every wine which the maker produces from every vintage. Individual wines may be distinctly better or distinctly worse than the ratings would indicate.

NR means the winery is not rated, usually because I have not recently tasted its wines, occasionally because it is too recent on the scene (and in the case of Coldstream Hills because it is my winery). In this (1993) edition I have increased the number of NR ratings for newer wineries (some of which were previously given specific quality ratings) simply because I have come to realise it is dangerous to assess a winery on the evidence of only one or two vintages.

## YEAR OF ESTABLISHMENT                    Est 1985

A more or less self-explanatory item, but you should be aware that some makers choose the year in which they purchased the land, others the year in which they first planted grapes, others the year they first made wine, others the year they first offered wine for sale . . . and so on. There may also be minor complications where there has been a change of ownership or a break in production; varying practices exist here – I have not attempted to arbitrate or adjudicate between them.

## METHODS OF DISTRIBUTION            NFR/CD/ML
(WHICLAR & GORDON)

It is in this section that a number of abbreviations occur, and these are explained on page 8. Remember, if you are trying to find a wine in a retail outlet and are unsuccessful, a phone call or letter to the winery concerned should direct you to your nearest supplier (and will probably ensure that you go on the winery mailing list if it has one).

UNITED KINGDOM DISTRIBUTION

For United Kingdom readers, 'UK' indicates the wines are distributed in the United Kingdom, and I have provided the distributor's name in brackets before the price. For further information on United Kingdom distributors, contact The Australian Wine Bureau, Australia House, Strand, London, WC2B 4LA, ph 071 438 8259; fax 071 836 4250.

## PRICE                                   $10—22

PRICES GIVEN FOR AUSTRALIAN WINES ARE FOR PURCHASE IN AUSTRALIA, IN AUSTRALIAN DOLLARS; THOSE FOR NEW ZEALAND ARE IN NEW ZEALAND DOLLARS AND FOR PURCHASE THERE.

1. In each instance I have indicated whether the price is cellar door or retail; by and large the choice has been determined by which of the two

methods of sale is most important to the winery, ie it will reflect the way you will most probably purchase the wine. In this day and age it is hazardous in the extreme to try and predict the difference between the retail price and the cellar-door price, but most wineries would seek to offer the wine cellar-door (or by mailing list — the price will be one and the same except for freight) at about 15% less than the normal single bottle retail price.

2. The concept of normal retail price was once a simple matter, but is no longer so. Whether or not encouraged by the winery (some do, some don't) discounting is a way of life, so much so that there are three or four different retail prices for any given wine. The first is the recommended retail price, arrived at by applying a full margin (according to various formulae — one is to multiply the wholesale price per case by 0.154, thereby arriving at the recommended retail price for a single bottle). Some wine is sold at that price these days, but not much. The next price (lower than the recommended) is sometimes called the real retail price; it does not assume any special promotional deal, but does in all probability reflect a less than full margin being obtained by the retailer. The third price is the so-called promotional price, a price arrived at by virtue of the wholesaler/distributor (or the winery where it deals direct with retailers) giving a percentage reduction in the case price, usually for a multi-case purchase, matched by a reduced retailer margin. These three levels of price all exist, and may give rise to a $5 variation in the price of a $15 bottle of wine.

Fourthly and finally, there is the super discount price, which bears little or no relationship to the recommended price, and little or no relationship to the price which prevailed when the wine was first released. It may either reflect a retailer quitting stock at or below cost as a loss leader, or as a means of getting cash flow, or it may represent a special incentive from the wine company or distributor anxious to get rid of the last remaining stocks of a particular wine. In almost all instances, the retail prices quoted are the recommended retail prices, and it should not take a great deal of ingenuity on your part for you to find wines at lower prices.

3. The price range is simply for the cheapest and most expensive table wine being sold by the winery in mid 1992. The letter 'R' of course means that it is the retail price, 'ML' or 'CD' indicates that it is the cellar-door price. In almost all instances I have not reflected the cost of fortified wines or sparkling wines, simply because these tend to distort the relative pricing as between those wineries which do sell fortified wines (which are more expensive) and those which do not. The only exception is in respect to the producers in North East Victoria who specialise in fortifieds, Muscats and Tokays, and the top prices of these are quoted. There the maximum will be for fortified wines, the minimum for table wines.

4. Space does not permit a wine-by-wine pricing, and the span of prices is there simply for an approximate indication of the pricing structure of each winery.

## Pricing Notes for United Kingdom Readers*

1. The price of wine in the United Kingdom is affected by a number of factors, including excise and customs duty rates, VAT, and the level of mark-up applied at the various stages of distribution. At present, a bottle of Australian wine entering the United Kingdom attracts approximately £1 (£2 for sparkling wines) in duties and 17.5% VAT on its retail price. The importer of the wine will mark up the price by up to 25% before selling to the retailer, who in turn will add 30–35%. Any additional links in the distribution chain will add further to the eventual cost of the wine. Importers selling direct to the public cut out at least one of these margins.

2. Generally most prices in the United Kingdom are comparable with the

full retail, ie non-discounted, price in Australia once the tax differential and importer's mark up has been removed. Some wines are less expensive in the United Kingdom; for example, Penfolds' Grange Hermitage can be 20% cheaper. Certainly Australian wines represent very good value in the United Kingdom, compared not only with other regional and varietal wines but even with those in Australia. As a rule, the general starting price for wine from a known producer is about £3.50. New Zealand wines also offer good value at present, due to the weakness of the New Zealand dollar. As a result of heavy discounting/ loss leading in Australia and the very high duty rates on sparkling wines in the United Kingdom, these wines appear to be very much more expensive in the United Kingdom than in Australia.

* Information by courtesy of Philip Reedman, The Australian Wine Centre, London.

| REGION | YARRA V |
| --- | --- |

At the end of the first line or on the second line, I give the region of the winery, often abbreviated for space reasons, but hopefully decipherable without the need of any special key.

| **ADDRESS AND PHONE NUMBER** |
| --- |
| Lot 6, Maddens Lane, Coldstream, Vic 3770 (059) 649 389 |

Largely self-explanatory; the address is that of the winery and cellar door; in a few instances it is the vineyard — this occurs when the wine is made at another winery under contract, and is sold only through retail.

| CELLAR DOOR SALES HOURS | OPEN W'ends 10-5 |
| --- | --- |

These appear after the words 'Open' in the third or fourth line of the text. Where the winery is either shown as not open, or (for example) only open on weekends, a telephone call will quickly tell you whether it is in fact prepared to open by appointment. Many will, some won't. Also, virtually every winery which is shown as being open only for weekends is in fact open for public holidays. Once again, a phone call will put that matter beyond doubt.

| PRODUCTION | 20 000 cases |
| --- | --- |

The figure is given merely to give you an indication of the size of the operation. Some wineries (principally but not exclusively the large companies), regard the information as confidential, and in that event 'NFP' (not for publication) will appear.

| WINEMAKERS | James Halliday and Phillip Dowell |
| --- | --- |

In the large companies, the winemaker is simply the head of a team; there may be many executive winemakers actually responsible for specific wines.

| **PRINCIPAL WINES** |
| --- |
| Steels Range (second label) Chard, Pinot; varietal range Chard, Fumé, Pinot, Cab Sauv, Cab Merl; Reserve range Chard, Pinot, Merl. |

Abbreviations once again raise their ugly head, but hopefully you will quickly become familiar with them. Particularly with the larger companies, it is not possible to give a complete list of the wines; the saving grace is that these days most of the wines are simply identified on their label by their varietal composition.

| BEST VINTAGES | W '86, '88, '90, '91 |
| | R '87, '88, '90, '91 |

This is the only area in which I defer to the winemaker's judgement. While I may well have tasted many of the wines from a given winery over the years, I do not have the opportunity that the maker does of constantly undertaking vertical tastings (ie tastings of successive vintages) — when I say constantly, I mean once or twice a year. There really is no option but to defer to the winemaker's view of such matters. It should also be realised that these judgements are a generalisation within themselves: if a winery has three white wines and three red wines, there might well be a different vintage rating for each wine if space permitted. The problem becomes acute for some producers who, for example, produce both Pinot Noir and Cabernet Sauvignon, or Rhine Riesling and Chardonnay.

**SUMMARY**  The author's own winery, and therefore not rated; however, from 231 entries in 29 shows, Coldstream Hills has won 33 trophies, 63 gold medals, 45 silver medals and 67 bronze medals in Australian wine shows, with a medal success rate of over 75%, twice the national average.

My summary of the winery; little needs to be said, except that I have tried to mix up the subjects I have touched on.

## KEY TO ABBREVIATIONS

| | | | |
|---|---|---|---|
| CD | Cellar door/Cellar door price | NFR | National Fine Retail |
| LR | Limited Retail | NR | National Retail |
| M | Meals or food available | R | Retail |
| ML | Mailing List | UK | Distributed in the |
| NFP | Not for publication | | United Kingdom |

| | | | |
|---|---|---|---|
| Cab Franc | Cabernet Franc | Meth Champ | Méthode |
| Cab Merl | Cabernet Merlot | | Champenoise |
| Cab Sauv | Cabernet Sauvignon | Muller | Muller Thurgau |
| Cab Sauv | Cabernet Sauvignon | P Gris | Pinot Gris |
| Malb | Malbec | Pinot | Pinot Noir |
| Cab Shir | Cabernet Shiraz | Ries | Riesling |
| Chab | Chablis | Rosé | Rosé |
| Chard | Chardonnay | Sauv Bl | Sauvignon Blanc |
| Chenin | Chenin Blanc | Sem | Semillon |
| Colomb | Colombard | Shir | Shiraz |
| Fronti | Frontignac | Sparkl | Sparkling |
| Fumé | Fumé Blanc | Sylv | Sylvaner |
| Gewurz | Gewurztraminer | Tram Ries | Traminer Riesling |
| Herm | Hermitage | Verd | Verdelho |
| LH | Late Harvest | Viog | Viognier |
| LP | Late Picked | Wh Burg | White Burgundy |
| Merl | Merlot | | |

## 1992 VINTAGE

### AUSTRALIA

From a viticultural standpoint, 1992 was one of the most difficult vintages in the past 20 years, which makes generalisations hazardous. Remember, too, that a vintage report is just that: a description of the weather which prevailed in the lead up to and during the harvest. When written in the months following vintage, only the broadest generalisations about wine quality can be made at the best of times — and 1992 was not the best of times.

NEW SOUTH WALES split in two: the Hunter Valley, having been decimated by a severe drought through the second half of 1991, received a deluge during vintage, particularly affecting the Lower Hunter Valley. As always, some good wines will be made, but extreme care will be needed in selection. Further south, the Murrumbidgee Irrigation Area came under the weather pattern which prevailed across southern Australia, and had a very cool vintage which will produce elegant, intensely flavoured wines with lower than usual alcohol levels. SOUTH AUSTRALIA had the coolest summer since records began, leading to uneven ripening and to widespread outbreaks of powdery mildew in areas such as Coonawarra. Three periods of rain — in early March, late March and mid-April — turned the vintage into a viticultural version of Russian roulette, affecting some areas and vineyards more than others. Viticultural expertise was rewarded, and carelessness severely punished; having a crystal ball also helped. The potential for great wine was always there, and in some cases — particularly with the red wines — will be realised. VICTORIA shared the freakishly cool summer, but missed the rain. From North East Victoria, where some of the greatest Muscats and Tokays for decades were made, through central Victoria and thence to the southern regions, a cool but sunny vintage produced many wines of exceptional quality. The only problems were some instances of excessive yield and a few outbreaks of powdery mildew. The red wines seem likely to be remembered for years, with intense colour and flavour, the early ripening varieties (especially Pinot Noir and Chardonnay) revelling in the cool conditions. WESTERN AUSTRALIA shared South Australia's problems, vintage-time rain causing particular problems in a year of generally high yields, with the Lower Great Southern region most affected, Margaret River less so, and the Swan Valley escaping altogether. As in other regions, the red wines will be the most successful, the Rhine Rieslings least successful. TASMANIA always struggles in cool vintages, and this year was no exception; spring frosts in the Pipers Brook region also devastated several vineyards, though most were spared. QUEENSLAND'S Granite Belt suffered the same drought as the Hunter Valley, but was spared the vintage deluge, and had an early harvest of high quality, albeit low yield.

### NEW ZEALAND

The same cool weather — attributed variously to El Nino and Mount Pinatubo — dominated the season in New Zealand. A particularly cold spell during flowering reduced yields in many regions, and a cloudy summer delayed ripening to a frightening degree.

GISBORNE and HAWKE'S BAY did best overall, with the red wines to the fore: however, as in South Australia, selection (both by winemaker and the consumer) will be all-important. MARTINBOROUGH had its worst vintage ever, with spring and autumn frosts causing severe damage. MARLBOROUGH had its coolest summer for 54 years; some magnificent sparkling wine based from Pinot Noir and Chardonnay will be the high point of the vintage, but the Sauvignon Blanc will not be in the same class as '91. CANTERBURY was hit by three days of hail in early April while CENTRAL OTAGO, which depends heavily on a warm summer, had a year it would prefer to forget.

**AFFLECK**  C–CB Est 1976 ML $9.50–12 ML  CANBERRA
RMB 244 Gundaroo Road, Bungendore, ACT 2621  (06) 236 9276
**OPEN** By appointment  **PRODUCTION**  200 cases
**WINEMAKER** Ian Hendry
**PRINCIPAL WINES** Chard, Pinot, LH Sauv Bl, Cab Shir.
**SUMMARY** A strictly weekend and holiday interest for busy
professionals Ian and Sue Hendry; a firm, herbaceous 1990 Chardonnay
shows competent winery skills.

**ALKOOMI**  A–B A Est 1971 NFR/CD/ML $9–19 CD  LWR GRT
STHN
Wingeballup Road, Frankland, WA 6396  (098) 55 2229  fax (098) 55 2284
**OPEN** 7 days 10.30–5  **PRODUCTION**  15 000 cases
**WINEMAKER** Kim Hart
**PRINCIPAL WINES** Ries, Chard, Sauv Bl, Classic DW, Shir, Cab Sauv,
Malb.
**BEST VINTAGES W** '82, '88, '90 **R** '83, '84, '86, '89
**SUMMARY** Consistently makes some of the region's best wines, with
Malbec a specialty, avoiding jaminess but packed with flavour. Long-lived,
fine-structured Rhine Riesling and deeply coloured, potent Cabernet
Sauvignon are excellent, with all the 1989 reds showing great style.

**ALLANDALE**  BA–B Est 1977 LR/CD/ML/UK
(Aust Wine Centre) $11–12 CD  HUNTER V
Lovedale Road, Pokolbin via Maitland, NSW 2321  (049) 90 4526
fax (049) 90 1714
**OPEN** Mon–Sat 9–5, Sun 10–5  **PRODUCTION**  8000 cases
**WINEMAKER** Bill Sneddon
**PRINCIPAL WINES** Meth Champ, Sauv Bl, Sem, Chard, Tram, Pinot,
Shir, Cab Sauv.
**BEST VINTAGES W** '85, '87, '90, '91 **R** '83, '85, '86, '91
**SUMMARY** Has bounced back to top form with a good, barrel-ferment
style '90 Chardonnay and a quite superb, intense grapefruit/melon
accented '91 Special Release Chardonnay.

**ALLANMERE**  A–A Est 1984 LR/CD/ML $12.50–20 CD
HUNTER V
Allandale Road, Allandale via Pokolbin, NSW 2321  (049) 30 7387
**OPEN** Mon–Fri 11–4, w'ends 10–5  **PRODUCTION**  2500 cases
**WINEMAKER** Newton Potter
**PRINCIPAL WINES** Chard, Sem, Cab Sauv, Cab Shir, Herm.
**BEST VINTAGES W** '86, '88, '90, '91 **R** '85, '86, '87, '91
**SUMMARY** Owner Dr Newton Potter has placed Allanmere on the
market, threatening to end a brief but scintillating era during which he
and his winemakers produced gloriously flavoured and balanced white
wines, especially Chardonnay and Semillon, and clean, generous regional
reds. Any purchaser will gain a fine inheritance.

**ALL SAINTS**  NR Est 1864 NR/CD $6.85–35 R  NE VIC
All Saints Road, Wahgunyah, Vic 3687  (060) 33 1922
**OPEN** Mon–Sat 9–5, Sun 11–5  **PRODUCTION**  30 000 cases
**WINEMAKER** A. Sutherland Smith
**PRINCIPAL WINES** Chard, Tram Ries, Chenin, Ries, Shir, Cab Merl,
Muscat, Tokay, Port.
**SUMMARY** The purchase of All Saints by Brown Brothers in 1991 is an
almost fairy tale ending to what promised to be a disaster. It makes great
sense, and should ensure the future of the historic All Saints Winery as a
major cellar door and tourist attraction — as well as giving Brown
Brothers some fabulous fortified wine stocks.

**AMBERLEY ESTATE** NR Est 1987 NFR/CD/ML/UK
(Wine Australia) $10–17 CD MARGARET R
Wildwood and Thornton Road, Yallingup, WA 6282 (097) 55 2288
fax (097) 55 2171
**OPEN** 7 days 10–4.30 **PRODUCTION** 20 000 cases
**WINEMAKER** Eddie Price
**PRINCIPAL WINES** Wh Burg, Sauv Bl, Chenin, Sem, Sauv Blanc Sem,
Cab Sauv, Merl.
**SUMMARY** An ambitious venture owned by South African-born Albert
Haak with ex-Brown Bros winemaker Eddie Price in charge of pro-duction.
Still early days, but the first white wines are very light bodied with the
exception of the tangy, lively top-of-the-range Sauvignon Blanc Semillon.

**ANDREW GARRETT** B–B Est 1983 NR/CD/ML
$10.90–13.90 R STHN VALES
Kangarilla Road, McLaren Vale, SA 5171 (08) 323 8853 fax (08) 323 8550
**OPEN** Sum 10–5, Wint 11–4
**PRODUCTION** 4500 tonnes (288 000 case equivalent)
**WINEMAKER** Warren Randall
**PRINCIPAL WINES** Chard, Ries, Fumé, Sem, Gewurz, Pinot, Cab Merl,
Shir, sparkl.
**BEST VINTAGES** **W** '89, '90, '91 **R** '88, '90, '91
**SUMMARY** Now controlled by Suntory of Japan, this high-flying winery
was a major topic of conversation in the second half of the 1980s as its
production soared and its aggressive purchasing helped push grape prices
to unsustainable heights. Well-crafted wines are sourced from all the major
South Australian regions, with Padthaway Rhine Riesling consistently
good, and 1991 Barrel Fermented Chardonnay a tour de force.

**ANGOVE'S** CB–A Est 1886 NR/CD/ML $2.99–19 R
RIVERLANDS
Bookmark Avenue, Renmark, SA 5341 (085) 85 1311 fax (085) 85 1583
**OPEN** Mon–Fri 9–5 **PRODUCTION** 500 000 cases
**WINEMAKER** Frank J. Newman
**PRINCIPAL WINES** Four ranges: at the top, Limited Editions Chard and
Cab Sauv; then a complete range of white and red varietal wines; next the
export-oriented Butterfly Ridge wines and at the bottom the Misty Vineyards
generic range. Also Premium Brandy St Agnes and Stones Ginger Wine.
**BEST VINTAGES** **W** '88, '89, '90, '91 **R** '85, '86, '88, '89
**SUMMARY** Exemplifies the economies of scale achievable in the
Australian Riverlands without compromising potential quality. Very
good technology provides wines which are never poor and which can
sometimes exceed their theoretical station in life. The white varietals are
best, eg fruity, well balanced 1991 Chardonnay.

**ARROWFIELD** CB–B Est 1969 NR/CD/ML/UK
(Pacific Wines, Alliance Wines) $9.90–21 UPPER HUNTER V
Highway 213, Jerrys Plains, NSW 2330 (065) 76 4041 fax (065) 76 4144
**OPEN** 7 days 10–4 **PRODUCTION** 120 000 cases
**WINEMAKER** Simon Gilbert
**PRINCIPAL WINES** There are now six distinct lines, all ultimately
under the Arrowfield umbrella: Arrowfield, Arrowfield Cowra Selection,
Arrowfield Reserve, Simon Whitlam, Simon Gilbert, Wollombi Brook,
Hunter Gold and Hunter Red.
**BEST VINTAGES** **W** '86, '87, '91 **R** '86, '87, '91
**SUMMARY** After a brief flirtation with the Mountarrow name, this
Japanese-owned company is now reviving Arrowfield as its flagship, although
the brand positioning of its various wines is still obscure. Oak plays a major
and sometimes heavy-handed role in white wines, but an outstanding 1990

Cabernet Sauvignon shows that Simon Gilbert can produce the goods.

**ASHBROOK ESTATE** BA–A Est 1975 LR/CD/ML/UK
(Milton Sandford) $15–20 R MARGARET R
Harman's South Road, Willyabrup, WA 6284 (097) 55 6262
fax (09) 481 3836
**OPEN** W'ends 11–5 **PRODUCTION** 6000 cases
**WINEMAKERS** T. & B. Devitt
**PRINCIPAL WINES** Sem, Sauv Bl, Ries, Chard, Verd, Cab Sauv.
**BEST VINTAGES W** '87, '89, '90, '91 **R** '82, '84, '85, '86, '90
**SUMMARY** A fastidious maker of outstanding table wines but which
shuns publicity and the wine show system alike, and is less well known
than it deserves to be. Richly tropical 1991 Verdelho and ripe, gooseberry
flavoured and sculptured Sauvignon Blanc are especially good.

**ASHTON HILLS** CA–CB Est 1982 LR/CD/ML $9–13 CD
ADELAIDE HILLS
Tregarthen Road, Ashton, SA 5137 phone and fax (08) 390 1243
**OPEN** Fri/Sat/Sun 10–5 **PRODUCTION** 1500 cases
**WINEMAKER** Stephen George
**PRINCIPAL WINES** Chard, Ries, Cab Sauv, Pinot.
**BEST VINTAGES W** '89, '90 **R** '88, '89, '90
**SUMMARY** In its infancy and still to achieve anything like its full potential,
but the beautifully fresh, passionfruit-lime 1990 Rhine Riesling had developed
superbly by 1992, and points the way. The reds tend to lightness except
for wines such as the weighty, slightly tough, 1991 Pinot Noir.

**AUGUSTINE** CB–B Est 1918 LR/CD $5.95–9.95 CD MUDGEE
George Campbell Drive, Mudgee, NSW 2850 (063) 72 3880
**OPEN** 7 days 10–4 **PRODUCTION** 2500 cases
**WINEMAKER** Jon Reynolds
**PRINCIPAL WINES** Chard, Tram Ries, Pinot, Cab Sauv.
**BEST VINTAGES W** '88, '89, '90, '91 **R** '87, '88, '89, '91
**SUMMARY** The moribund fortunes of this long-established winery have
been revived under the stewardship of Sydney wine identity Dr Ray
Healey, and with competent contract winemaking now in place, even
better things can be expected.

**AULDSTONE** NR Est 1989 CD/ML $8–12 CD NE VIC
Booth's Road, Taminick via Glenrowan, Vic 3675 (057) 66 2237
**OPEN** Thurs–Sun 9–5 **PRODUCTION** 1600 cases
**WINEMAKER** Contract
**PRINCIPAL WINES** Taminick Dry, Ries, Chard, Cab Sauv, Port, Muscat.
**SUMMARY** Michael and Nancy Reid have restored a century old stone
winery and are replanting the largely abandoned vineyard around it. The
table wines tasted to date have not impressed, but the Boweya Muscat
shows good varietal character in a youthful mould.

**AUSTIN'S BARRABOOL WINES** NR Est 1984 LR/ML
$10–16 CD GEELONG
50 Lemins Road, Waurn Ponds, Vic 3221 (052) 43 3014
**OPEN** By appointment **PRODUCTION** 750 cases
**WINEMAKER** John Ellis (Contract)
**PRINCIPAL WINES** Reis, Chard, Cab Sauv.
**SUMMARY** A tiny winery which has made its mark with a gold medal
winning, full-flavoured and intense 1990 Rhine Riesling.

**AVALON VINEYARD** C–C Est 1981 LR/CD/ML $8–11 CD
NE VIC
RMB 9556 Whitfield Road, Wangaratta, Vic 3678 (057) 29 3629
**OPEN** 7 days 9–5 **PRODUCTION** 650 cases

**WINEMAKER** Doug Groom
**PRINCIPAL WINES** Chard, Sem, Cab Sauv, Pinot.
**BEST VINTAGES** **W** '87, '89, '90, '91 **R** '87, '88, '90, '91
**SUMMARY** Despite winemaker Doug Groom's Roseworthy training and degree, wine quality — particularly white wine quality — has been extremely variable.

**AVALON WINES** NR Est 1986 LR/CD $10–12 CD
PERTH HILLS
Lot 156 Bailey Road, Glen Forrest, WA 6071 (09) 298 8049
**OPEN** By appointment only **PRODUCTION** 500 cases
**WINEMAKER** Candy Johnsson (Contract)
**PRINCIPAL WINES** Chard, Sem, Cab Sauv.
**SUMMARY** One of the newest wineries in the Perth Hills; the appointment of Candy Johnsson (of Jane Brook Winery) as contract winemaker should lift quality.

**BAILEYS** CA–BA Est 1870 NFR/CD/ML/UK (Australian Wineries) $7.95–47 CD NE VIC
Cnr Taminick Gap Road and Upper Taminick Road, Glenrowan, Vic 3675 (057) 66 2392 fax (057) 66 2596
**OPEN** Mon–Fri 9–5, w'ends 10–5 **PRODUCTION** 35 000 cases
**WINEMAKER** Steve Goodwin
**PRINCIPAL WINES** Colomb, Ries, Sauv Bl, Chab, Chard, Chasselas, Cab Sauv, Shir, Classic Herm, Muscat, Tokay, Port.
**BEST VINTAGES** **W** '88, '90, '91 **R** '83, '88, '89, '91
**SUMMARY** One of the great names of North East Victoria, justifiably famous for its textured, opulent Muscats and Tokays; the ferruginous red table wines have a devoted following but, while better than the white table wines, are not in the same class as the fortifieds.

**BALDIVIS ESTATE** B–B Est 1982 LR/CD/ML/UK (Richard Sandford) $9–12 CD SW COASTAL
Lot 165 River Road, Baldivis, WA 6171 (09) 525 2066 fax (09) 525 2411
**OPEN** Mon–Sun 10–4 **PRODUCTION** 5500 cases
**WINEMAKER** John Smith
**PRINCIPAL WINES** Chard, Sem, Sauv Bl, Cab Merl, Nouveau Rouge.
**SUMMARY** The 1990 vintage marked a turning point for Baldivis Estate; the 1991 white wines, led by a vibrant, spicy and sophisticated Chardonnay, are in another class again. Given the financial strength and marketing skills of owner Peter Kailis and the skills of John Smith we shall hear more of Baldivis Estate in the future.

**BALD MOUNTAIN** CB–BA LR/CD/ML $13.90–15.60 R
GRANITE BELT
Old Wallangarra Road, Wallangarra, Qld 4383 (076) 84 3186
**OPEN** W'ends, hols 10–4 **PRODUCTION** 2500 cases
**WINEMAKER** John Cassegrain
**PRINCIPAL WINES** Sauv Bl, Chard, Shir.
**SUMMARY** Denis Parsons is a self-taught but exceptionally competent vigneron who, in a few short years, has turned Bald Mountain into the viticultural showpiece of the Granite Belt. Wine quality has yet to consistently reflect that success, but the '89 Shiraz once again shows the suitability of the wine to the district.

**BALGOWNIE** B–B Est 1969 NFR/CD/ML/UK (Lawlers, Champagne Henriot) $12.50–16.50 CD BENDIGO
Hermitage Road, Maiden Gully, Vic 3551 (054) 49 6222
fax (054) 49 6506
**OPEN** Mon–Sat 10–5 **PRODUCTION** 4000 cases
**WINEMAKER** Lindsay Ross

**PRINCIPAL WINES** Chard, Herm, Pinot, Cab Sauv.
**BEST VINTAGES W** '82, '84, '87, '89 **R** '80, '85, '88, '90
**SUMMARY** Once in a class on its own, Balgownie has come back into the pack in recent years, in part living on the long term record of its intense, long-lived Cabernet Sauvignon. What impact the departure of founder Stuart Anderson will have remains to be seen.

**BALLANDEAN ESTATE** CB–B Est 1970 CD/ML $8–15 CD GRANITE BELT
Sundown Road, Ballandean, Qld 4382 (076) 84 1226
**OPEN** 7 days 9–5 **PRODUCTION** 8000 cases
**WINEMAKER** Angelo Puglisi, Adam Chapman
**PRINCIPAL WINES** Chard, Sem Sauv Bl, Aus Sylv, Shir, Cab Sauv.
**BEST VINTAGES W** '83, '86, '89, '90 **R** '83, '87, '89, '90
**SUMMARY** The senior winery of the Granite Belt, and by far the largest. The white wines are of diverse but interesting styles (witness the peachy 1991 Sylvaner), the red wines smooth and usually well made, with the 1987 Cabernet Sauvignon of special merit.

**BALNARRING** CB–CB Est 1982 LR/CD/ML $11–15 CD MORNINGTON P
Bittern-Dromana Road, Balnarring, Vic 3926 (059) 83 5258
**OPEN** 7 days 10–4 **PRODUCTION** 2000 cases
**WINEMAKER** Various contract
**PRINCIPAL WINES** Chard, Ries, Gewurz, Pinot, Cab Merl, Merl.
**BEST VINTAGES W** '85, '86, '88, '91 **R** '85, '87, '89, '90, '91
**SUMMARY** The powerful extractive red wines of Balnarring are unlike those of any other Mornington producer, and certainly offer another face for the Peninsula. The white wines have been variable, but are improving; the 1991 Pinot Noir is a lovely, intense cherry-flavoured wine.

**BALNAVES OF COONAWARRA** NR Est 1975 LR/CD/ML $14.20–15.75 CD COONAWARRA
Main Road, Coonawarra, SA 5263
**OPEN** 7 days 10–5 **PRODUCTION** 1400 cases
**WINEMAKER** Ralph Fowler (Contract)
**PRINCIPAL WINES** Chard, Shir, Cab Sauv, Cab Merl.
**SUMMARY** Former Hungerford Hill vineyard manager and now viticultural consultant-cum-grape grower Doug Balnaves established his vineyard in 1975, but did not launch into winemaking until 1990, with colleague Ralph Fowler as contract maker. The first releases are of exemplary quality, with a gold and trophy-winning 1990 Cabernet Merlot with abundant cassis/blackcurrant fruit and great tannin structure, and a ripe, buttery 1991 Chardonnay suggesting a high rating in future editions of this book.

**BANNOCKBURN** A–AB Est 1974 NFR/UK (Geoffrey Roberts) $15–27 R GEELONG
Midland Hwy, Bannockburn, Vic 3331 (052) 81 1363 fax (052) 81 1349
**OPEN** By appointment only **PRODUCTION** 9000 cases
**WINEMAKER** Gary Farr
**PRINCIPAL WINES** Sauv Bl, Ries, Chard, Pinot, Shir, Cab Sauv.
**BEST VINTAGES W** '85, '86, '88, '89, '90 **R** '85, '86, '87, '88, '91
**SUMMARY** One of Australia's foremost producers of Pinot Noir, made in an uncompromising style which owes much to Gary Farr's extensive Burgundian winemaking experience gained at Domaine Dujac; the viticulture, too, is strongly French-influenced. An equally powerful and complex Chardonnay also demands the utmost respect.

**BARONGVALE** NR Est 1988 CD/ML $8–10 CD GEELONG
East West Road, Barongarook, Vic 3249 (052) 33 8324

**OPEN** By appointment only   **PRODUCTION** NFP
**WINEMAKER** Stuart Walker
**PRINCIPAL WINES** Chard, Colomb, Sem, Ries, Cab Sauv, Pinot Cab.
**SUMMARY** One of the most remote wineries in the West Geelong region, making a surprisingly wide range of wines of (to me) unknown quality.

## BAROSSA SETTLERS CB–B Est 1983 CD/ML $9.50–12.50 CD BAROSSA V

Trial Hill Road, Lyndoch, SA 5351   (085) 24 4017
**OPEN** Mon–Sat 10–4, Sun 1–4   **PRODUCTION** 1400 cases
**WINEMAKER** Doug Lehmann
**PRINCIPAL WINES** Champ, Chard, Ries, Ausl Ries, Shir Claret, Cab Sauv, Port.
**BEST VINTAGES W** '84, '87, '90, '91 **R** '80, '83, '84, '86, '90
**SUMMARY** A superbly located cellar door is the only outlet (other than mail order) for the wines from this excellent vineyard owned by the Haese family. Contract winemaking by Doug Lehmann has produced some attractive Rhine Rieslings and Cabernets, and a voluptuous, forward '90 Chardonnay.

## BAROSSA VALLEY ESTATES CB–BA Est 1984 NR/CD/ML/UK (Berri Renmano) $9–19.95 R  ADELAIDE PLAINS

Heaslop Road, Angle Vale, SA 5117  (08) 284 7000  fax (08) 284 7219
**OPEN** Mon–Fri 9–5, Sat 11–5, Sun 1–5   **PRODUCTION** NFP
**WINEMAKER** Colin Glaetzer
**PRINCIPAL WINES** Chard, Sauv Bl, Sem Ries, Front, Spat, Shir, Cab Sauv.
**BEST VINTAGES W** '86, '89, '90, '91 **R** '85, '88, '90, '91
**SUMMARY** This is a stand-alone brand of the Berri Renmano cooperative group, using the best grapes from grower members in the Barossa Valley, but made at the Lauriston winery. Quality is reliably sound to good, and value undoubted. Watch for the special E & E Black Pepper Shiraz.

## BARRETTS NR Est 1986 CD $9–14 CD  SW VIC

Portland-Nelson Highway, Portland, Vic 3305  (055) 26 5257
**OPEN** 7 days 10–6   **PRODUCTION** 1000 cases
**WINEMAKER** Bests (Contract), others by Rod Barrett
**PRINCIPAL WINES** Ries, Tram Ries, Pinot, Cab Sauv.
**SUMMARY** The second (and newer) winery in the Portland region; the '89 Cabernet Sauvignon (briary, red berry and elegant), '90 Riesling (passionfruit and lime) and '91 Traminer (in similar style) all showed well in 1992.

## BASEDOW BA–A Est 1896 NR/CD/ML/UK (Bibendum Ltd) $5.45–9.35 CD  BAROSSA V

161-165 Murray Street, Tanunda, SA 5352  (085) 63 2060
fax (085) 633 3597
**OPEN** Mon–Fri 9–5, Sat 10–5, Sun 12–4
**PRODUCTION** 38 000 cases
**WINEMAKERS** Doug Lehmann, Roger Harbord
**PRINCIPAL WINES** Front Spatlese, Chard, Wh Burg, Ries, Herm, Cab Sauv, Port.
**BEST VINTAGES W** '83, '86, '88, '90 **R** '81, '82, '84, '88
**SUMMARY** The most consistent over-achiever in Australia during the past five years, making invariably excellent white wines at absurdly low prices. The White Burgundy (a deliciously oaked Semillon) is the flag-bearer, but the equally seductive Chardonnay and smoothly rich Rhine Riesling are often in the same class.

## BASKET RANGE WINE NR Est 1980 LR/ML $12 ML ADELAIDE HILLS

Blockers Road, Basket Range, SA 5138 (vineyard only); postal PO Basket Range, SA 5138
**OPEN** Not **PRODUCTION** 300 cases
**WINEMAKER** Phillip Broderick
**PRINCIPAL WINES** A single Bordeaux-blend of Cab Sauv/Cab Fr/Merl/Mal.
**SUMMARY** Both the 1988 and 1989 vintages (the only wines released to date) have appealed at various times; the 1988 has not come on so well in bottle, but the red berry, plum and spice of '89 is attractive.

**BASS PHILLIP** NR Est 1979 LR/ML $18–24 R STH GIPPSLAND
Tosch's Road, Leongatha Sth, Vic 3953 (056) 64 3341
**OPEN** By appointment summer **PRODUCTION** 1000 cases
**WINEMAKER** Phillip Jones
**PRINCIPAL WINES** Pinot.
**BEST VINTAGES R** '84, '86, '88, '89, '91
**SUMMARY** The Pinots of Bass Phillips have attracted much deserved publicity; at their best they are quite superb, but a now-discontinued policy of individual cask bottling led to disconcerting variability with the initial releases. The potential is exceptional, particularly for the Reserve bottlings.

**BELBOURIE** NR Est 1963 LR/CD/ML $12–20 CD HUNTER V
Branxton Road, Rothbury, NSW 2330 (049) 38 1556
**OPEN** Sat–Mon 9–5 **PRODUCTION** 1100 cases
**WINEMAKER** John Roberts
**PRINCIPAL WINES** Tram, Sem Chard, Cab Malb.
**SUMMARY** Not rated simply because the idiosyncratic wines of Belbourie cannot be judged by conventional yardsticks. Try them for yourself.

**BELLINGHAM** NR Est 1984 LR/CD/ML $10 ML TAS
Pipers Brook, Tas 7254 (003) 82 7149
**OPEN** By appointment **PRODUCTION** 1000 cases
**WINEMAKER** Greg O'Keefe (Contract)
**PRINCIPAL WINES** Ries, Chard, Cab Sauv.
**SUMMARY** Dallas Targett sells part of the grapes from his substantial vineyard, and has part contract-made. The 1991 Rhine Riesling has intense, perfumed lime juice aroma and flavour, and is a good wine by any standards. The 1991 Pinot shows quite stylish sappy/berry aroma, but is a little volatile and a little prematurely developed. Nonetheless, the promise is there.

**BELUBULA VALLEY VINEYARDS** NR Est 1986 CENTRAL HIGHLANDS
Golden Gully, Mandurama, NSW 2798 (063) 67 5236 or (02) 25 86024
**OPEN** Not **PRODUCTION** 100 cases
**WINEMAKER** D. R. Somervaille
**PRINCIPAL WINES** Chard, Sem, Cab Sauv.
**SUMMARY** Belubula Valley is a foundation member of the Central Highlands Grapegrowers Association, centred on Orange; the vineyard is located on the Belubula River, near Carcoar, and the small amounts of wine made to date have not yet been commercially released.

**BENFIELD ESTATE** CB–B Est 1985 LR/CD/Ml $7–12 CD CANBERRA DISTRICT
Fairy Hole Road, Yass, NSW 2582 (06) 226 2427
**OPEN** W'ends, pub hols 10–5 **PRODUCTION** 850 cases
**WINEMAKER** David Featherstone
**PRINCIPAL WINES** Ries, Chard, Sem, Mer, Cab Sauv.

**SUMMARY** After a hiatus, Benfield Estate has returned to active winemaking and marketing with a most attractive soft, minty/berry 1990 Merlot and a light, elegant and faintly limey 1991 Rhine Riesling leading the way.

**BERESFORD** CB–B Est 1985 NFR/CD/ML $10.50–12 R STHN VALES
Old Heritage Horndale Winery, Fraser Avenue, Happy Valley, SA 5067
(08) 322 3611 fax (08) 322 2402
**OPEN** 7 days 9–5 **PRODUCTION** 12 000 cases
**WINEMAKER** Robert Dundon
**PRINCIPAL WINES** Chard, Sauv Bl, Pinot, Cab Sauv.
**BEST VINTAGES W** '87, '88, '89, '90 **R** '82, '86, '88, '90
**SUMMARY** The Chardonnays have been the most consistent performers showing good oak handling and complexity. Rob Dundon prefers light, understated red wines, although his carbonic maceration Pinot Noir has positive flavour and attracts a loyal following.

**BERRI ESTATES** C–B Est 1922 NR/CD/ML/UK (Berri Renmano) $4.50 R RIVERLAND
Sturt Highway, Glossop, SA 5344 (085) 83 2303 fax (085) 83 2224
**OPEN** Mon–Sat 9–5 **PRODUCTION** 35 million litres
**WINEMAKER** Reg Wilkinson
**PRINCIPAL WINES** Brentwood Ries, Chab, Moselle, Claret.
**BEST VINTAGES W** '85, '88, '89, '90 **R** '85, '88, '90, '91
**SUMMARY** The Brentwood label is a very modest tip of the vast iceberg; most of the production is sold in bulk on both export and local markets. The premium wines appear under the Renmano banner.

**BEST'S** BA–A Est 1866 NFR/CD/UK (Chennel & Armstrong) $8.20–20 CD GRT WESTERN
2km off Western Highway, Great Western, Vic 3377 (053) 56 2250 fax (053) 56 2430
**OPEN** Mon–Fri 9–5, Sat 9–4, Sun 12–4 on long w'ends & sch hols
**PRODUCTION** 12 000 cases
**WINEMAKER** Viv Thomson, Simon Clayfield
**PRINCIPAL WINES** Chard, Ries, Gewurz, Shir, Cab Sauv, sparkl, fortifieds.
**BEST VINTAGES W** '84, '87, '89, '91 **R** '84, '87, '88, '89, '91
**SUMMARY** Crystal clear and silky smooth cherry (sometimes with a touch of mint) Hermitage and a suave, fruit-driven Chardonnay set the pace for this historic winery which deserves far greater recognition than it is usually given.

**BETHANY** B–B Est 1977 LR/CD/ML $8.50–13 CD BAROSSA V
Bethany Road, Bethany via Tanunda, SA 5352 (085) 63 2086 fax (085) 63 0046
**OPEN** Mon–Sat 10–5, Sun 1–5 **PRODUCTION** 12 000 cases
**WINEMAKERS** G. & R. Schrapel
**PRINCIPAL WINES** Ries, Chard, Sem (Wood Mat), Ausl Ries, Cab Sauv, Cab Merl, Shir, Port.
**BEST VINTAGES W** '86, '90, '91 **R** '87, '88, '89, '90
**SUMMARY** Once known principally for its full-flavoured, sometimes sweet, Rhine Rieslings, but has since also shown a deft hand with buttery, honeyed, oaky Chardonnay and a fresh, modern-style Cabernet Merlot.

**BIANCHET** CB–B Est 1976 LR/CD/ML $10–18 CD YARRA V
Lot 3 Victoria Road, Lilydale, Vic 3140 (03) 739 1779
**OPEN** W'ends 10–6 **PRODUCTION** 2000 cases

**WINEMAKER** Lou Bianchet
**PRINCIPAL WINES** Chard, Gewurz, Verduzzo, Sem, Pinot, Shir, Cab Sauv, Merl.
**BEST VINTAGES W & R** '85, '86, '88, '90
**SUMMARY** Makes invariably full–flavoured wines in a traditional and at times rustic style, with little or no reliance on oak. Verduzzo, an Italian white grape, is an interesting winery specialty.

## BIRDWOOD ESTATE NR Est 1990 ML $9–13 CD
ADELAIDE HILLS
Narcoonah Road, Birdwood, SA 5234  (08) 263 0986
**OPEN** Not  **PRODUCTION** 900 cases
**WINEMAKER** Oli Cucchiarelli
**PRINCIPAL WINES** Chard, Ries, Cab Sauv.
**SUMMARY** Italian-born Oli Cucchiarelli, an engineer by trade, graduated from Charles Sturt University in Wine Science in 1986, and now pursues a part-time career as vigneron. The initial releases from 1990 showed promising fruit flavour but were marred by rather raw, splintery oak.

## BLACKWOOD CREST C–B Est 1976 LR/CD $10.95–12.95
R LWR GRT STHN
RMB 404A Boyup Brook, WA 6244  (097) 67 3029
**OPEN** 7 days 10–5  **PRODUCTION** 830 cases
**WINEMAKER** Kim Hart, Max Fairbrass
**PRINCIPAL WINES** Ries, Sem Sauv Bl, Shir, Cab Sauv, Port.
**SUMMARY** A remote and small winery which has produced one or two striking red wines full of flavour and character; worth watching.

## BLANCHE BARKLY DC–C Est 1972 CD/ML
BENDIGO
Rheola Road, Kingower, Vic 3517  (054) 43 3664
**OPEN** 7 days 10–5; please phone  **PRODUCTION** NFP
**WINEMAKER** David Reimers
**PRINCIPAL WINES** Mary Eileen Shir, Alexander Cab Sauv, George Henry Cab Sauv.
**SUMMARY** Sporadic but small production and variable quality seem to be the order of the day; the potential has always been there.

## BLEASDALE C–B Est 1850 LR/CD/ML/UK
(Wine Schoppen, Sheffield) $5–9.90 CD  LANGHORNE CREEK
Wellington Road, Langhorne Creek, SA 5255  (085) 37 3001
**OPEN** Mon–Sat 9–5, Sun 11–5  **PRODUCTION** 40 000 cases
**WINEMAKER** Michael Potts
**PRINCIPAL WINES** Ries, Chard, Verd, Colomb, Cab Sauv, Cab Malb Merl, Shir Cab.
**BEST VINTAGES W** '82, '84, '86, '87 **R** '82, '84, '86, '87
**SUMMARY** Supremely honest, soft, bottle-aged red wines are the winery specialty, usually with a particular gamey edge which may or may not appeal; full-flavoured, buttery Verdelho is also recommended.

## BLEWITT SPRINGS B–B Est 1987 LR/ML $8–14 R
STHN VALES
Fraser Avenue, Happy Valley, SA 5159  (08) 322 3611  fax (08) 322 3610
**OPEN** Not  **PRODUCTION** 4000 cases
**WINEMAKER** Brett Howard
**PRINCIPAL WINES** Chard, Sem, Shir, Cab Sauv.
**BEST VINTAGES W** '88, '89, '90 **R** '86, '87, '89, '90
**SUMMARY** A newcomer to the scene which has attracted much attention and praise for its voluptuous Chardonnays, crammed full of peachy, buttery fruit and vanillan American oak. Oak also plays a major role in the

Semillon and the red wines; a lighter touch might please some critics.

**BLOODWOOD ESTATE** NR Est 1983 CD/ML $12.95–16 CD  CENTRAL TABLELANDS
4 Griffith Road, Orange, NSW 2800  (063) 62 5631
**OPEN** By appointment  **PRODUCTION** 2000 cases
**WINEMAKER** Stephen Doyle
**PRINCIPAL WINES** Chard, Ries, Rosé, Cab Sauv.
**SUMMARY** A relative newcomer from an extremely interesting region; cask samples of the 1991 vintage red wines showed massive, minty/berry/cassis flavours and strong, scented bouquets.

**BONNEYVIEW** NR Est 1975 CD/ML $6–9 CD  RIVERLAND
Sturt Highway, Barmera, SA 5345  (085) 88 2279
**OPEN** 7 days 9–5.30  **PRODUCTION** 2000 cases
**WINEMAKER** Robert Minns
**PRINCIPAL WINES** Tram Ries, Front, Chard, Shir, Cab Merl, fortifieds.
**SUMMARY** The smallest Riverland winery selling exclusively cellar door, with an ex-Kent cricketer and Oxford University graduate as its owner/winemaker.

**BOOTH'S TAMINICK** C–CB Est 1900 CD/ML $5–12 CD NE VIC
Taminick via Glenrowan, Vic 3675  (057) 66 2282
**OPEN** Mon–Sat 9–5, Sun 10–5  **PRODUCTION** NFP
**WINEMAKER** Cliff Booth
**PRINCIPAL WINES** Chard, Shir, Cab Sauv, Cab Merl, Port, Muscat.
**SUMMARY** Ultra-conservative producer of massively flavoured and concentrated red wines, usually with more than a few rough edges which time may or may not smooth over.

**BOROKA** DC–C Est 1974 CD/ML $6.50–10 CD  GRT WESTERN
Pomonal Road, Halls Gap, Vic 3381  (053) 56 4252
**OPEN** Mon–Sat 9–5  **PRODUCTION** 1500 cases
**WINEMAKER** Bernard Breen
**PRINCIPAL WINES** Chab & Ries blends, Rosé, Shir, Cab Sauv.
**SUMMARY** Out of the mainstream in terms of both wine quality and location, but does offer light lunches or picnic takeaways, and the views are spectacular.

**BOSANQUET ESTATE** C–B Est 1989 NR/CD/ML $6.99 R STHN VALES
Old Heritage Horndale Winery, Fraser Avenue, Happy Valley, SA 5067
(08) 322 3611  fax (08) 322 2402
**OPEN** 7 days 9–5  **PRODUCTION** 50 000 cases
**WINEMAKER** Robert Dundon
**PRINCIPAL WINES** Sem Chard, Fumé, Ries, Cab Shir.
**BEST VINTAGES W** '89, '90 **R** '87, '88, '89
**SUMMARY** The strikingly labelled wines compete against the major wine companies in the most competitive sector of an overly competitive market; the quality is all one could reasonably hope for, the softly fruity style precisely aimed at the target market.

**BOSTON BAY** B–B Est 1986 LR/CD/ML $9.90–12.90 CD PORT LINCOLN
Lincoln Highway, Port Lincoln, SA 5606  (086) 84 3600
**OPEN** W'ends/sch/pub hols 11.30–4.30  **PRODUCTION** 2500 cases
**WINEMAKER** R. Harbord
**PRINCIPAL WINES** Ries, Spat Ries, Cab Merl.
**BEST VINTAGES W** '88, '90, '91 **R** '89, '91

**SUMMARY** While strongly tourist-oriented, wine quality is good by any standards, thanks to competent contract winemaking by Basedow's Roger Harbord.

**BOTOBOLAR** B–BA Est 1971 LR/CD/ML/UK (Vintage Roots, Berks) $4.50–11.50 CD MUDGEE
Botobolar Lane, Mudgee, NSW 2850 (063) 73 3840
**OPEN** 7 days 10–5 **PRODUCTION** 9000 cases
**WINEMAKER** Gil Wahlquist
**PRINCIPAL WINES** Crouchen, Ries Tram, Mars, Chard, Ries, Shir, Cab Sauv, St Gilbert.
**BEST VINTAGES W** '86, '87, '88, '89, '91 **R** '82, '84, '85, '89, '91
**SUMMARY** Now that Carlo Corino (ex Montrose winemaker) has returned to Italy (or to be precise, Sicily) Gil Wahlquist is unchallenged as Godfather of Mudgee, a district he has tirelessly promoted through his handsome winery newsletter *Botobolar Bugle*, through the sheer quality of his red wines, through his organic grapes and occasional preservative-free wines.

**BOWEN ESTATE** BA–BA Est 1972 NFR/CD/ML $9–12 CD COONAWARRA
Main Penola-Naracoorte Road, Penola, SA 5277 (087) 37 2229
**OPEN** Mon–Sat 9–5, Sun, long w'end **PRODUCTION** 7000 cases
**WINEMAKER** Doug Bowen
**PRINCIPAL WINES** Ries, Chard, Shir, Cab Sauv.
**BEST VINTAGES W** '82, '84, '86, '90 **R** '80, '84, '89, '90
**SUMMARY** For long regarded as the best of the small wineries in Coonawarra, with its often peppery, rich Shiraz and classically restrained Cabernet Sauvignon vying against each other for supremacy.

**BOYNTON'S OF BRIGHT** CA–B Est 1987 CD/ML $8–14 CD NE VIC
Ovens Valley Highway, Bright, Vic 3747 (057) 56 2356
**OPEN** 7 days 10–5 **PRODUCTION** 9000 cases
**WINEMAKER** Kel Boynton
**PRINCIPAL WINES** Chard, Ries, Sauv Bl, Cab Sauv, Shir, Mataro.
**SUMMARY** Boynton's 1989 and 1990 red wines have had spectacular success at some wine shows; American oak aroma and flavour is pronounced, and may not appeal to all, but there is no doubting the strength and depth of flavour.

**BRAHAMS CREEK WINERY** NR Est 1990 LR/CD/ML $Not fixed YARRA V
Woods Point Road, East Warburton, Vic 3799 (059) 66 2802 ; postal PO Box 105, Oakleigh, Vic 3166
**OPEN** W'ends 10–5 **PRODUCTION** 800 cases
**WINEMAKER** Geoffrey Richardson
**PRINCIPAL WINES** Pinot, Cab Sauv.
**SUMMARY** No wines have been released at the time of writing; they were due to come onto the market in late 1992.

**BRANDS LAIRA** B–B Est 1965 NFR/CD/ML $12.05–20 R COONAWARRA
Penola-Naracoorte Highway, Coonawarra, SA 5263 (087) 36 3260
fax (087) 363 208
**OPEN** 7 days 8–5 **PRODUCTION** 18 000 cases
**WINEMAKERS** Bill and Jim Brand
**PRINCIPAL WINES** Chard, Shir, Cab Sauv, Cab Merl; limited release of Original Vineyard Shir.
**BEST VINTAGES R** '84, '86, '88, '90
**SUMMARY** Now 50% owned by McWilliams, the technical experience

of which may well see the Brand's red wines recover the exalted reputation they once had; while they have recovered from a particularly bad patch, they can be a little pedestrian.

**BREAM CREEK** NR Est 1975 LR/ML $12–14 R
EAST COAST TAS
Marion Bay Road, Bream Creek, Tas 7175 (vineyard only); postal 655 Main Road, Berriedale, Tas 7011 (002) 492 2949
**OPEN** Not **PRODUCTION** 2200 cases
**WINEMAKER** Julian Alcorso (Contract)
**PRINCIPAL WINES** Ries, Chard, Cab Sauv (light and wooded), Pinot.
**SUMMARY** Fred Peacock, long-time vineyard manager of Moorilla Estate, purchased the Bream Creek vineyard (which had hitherto sold its grapes to Moorilla) in 1990 and in that year had the first wines made for him by Julian Alcorso at Moorilla. Since then, every wine made has won at least one medal at the Royal Hobart Wine Show; the best to-date is undoubtedly the 1991 Rhine Riesling with lime aromas and flavours, and appreciable sweetness giving the wine weight and flesh.

**BRIAGOLONG ESTATE** CB–CB Est 1979 LR ML
$16.50–18 ML  GIPPSLAND
Valencia-Briagolong Road, Briagolong, Vic 3860  (051) 47 2322
**OPEN** Not **PRODUCTION** 200 cases
**WINEMAKER** Gordon McIntosh
**PRINCIPAL WINES** Chard, Pinot.
**BEST VINTAGES** **W** '83, '89, '90 **R** '83, '84, '88, '90
**SUMMARY** This is very much a weekend hobby for medical practitioner Gordon McIntosh, who nonetheless tries hard to invest his wines with Burgundian complexity, with mixed success; the stylish, tangy 1989 Pinot Noir is the best yet.

**BRIAR RIDGE** CB–CB Est 1972 CD/ML $12.50–15 CD
HUNTER V
Mount View Road, Mount View, NSW 2325  (049) 90 3670
**OPEN** Mon–Fri 9–5, w'ends 10–5 **PRODUCTION** 7000 cases
**WINEMAKER** Kees Van De Scheur
**PRINCIPAL WINES** Sem, Chard, Herm, Cab Sauv, sparkl.
**BEST VINTAGES** **W** '84, '87, '89, '91 **R** '85, '86, '87, '91
**SUMMARY** Originally the Robson Vineyard, Briar Ridge has gradually assumed its own identity, with winemaking and style continuity provided by Kees Van De Scheur, and future promise of even better things through the consultancy of ex-Lindemans winemaker Karl Stockhausen.

**BRIARS, THE** NR Est 1989 LR/CD/ML $14.50 CD/ML
MORNINGTON P
Nepean Highway, Mount Martha, Vic 3934 (059) 743 686
**OPEN** W'ends 11–4.30 **PRODUCTION** 1000 cases
**WINEMAKER** Brian Fletcher (Contract)
**PRINCIPAL WINES** Chard, Pinot, Cab Sauv.
**SUMMARY** An enterprising venture of the Mornington Shire Council, with grapes grown at and sold from the historic Briars Homestead, marketed cellar door, through a few Mornington Peninsula restaurants and through The Briars Wine Club mailing list. The wine is not exported, and has no connection with the Dromana Estate export brand also called The Briars.

**BRIDGEWATER MILL** BA–A Est 1985 NFR/CD/UK
(Geoffrey Roberts) $10.70–15.50 R  ADELAIDE HILLS
Mount Barker Road, Bridgewater, SA 5155  (08) 339 3422
fax (08) 339 5253
**OPEN** Mon–Fri 9.30–5, w'ends 10–5 **PRODUCTION** NFP

**WINEMAKER** Brian Croser
**PRINCIPAL WINES** Chard, Ries, Sauv Bl, Cab Malb.
**BEST VINTAGES W** '87, '88, '90 **R** '86, '88, '90, '91
**SUMMARY** The second label of Petaluma, which consistently provides wines most makers would love to have as their top label. Tangy, intense gooseberry Sauvignon Blanc has been exceptionally good, which is not to disparage the Riesling or the Chardonnay. The vineyard sources, incidentally, are diverse.

## BRINDABELLA HILLS NR Est 1989 LR/CD/ML $9–16 CD
CANBERRA
Woodgrove Close via Hall, ACT 2618  (06) 230 2583
**OPEN** W'ends 10–5  **PRODUCTION** 2000 cases
**WINEMAKER** Dr Roger Harris
**PRINCIPAL WINES** Ries, Chard, Sauv Bl Sem, Pinot, Cab Merl.
**SUMMARY** Barrel samples of Brindabella Hills red wines consistently show outstanding promise, but Roger Harris has had problems in getting the wine safely into bottle. The 1991 white wines made the transition safely, with a crisp Rhine Riesling and Chardonnay appealing most.

## BROKE ESTATE NR Est 1989 HUNTER V
Wollombi Road, Broke, NSW 2330  phone and fax  (065) 79 1065
**OPEN** Not  **PRODUCTION** 2000 cases
**WINEMAKER** Simon Gilbert (Contract)
**PRINCIPAL WINES** Chard, Sauv Bl, Cab Sauv, Franc.
**SUMMARY** Viticultural consultancy advice from Dr Richard Smart and contract winemaking by Simon Gilbert got Broke Estate away to a flying start with its 1991 vintage, producing wines which, tasted as cask samples, were consistently excellent, if somewhat oaky. If the wines make the transition to bottles safely, Broke Estate will bring owners Bliss and Bill Ryan considerable satisfaction.

## BROKEN RIVER DC–C Est 1984 LR/CD/ML $8–11 CD
NTH GOULBURN R
Cosgrove Road, Lemnos, Vic 3631  (058) 29 9486
**OPEN** Thur–Sun 10–5  **PRODUCTION** 1500 cases
**WINEMAKER** David Traeger
**PRINCIPAL WINES** Meth Champ, Chenin, Ries, Cab Franc, Cab Franc Cab Sauv.
**BEST VINTAGES W** '84, '90 **R** '85, '88, '89
**SUMMARY** Frank and Helen Dawson are dedicated vignerons and wine lovers; given the experience of contract winemaker David Traeger the frankly disappointing quality of the initial releases will surely be remedied in due course.

## BROKENWOOD A–A Est 1970 NFR/CD/ML/UK
(Aust Wine Centre) $14–22 CD  HUNTER V
McDonalds Road, Pokolbin, NSW 2321  (049) 98 7559  fax (049) 98 7893
**OPEN** 7 days 10–5  **PRODUCTION** 17 000 cases
**WINEMAKER** Iain Riggs
**PRINCIPAL WINES** Sem (unwooded and oak-matured) Chard, Pinot, Herm, Cab Sauv, 'Graveyard' top of the range release.
**BEST VINTAGES W** '83, '84, '86, '89, '91 **R** '83, '86, '89, '91
**SUMMARY** Deservedly fashionable winery producing consistently excellent wines. Unwooded Sauvignon Blanc Semillon has especially strong following (the 1991 outstanding), as has Cabernet Sauvignon; the three Graveyard releases are well worth the extra money, the red wines being exceptionally long-lived. The Graveyard Hermitage is one of the best Hunter reds available today.

**BROOKLAND VALLEY** B–CB Est 1984 LR/CD/ML
$13–15.90 CD MARGARET R
Caves Road, Willyabrup, WA 6284 (097) 55 6250
**OPEN** Tues–Sun 11–4.30 **PRODUCTION** 5000 cases
**WINEMAKER** Gary Baldwin (Consultant)
**PRINCIPAL WINES** Chard, Sauv Bl, Cab Sauv, Cab Franc.
**SUMMARY** The strikingly labelled first wines (from the 1990 vintage)
show skilled winemaking but, perhaps because of the youth of the vines,
not a great deal of varietal character; nonetheless, the wines — and the
lovely winery restaurant — have enjoyed great success.

**BROOKS CREEK WINES** NR Est 1973 LR/CD/ML
$7.50–19 CD CANBERRA
RMB 209 Brooks Road, Bungendore, NSW 2621 (06) 236 9221
**OPEN** Sat–Sun 9–5 **PRODUCTION** 1300 cases
**WINEMAKER** Lawrie Brownbill
**PRINCIPAL WINES** Ries, Chard, Mataro, Cab Mal, Cab Sauv.
**SUMMARY** The Brownbill family purchased what was then known as
Shingle House from Max and Yvonne Blake in early 1990, and have re-
named it Brooks Creek Vineyard. Production varies, as the vineyard can
be prone to frost, but one of the continuing specialties is the Mataro,
which in 1991 produced a light-bodied wine, but one which is crammed
with vibrant pepper and spice. The same year produced a pleasant
botrytis-affected Rhine Riesling.

**BROUSSARDS CHUM CREEK WINERY** NR Est
1977 CD/ML $16 CD YARRA V
Cunninghams Road, Chum Creek via Healesville, Vic 3777 (059) 62 5551
**OPEN** W'ends, hols 10–6 **PRODUCTION** 350 cases
**WINEMAKER** Contract made
**PRINCIPAL WINES** Chard, Pinot, Cab Sauv.
**SUMMARY** One of the more remote and smallest of the Yarra Valley
wineries, quietly selling all of its wine through the cellar door.

**BROWN BROS** B–BA Est 1889 NR/CD/ML/UK $8–25 R NE VIC
Off main Glenrowan-Myrtleford Road, Milawa, Vic 3678 (057) 27 3400
**OPEN** Mon–Sat 9–5, Sun 10–6 **PRODUCTION** NFP
**WINEMAKER** John G. Brown
**PRINCIPAL WINES** An immense range of varietal wines in various
price categories; at the bottom Victorian range, then Limited Production,
then Regional Releases including Koombahla, Meadow Creek and
Whitlands, next Family Reserve and, finally, Classic Vintage Releases.
**BEST VINTAGES W** '82, '86, '87, '90, '91 **R** '85, '86, '88, '90, '91
**SUMMARY** The parallels with Tyrrells abound; each has enjoyed
tremendous growth since 1960, providing absolutely reliable wines at big
company prices but with a small company image. Each company enjoys
tremendously strong markets in its home state but each has also prospered in
export markets; here in fact Brown Bros have led the way, particularly in the
United Kingdom. Brown Bros has also showed great enterprise in developing
new varietal styles, new high-country vineyards and in establishing a
commercial-scale experimental high-tech winery adjacent to the main winery.

**BUCHANAN** CB–CB Est 1985 LR/CD/ML/UK
(Haughton Fine Wines) $10.90–15.20 CD TAMAR V
Glendale Road, Loira, West Tamar, Tas 7275 (003) 94 7488
**OPEN** 7 days 10–4 **PRODUCTION** 2500 cases
**WINEMAKER** Don Buchanan
**PRINCIPAL WINES** Chard, Ries, Pinot, Cab Sauv.
**BEST VINTAGES W** '90, '91 **R** '87, '88, '91
**SUMMARY** Don Buchanan has considerable experience in both

winemaking and viticulture, and there is no reason why he should not leave his mark on Tasmanian winemaking. My reservations about his wines stem from what strikes me as heavy-handed and not always sympathetic use of oak; other critics, it must be said, have no problems on this score.

## BULLERS BEVERFORD  DC–CB Est 1952 LR/CD/ML
$7–13 CD  MURRAY R
Murray Valley Highway, Beverford, Vic 3590  (050) 37 6305
**OPEN** Mon–Sat 9–5  **PRODUCTION** 26 000 cases
**WINEMAKER** Richard Buller (Jnr)
**PRINCIPAL WINES** Wh Front, Ries, Chenin, Chab, Sem, Chard, Cab Sauv, Shir, Cab Merl.
**SUMMARY** Traditional wines, principally white, which in the final analysis reflect both their Riverland origin and a fairly low-key approach to style in the winery.

## BULLERS CALLIOPE  CB–B Est 1921 LR/CD/ML
$6.50–12.50 CD  NE VIC
Three Chain Road, Rutherglen, Vic 3685  (060) 32 9660
**OPEN** Mon–Sat 9–5, Sun 10–5  **PRODUCTION** 10 000 cases
**WINEMAKER** Andrew Buller
**PRINCIPAL WINES** Shir, Cab Sauv, Tawny Port, Vintage Port, Muscat, Tokay, Madeira.
**SUMMARY** The dry red table wines and the range of fortifieds are well priced; the Vintage Port has a style all of its own, but the fresh, medium-weight Tokay and Muscat are particularly easy to drink.

## BUNGAWARRA  NR Est 1975 LR/CD/ML $14–17 CD
GRANITE BELT
Bents Road, Ballandean, Qld 4382  (076) 84 1128
**OPEN** 7 days 9–5  **PRODUCTION** 600 cases
**WINEMAKER** Philip Christensen
**PRINCIPAL WINES** Chard, Shir, Cab Sauv.
**BEST VINTAGES** W '86, '87, '89, '91  R '82, '85, '88, '91
**SUMMARY** Oak-derived volatility runs through the Bungawarra red wines to an unacceptable degree; a 1991 Shiraz Cabernet Malbec tasted from a sound oak barrel had excellent ripe, spicy fruit. Some hard decisions on oak replacement are needed.

## BURGE FAMILY  BA–B Est 1928 CD/ML $7.80–12.80 CD
BAROSSA V
Barossa Way, Lyndoch, SA 5351  (085) 24 4644
**OPEN** 7 days 10–5  **PRODUCTION** 3000 cases
**WINEMAKER** Rick Burge
**PRINCIPAL WINES** Sem, Chard, Ries, Herm, Clochmerle Pinot, Homestead Blend, Tawny Port.
**SUMMARY** Rick Burge came back to the family winery after a number of years successfully running St Leonards; there was much work to be done, but he has achieved much, using the base of very good fortified wines and markedly improving table wine quality with wines such as the quite suprising 1990 Clochmerle Pinot Noir.

## BURNBRAE  DB–C Est 1976 CD/ML $7.50–12 CD  MUDGEE
The Hargraves Road, Erudgere via Mudgee, NSW 2850  (063) 73 3504
**OPEN** 7 days 9.30–5  **PRODUCTION** 1800 cases
**WINEMAKER** R. B. Mace
**PRINCIPAL WINES** Chard, Wh Burg, Tram Ries, Gren Rosé, Shir, Shir Cab Malb, Port, Muscat.
**SUMMARY** Burnbrae's red wines can only be described as formidable, as exemplified by the 15.5% alcohol of the massively extractive 1990

Cabernet Sauvignon, a wine for bigger men than I. The 1988 Vintage Port is, however, an attractive spicy style.

## CALAIS ESTATES CB–CB Est 1987 LR/CD/ML $9–15 CD HUNTER V

Palmers Lane, Pokolbin, NSW 2321    (049) 98 7654
**OPEN** Mon–Fri 9–5, w'ends 10–5    **PRODUCTION** 11 000 cases
**WINEMAKER** Colin Peterson
**PRINCIPAL WINES** Sem, Chard, Chard Sem, Tram Ries, Pinot, Shir, Cab Sauv.
**BEST VINTAGES W** '88, '89, '90, '91 **R** '87, '88, '90, '91
**SUMMARY** The former Wollundry vineyards are now fully mature and are among the best in the Hunter Valley; a little more sophistication in the winemaking could see outstanding wines under the Calais label. Colin Peterson, incidentally, is the son of Ian and Shirley Peterson of Petersons.

## CALLATOOTA ESTATE DC–C Est 1972 LR/CD/ML $8–12 CD UPPER HUNTER V

Wybong Road, Wybong, NSW 2333   (065) 47 8149
**OPEN** Sum 9–6, Wint 9–5    **PRODUCTION** 6500 cases
**WINEMAKER** Andrew Cruickshank
**PRINCIPAL WINES** Rosé, Cab Sauv identified by cask and vat numbers.
**SUMMARY** Trenchantly regional wines which appeal to others more than to me.

## CAMDEN ESTATE CA–B Est 1980 LR/ML $9.75–18 SYDNEY DISTRICT

Lot 32 Macarthur Road, Camden, NSW 2570   (046) 58 1237
**OPEN** 11–4 by appointment **PRODUCTION** 5000 cases
**WINEMAKER** Norman Hanckel
**PRINCIPAL WINES** Chard, Chab Tram Ries, Cab Sauv.
**BEST VINTAGES W** '83, '88, '89
**SUMMARY** Situated on the banks of the Nepean River opposite one of the birthplaces of Australian wine, and has produced some outstanding buttery, mouthfilling Chardonnays. The other wines are not in the same class, reflecting a humid and often rather wet autumn.

## CAMPBELLS CA–B Est 1870 NFR/CD/ML/UK (Walter Siegel) $10.30–14.50 CD NE VIC

Murray Valley Hwy, Rutherglen, Vic 3685   (060) 32 9458 fax (060) 32 9870
**OPEN** Mon–Sat 9–5, Sun 10–5    **PRODUCTION** 30 000 cases
**WINEMAKER** Colin Campbell
**PRINCIPAL WINES** Chard Sem, Ries, Shir, Durif, Malb, Cab Sauv, Muscat, Tokay, Port.
**BEST VINTAGES W** '80, '86, '88, '90 **R** '86, '88, '90, '91
**SUMMARY** A wide range of table and fortified wines of ascending quality and price, which are always honest; as so often in this part of the world, the fortified wines are by far the best, with the extremely elegant Isabella Tokay and Merchant Prince Muscat at the top of the tree.

## CANOBLAS-SMITH NR Est 1986 CENTRAL TABLELANDS

Boree Lane, off Cargo Road, Lidster via Orange, NSW 2800
(063) 656 113
**OPEN** By appointment **PRODUCTION** 300 cases
**WINEMAKER** Murray Smith
**PRINCIPAL WINES** Chard, Cab Sauv.
**SUMMARY** Murray Smith expects to be open for cellar door sales by late 1992; the wines are produced from a close-planted vineyard at an elevation of 820 metres, and as from 1992 will be made on-site. It would be unfair to draw any conclusions from the only wine tasted — an

experimental, foot-stamped Pinot from the 1990 vintage.

**CAPE CLAIRAULT** B–B Est 1976 LR/CD/ML/UK
(Villeneuve) $12–19 CD   MARGARET R
Henry Road, Willyabrup, WA 6284   (097) 55 6225
**OPEN** 7 days 10–5   **PRODUCTION** 3500 cases
**WINEMAKER** Ian Lewis
**PRINCIPAL WINES** Sauv Bl, Sem Sauv Bl, Ries, Cab Sauv.
**BEST VINTAGES** **W** '85, '86, '88, '90 **R** '85, '86, '87, '90
**SUMMARY** Ian and Arni Lewis have the great gift of not taking themselves (or their wines) too seriously, which is not to deny they are committed to quality: they are, and are always seeking to improve on the impressive record of crisp, herbaceous Sauvignon Blanc and finely structured, berry-flavoured Cabernet Sauvignon, not to mention a tangy, passionfruit-accented 1991 Rhine Riesling and a complex, textured, spicy 1991 Semillon.

**CAPE MENTELLE** A–A Est 1970 NFR/CD/ML/UK
(Paragon Vintners) $15–22 R   MARGARET R
Off Wallcliffe Road, Margaret River, WA 6285   (097) 57 2070
**OPEN** 7 days 10–4.30   **PRODUCTION** 25 000 cases
**WINEMAKER** John Durham
**PRINCIPAL WINES** Chard, Sem Sauv Bl, Cab Sauv, Shir, Zinfan.
**BEST VINTAGES** **W** '82, '86, '88, '90, '91 **R** '82, '83, '88, '90
**SUMMARY** One of Australia's foremost premium wineries, now majority owned by Veuve Clicquot but still firmly under the control of founder David Hohnen. Its red wines are legends in their own lifetime: while Cabernet Sauvignon attracts most attention, I often prefer the spicy Shiraz (labelled Hermitage) and the voluptuous Zinfandel. The textured, peachy 1990 Chardonnay and floral, fruity 1991 Semillon Sauvignon Blanc are the best white wines to date.

**CAPEL VALE** A–A Est 1979 NFR/CD/ML/UK
(Roxborough, Kelso, Scotland) $13.50–18 R   SW COASTAL
Lot 5 Capel North West Road, Stirling Estate, Capel, WA 6271
(097) 27 2439
**OPEN** 7 days 10–4.30   **PRODUCTION** 15 000 cases
**WINEMAKER** Rob Bowen
**PRINCIPAL WINES** Ries, Gewurz, Tram Ries, Sem Sauv Bl, Chard, Shir, Cab Sauv, Baudin.
**BEST VINTAGES** **W** '86, '89, '90, '91 **R** '85, '88, '90, '91
**SUMMARY** Always an outstanding maker of pungent and intense white wines, Capel Vale has now lifted its red wines (with the '87 and '88 vintages, the latter in particular) into the same high class. The arrival of Rob Bowen as winemaker should see even greater things, if this is indeed possible.

**CAPOGRECO** DC–C Est 1976 CD/ML $7–10 CD   MURRAY R
Riverside Avenue, Mildura, Vic 3500 · (050) 23 3060
**OPEN** Mon–Sat 10–6   **PRODUCTION** NFP
**WINEMAKER** Bruno Capogreco
**PRINCIPAL WINES** Ries, Mos, Cab Sauv, Claret, Rosé, fortified and flavoured.
**SUMMARY** Italian-owned and run, the wines are a blend of Italian and Australian Riverland influences; the herb infused Rosso Dolce is a particularly good example of its kind.

**CAROSA** NR Est 1986 LR/CD/ML $9.70–14 CD   PERTH HILLS
Lot 3 Houston Street, Mount Helena, WA 6555   (09) 572 1603
**OPEN** W'ends 10–5   **PRODUCTION** 350 cases
**WINEMAKER** James Elson
**PRINCIPAL WINES** Sem, Chard, Cab Merl, Pinot.

**SUMMARY** Barrel samples tasted early in the piece were not in proper condition for judging, but winemaker (and consultant) Jim Elson has extensive Eastern states experience, so should succeed.

**CARTOBE** C–C Est 1980 LR/CD/ML $8–15 CD  HILLTOPS
Young Road, Boorowa, NSW 2586  (063) 85 3128
**OPEN** Fri–Sun 10–5  **PRODUCTION** 5000 cases
**WINEMAKER** Geoff Carter
**PRINCIPAL WINES** Chard, Chab, Sauv Bl, Ries, Noble Ries, Cab Sauv, Pinot.
**BEST VINTAGES W** '86, '88, '89, '91 **R** '87, '90
**SUMMARY** A full-flavoured 1990 Noble Riesling is one of the best wines in the portfolio of what is now the leading independent winery in the Hilltops region following the acquisition of Barwang by McWilliams.

**CASELLA** C/B Est 1969 LR/CD/ML MIA
Farm 1471 Yenda, NSW 2681  (069) 681 346
**OPEN** 7 days 9–5  **PRODUCTION** 9000 cases
**WINEMAKER** John Casella
**PRINCIPAL WINES** Sem, Chard, Gewurtz, Shir, Cab Sauv.
**SUMMARY** John Casella makes lush, soft, early maturing and full-flavoured white wines, and suprised with a highly-toned, ripe, spicy berry 1990 Cabernet Sauvignon.

**CASSEGRAIN** CA–B Est 1980 NFR/CD/ML $7.95–25 R
HASTINGS V
Hastings Valley Winery, Pacific Highway, Port Macquarie, NSW 2444 (065) 83 7777  fax (065) 84 0353
**OPEN** 7 days 9–5  **PRODUCTION** 45 000 cases
**WINEMAKERS** John Cassegrain, Drew Noon
**PRINCIPAL WINES** Chard, Sem, Shir, Cab Sauv, Pinot, Cab Merl, Chambourcin.
**BEST VINTAGES W** '85, '86, '89, '91 **R** '87, '88, '89, '91
**SUMMARY** Highly sophisticated viticulture together with the planting of varieties such as Chambourcin and Chardonnay help meet the challenges of a very wet and humid growing and harvest season in the north coast of New South Wales. Overall wine quality (some grapes are bought from the Hunter Valley) is excitingly variable.

**CASTLE ROCK ESTATE** BA–A Est 1983 NFR/CD/ML
$11.80–14.80 CD LWR GRT STHN
Porongurup Road, Porongurup, WA 6324   (098) 41 1037
**OPEN** Wed–Fri 10–4, w'ends 10–5  **PRODUCTION** 1500 cases
**WINEMAKER** Kim Hart
**PRINCIPAL WINES** Ries, Chard, Cab Sauv.
**BEST VINTAGES W** '86, '89, '90 **R** '87, '88
**SUMMARY** Spectacular views and first class wines are the rewards for those who find their way to this remote vineyard owned by the Diletti family; fine, elegant, lime-and-toast Riesling and Cabernet as finely strung as any racehorse are cellaring specials.

**CATHCART RIDGE** NR Est 1977 LR/ML $12–12.50 CD
GRT WESTERN
Byron Road, Cathcart via Ararat, Vic 3377   (053) 52 1997
fax (053) 52 1558
**OPEN** Not  **PRODUCTION** 16 000 cases
**WINEMAKER** David Farnhill
**PRINCIPAL WINES** Chard, Shir, Cab Merl.
**BEST VINTAGES W** '87, '88, '89, '90 **R** '87, '88, '91
**SUMMARY** Recently sold by Dr Graeme Bertuch to the Farnhill family,

which will no doubt once again actively promote this winery which has a fine reputation for fragrant, spicy/peppery Shiraz and elegant Cabernet Merlot not to mention the very smooth and well made 1990 Chardonnay.

**CHALK HILL**  NR Est 1973 CD/ML $5.90–9 CD  STHN VALES
Brewery Hill Road, McLaren, Vale, SA 5171   (08) 323 8815
**OPEN** 7 days 1–5  **PRODUCTION** Nil 1991
**WINEMAKER** Nancy Benko
**PRINCIPAL WINES** Ries, Rosé, Shir, Cab Sauv, Port.
**SUMMARY** The retirement hobby of distinguished research scientist Dr Nancy Benko; wines from numerous vintages back to 1978 are still available at very low prices.

**CHAPEL HILL**  A–A Est 1979 NFR/CD/ML/UK
(Aust Wine Centre) $11–30 R  STHN VALES
Chapel Hill Road, McLaren Vale, SA 5171   (08) 323 8429
fax (08) 323 9245
**OPEN** Mon–Fri 9–5, w'ends 11–5  **PRODUCTION** 13 500 cases
**WINEMAKER** Pam Dunsford
**PRINCIPAL WINES** Chard, Herm Cab, Cab Sauv.
**BEST VINTAGES W** '88, '89, '90 **R** '88, '89, '90
**SUMMARY** With new owners, and Pamela Dunsford in charge of winemaking, the once sleepy and tiny Chapel Hill has sprung into top gear, winning trophies almost at will with the Reserve Chardonnay and 1990 Reserve Shiraz, the latter with exceptional concentration and balance, loaded with dark chocolate fruit.

**CHARLES CIMICKY**  BA–B Est 1972 LR/CD/ML $9–15.50 CD BAROSSA V
Gomersal Road, Lyndoch, SA 5351   (085) 24 4025
**OPEN** 7 days 10–4  **PRODUCTION** 2500 cases
**WINEMAKER** Charles Cimicky
**PRINCIPAL WINES** Sauv Bl, Ries, Colomb, Cab Merl, Shir, Port.
**BEST VINTAGES W** '81, '82, '85, '89, '91 **R** '81, '84, '87, '88, '91
**SUMMARY** These wines are of very good quality, thanks to the lavish (but sophisticated) use of new French oak in tandem with high quality grapes. The intense, long-flavoured Sauvignon Blanc has been a particularly consistent performer.

**CHARLES MELTON**  BA–BA Est 1984 LR/CD/ML/UK
(Australian Wine Centre) $7.90–14 CD  BAROSSA V
Krondorf Road, Tanunda, SA 5352   (085) 63 3606
**OPEN** 7 days 11–5  **PRODUCTION** 3500 cases
**WINEMAKER** Charlie Melton
**PRINCIPAL WINES** Rosé, Shir, Pinot Herm, Nine Popes (Grenache Shir), Cab Sauv.
**BEST VINTAGES R** '84, '86, '89, '90
**SUMMARY** The wine world needs more Charlie Meltons and more wines like the wonderfully rich, velvety and absolutely unique Nine Popes, a blend of Grenache and Shiraz from old, low-yielding vines. A must-see on any visit to the Barossa Valley.

**CHARLES STURT UNI**  BA–B Est 1977 CD/ML
$8.20–14.50 CD  HILLTOPS
Boorooma Street, North Wagga Wagga, NSW 2650   (069) 22 2435
fax (069) 22 2107
**OPEN** Mon–Fri 10–4, w'ends 11–4  **PRODUCTION** 10 000 cases
**WINEMAKER** R. Hooper
**PRINCIPAL WINES** Chard, Sem, Meth Champ, Sauv Bl, Ries, Cab Shir, Port, Muscat.

**BEST VINTAGES W** '80, '88, '90, '91 **R** '87, '88, '90, '91
**SUMMARY** With the highly talented Rodney Hooper now in charge of winemaking, the erratic wines of the past are no more, and the regionally based styles are worthy of this tertiary wine-teaching institution, the 1990 white wines having matured beautifully, and the '91s showing the same promise.

## CHATEAU DORRIEN  NR Est 1983 CD/ML $7.90–9.90 CD
BAROSSA V
Cnr Seppeltsfield Road and Barossa Valley Way, Dorrien, SA 5352
(085) 62 2850
**OPEN** 7 days 10–5  **PRODUCTION** 1000 cases
**WINEMAKER** Fernando Martin
**PRINCIPAL WINES** Ries, Chab, Chard, Sem, Ausl Ries, Herm, Cab Sauv, fortified.
**SUMMARY** Unashamedly and successfully directed at the tourist trade.

## CHATEAU FRANCOIS  C–B Est 1969 CD/ML $9–10 CD
HUNTER V
Off Broke Road, Pokolbin, NSW 2321 (049) 98 7548
**OPEN** W'ends 10–5 or by appointment  **PRODUCTION** 1000 cases (800 cases 1992)
**WINEMAKER** Don Francois
**PRINCIPAL WINES** Sem, Chard, Shir Pinot.
**SUMMARY** The rating suggests a certain schizophrenia in the Chateau Francois wines; they are sometimes very good (and when they are, the value for money is exceptional), sometimes not — suffering from an excess of what used to be called regional character. The 1991 Mallee Semillon has the richness one expects from this vintage, balanced by pleasing acidity; the 1990 Shiraz Pinot Noir has exceptional power in a regional mould.

## CHATEAU LEAMON  B–BA Est 1977 LR/CD/ML $10–16
CD  BENDIGO
140 km post, Calder Highway, Bendigo, Vic 3550
(054) 47 7995  fax (054) 470 855
**OPEN** 6 days 10–5 (not Tues)  **PRODUCTION** 2000 cases
**WINEMAKER** Ian Leamon
**PRINCIPAL WINES** Sem, Ries, Chard, Shir, Cab Sauv.
**BEST VINTAGES W** '82, '83, '89, '90 **R** '80, '83, '84, '88
**SUMMARY** Produces ever-interesting red wines, sometimes showing spicy characters, sometimes minty, but always with balance and length.

## CHATEAU PATO  C–B Est 1978 CD/ML $6–12 CD
HUNTER V
Thompson's Road, Pokolbin, NSW 2321  (049) 98 7634
**OPEN** By appointment only
**PRODUCTION** 300 cases  (120 cases in 1992)
**WINEMAKER** David Patterson
**PRINCIPAL WINES** Gewurz, Herm.
**SUMMARY** Almost an underground winery owned and run by all-night ABC radio announcer David Patterson; the full flavoured, concentrated Hermitage is worth chasing (and cellaring), particularly the lush, concentrated red berry, spice and tannin-filled 1991 wine.

## CHATEAU REMY  B–B Est 1963 NFR/CD/UK (Eurobrands)
$11–20 R  PYRENEES
Vinoca Road, Avoca, Vic 3467  (054) 65 3202  fax (054) 65 3529
**OPEN** 7 days 10–4  **PRODUCTION** 40 000 cases
**WINEMAKER** Vincent Gere
**PRINCIPAL WINES** Meth Champ, Sem, Blue Pyrenees (Cabernet

blend); Fiddlers Creek is a recently introduced second label extending the table wine range.

**BEST VINTAGES W** '82, '86, '88, '90 **R** '82, '86, '88, '89, '90, '91

**SUMMARY** Making determined efforts to lift the quality (and style) of its Méthode Champenoise wines, and having success in so doing, however much the climate may be seen as more suited to making full flavoured red table wine, exemplified by the wholly seductive 1989 Blue Pyrenees Estate dry red.

## CHATEAU REYNELLA BA–B Est 1838 NR/CD/UK
(Whiclar & Gordon) $14–18 R STHN VALES
Reynella Road, Reynella, SA 5161 (08) 381 2266
**OPEN** 7 days 10–4.30 **PRODUCTION** NFP
**WINEMAKERS** David O'Leary, Tom Newton
**PRINCIPAL WINES** Chard, Cab Sauv, Cab Malb Merl under the Stony Hill label; also sparkling and Vintage Port.
**BEST VINTAGES W** '86, '88, '90, '91 **R** '82, '86, '87, '90
**SUMMARY** Now restricted to a severely pruned range of good table wines and one of the two truly great Australian Vintage Ports. The Reynella winery and homestead complex is both historic and extremely beautiful, one of the priceless treasures of the industry, and is the headquarters of the Thomas Hardy group.

## CHATEAU TAHBILK BA–A Est 1860 NFR/CD/ML/UK
(Nicks Wines Intern'l) $9.95–30 R GOULBURN V
Off Goulburn Valley Highway, Tahbilk, Vic 3607 (057) 94 2555
**OPEN** Mon–Sat 9–5, Sun 11–5 **PRODUCTION** 90 000 cases
**WINEMAKER** Alister Purbrick
**PRINCIPAL WINES** Chard, Ries, Mars, Shir, Cab Sauv, Private Bin and Original V'yd.
**BEST VINTAGES R** '81, '86, '87, '88, '90
**SUMMARY** A winery steeped in tradition (with high National Trust classification) which should be visited at least once by every wine conscious Australian, and which makes wines — particularly red wines — utterly in keeping with that tradition. There are no modern, trendy wines for immediate consumption made here, just wines for real men (and women), to be cellared for decades.

## CHATEAU XANADU CA–B Est 1977 LFR/CD/ML/UK
(TBA) $13.50–24 CD MARGARET R
Railway Terrace off Wallcliffe Rd, Margaret River, WA 6285
(097) 57 2581 fax (097) 57 3389
**OPEN** Mon–Sat 10–4.30, Sun 11–4.30 **PRODUCTION** 6500 cases
**WINEMAKER** Conor Lagan
**PRINCIPAL WINES** Chenin, Sem, Sauv Bl, Chard, Rosé, Cab Sauv, Cab Sauv Reserve.
**BEST VINTAGES W** '85, '87, '89, '90, '91 **R** '82, '83, '86, '89
**SUMMARY** The white wines are truly excellent, coming in an impressive array of style, ranging from pungently grassy 1991 Semillon to gooseberry/passionfruit 1991 Sauvignon Blanc and citric, smoky Chardonnay. Real progress is being made with the Reserve red wines, but there is still a way to go with the others.

## CHATEAU YALDARA CB–BA Est 1965 NR/CD/ML/UK
(Stratfords) $5.30–13 R BAROSSA V
Gomersal Road, Lyndoch, SA 5351 (085) 24 4200 fax (085) 24 4678
**OPEN** 7 days 8.30–5 **PRODUCTION** 450 000 cases
**WINEMAKER** Herman Thumm, Jim Irvine
**PRINCIPAL WINES** Chard, Sem Sauv Bl, Ries, Saut, Cab Sauv, Shir, Merl, sparkl.

**BEST VINTAGES W** '88, '89, '90, '91 **R** '87, '88, '89, '91
**SUMMARY** Acacia Hill, Lakewood, Mill Stream, Lyndoch Valley and (prosaically) Chateau Yaldara are all brands coming from this enterprising winery once best known for some rather unpleasant sweet red table wines. Acacia Hill and Lakewood, inspired by consultant Jim Irvine, can be exceptionally good value — both red and white, the latter outstanding in 1991.

## CHATSFIELD BA–BA Est 1976 LR/CD/ML $8–14 CD LWR GRT STHN
34 Albany Hwy, Mount Barker, WA 6324 (098) 51 1704
**OPEN** Tues–Sun 10.30–4.30 **PRODUCTION** 1000 cases
**WINEMAKER** Claudio Radenti (Contract)
**PRINCIPAL WINES** Ries, Tram Ries, Chard, Shir, Cab Franc, Cab Sauv.
**BEST VINTAGES W** '82, '85, '87, '90 **R** '88, '89
**SUMMARY** A long-established vineyard, an Irish-born medical practitioner-owner, and a contract winemaker of Italian parentage have coalesced to produce tangy, smoky Chardonnay, spicy Shiraz and red berry Cabernet Sauvignon/Cabernet Franc, all of high quality, the red wines particularly so in 1989.

## CHITTERING ESTATE CB-C Est 1982 LR/CD $16-20 R PERTH HILLS
Chittering Valley Road, Chittering, WA 6084 (09) 571 8144
**OPEN** Sun only **PRODUCTION** 12 000 cases
**WINEMAKER** Steven Schapera
**PRINCIPAL WINES** Chard, Sem Sauv Bl, Cab Sauv Merl.
**BEST VINTAGES W** '89, '90 **R** '88, '89
**SUMMARY** One of the most interesting winery operations in Australia, with wealthy owners, extreme marketing skills and an intensely motivated winemaker producing wines of varying quality and style which are mainly exported to Japan.

## CLARENDON HILLS NR Est 1989 LR/UK
(Negociants Australia) $19–22 R STHN VALES
38 Stuart Road, Dulwich, SA 5065 (08) 364 0227
**OPEN** Not **PRODUCTION** 1500 cases
**WINEMAKER** Roman Bratasiuk and Graham Ward
**PRINCIPAL WINES** Chard, Cab Sauv, Merl.
**SUMMARY** Released with a fanfare of trumpets and much excitement in 1991, with comparisons to '82 Ch Pichon-Lalande and '61 Ch Latour. The 1990 red wines certainly had tremendous depth of flavour and extract, and promised to be long-lived, which is the avowed aim of Roman Bratasiuk.

## CLEVELAND NR Est 1985 CD/ML/UK (planned) $9–15 CD MACEDON
Shannon's Road, Lancefield, Vic 3435 (054) 29 1449
**OPEN** By appointment only **PRODUCTION** 500 cases
**WINEMAKER** Keith Brien
**PRINCIPAL WINES** Chard, Pinot, Cab Sauv under Cleveland label; Brien Family Selection Chard is second label.
**SUMMARY** Cleveland made a promising debut with its 1989 vintage, and in particular with its sappy/strawberry Pinot Noir showing marked Burgundian character, even if the difficult vintage and the still relatively young vines meant a light-bodied wine was inevitable. Subsequent releases have been more variable, with the '90 Cabernet Sauvignon the best.

## CLIFF HOUSE NR Est 1988 LR/ML $10.95–11.95 R TAS
RSD 457, Kayena, Tas 7270
**OPEN** Not **PRODUCTION** NFP
**WINEMAKER** Geoff Hewitt

**PRINCIPAL WINES** Chard, Ries, Cab/Pinot.
**SUMMARY** Has made an impressive debut with a weighty, complex 1991 Chardonnay, which has unusual mouthfeel; the eccentric blend of Cabernet and Pinot from 1990 results in a pleasant, clean red cherry/berry wine which inevitably lacks varietal distinction, but which is without technical fault.

## CLONAKILLA CA–B Est 1971 LR/CD/ML $10–14 CD CANBERRA

Crisps Lane off Gundaroo Road, Murrumbateman, ACT 2582
(06) 251 1938
**OPEN** W'ends, hols 11–5 **PRODUCTION** 650 cases
**WINEMAKER** John Kirk
**PRINCIPAL WINES** Sauv Bl, Ries, Botrytis Sem, Cab Shir, Port.
**BEST VINTAGES W** '81, '83,' 86, '91 **R** '83, '86, '88, '91
**SUMMARY** While the production is very small, the Kirk family produce wines with an unexpected touch of sophistication and intense flavours: a peppery 1990 Shiraz outstanding, herbaceous 1990 Cabernet Sauvignon very good, and good 1991 Semillon Sauvingon Blanc.

## CLOUD VALLEY NR Est 1991 LR/ML $15 ML MORNINGTON P

15 Ocean View Avenue, Red Hill South, Vic 3937 (059) 89 2762
**OPEN** Not **PRODUCTION** 650 cases
**WINEMAKER** Stoniers Merricks (Contract)
**PRINCIPAL WINES** Chard, Cab Sauv.
**SUMMARY** A fine, crisp, almost Chablis-style 1991 Chardonnay with melon/grapefruit flavours marked the arrival of Cloud Valley, a partnership between Bill Allen and Peter and Judy Maxwell, whose vineyards are at Red Hill South.

## CLYDE PARK B–B Est 1980 LR/UK (Oddbins) $15–22 R GEELONG

Midland Hwy, Bannockburn, Vic 3331 (052) 81 1363
**OPEN** Not **PRODUCTION** 1500 cases
**WINEMAKER** Gary Farr
**PRINCIPAL WINES** Chard, Pinot, Cab Sauv.
**BEST VINTAGES W** '85, '86, '88, '89, '90 **R** '85, '86, '87, '88, '90, '91
**SUMMARY** Gary Farr's (of Bannockburn) own vineyard, producing small quantities of highly flavoured and distinctively styled wines, with Pinot a new addition to the line, and 1990 Chardonnay unctuous and complex.

## COBAW RIDGE NR Est 1985 LR/CD/ML $14 CD MACEDON

Perc Boyer's Lane, East Pastoria via Kyneton, Vic 3444 (054) 235 227
**OPEN** W'ends 10–5 **PRODUCTION** 1000 cases
**WINEMAKER** Alan Cooper
**PRINCIPAL WINES** Chard, Shir, Cab Sauv.
**SUMMARY** Nelly and Alan Cooper have established Cobaw Ridge at an altitude of 610 metres in the hills above Kyneton replete with self-constructed pole-framed mud brick house and winery. Their first releases (from 1989 and '90) show promise, not surpisingly reflecting some of the fruit characters found in Virgin Hills and Knights Granite Hills.

## COFIELD ANDERSON CB–B Est 1986 CD/ML $8.50–15.50 CD NE VIC

Distillery Road, Wahgunyah, Vic 3687 (060) 33 3798
**OPEN** Mon–Sat 9–5, Sun 10–5 **PRODUCTION** 2600 cases
**WINEMAKERS** Max Cofield and Howard Anderson
**PRINCIPAL WINES** Pinot, Chard Sparkl, Shir Sparkl Burg, Ries, Sem, Chenin, Chard, LH Tokay, Pinot, Cab Shir, Cab Sauv, Muscat, Port.

**BEST VINTAGES W** '88, '89, '90 **R** '86, '88, '90, '91
**SUMMARY** Ex-Jolimont winemaker Howard Anderson has joined forces with district veteran Max Cofield to produce an eclectic range of wines in inimitable style. Well worth visiting for something different.

## COLDSTREAM HILLS NR Est 1985 NFR/CD/ML/UK
(Whiclar & Gordon) $10–22 R YARRA V
Lot 6, Maddens Lane, Coldstream, Vic 3770 (059) 64 9388
fax (059) 649 389
**OPEN** W'ends 10–5 **PRODUCTION** 20 000 cases
**WINEMAKERS** James Halliday and Phillip Dowell
**PRINCIPAL WINES** Steels Range (second label) Chard, Pinot; varietal range Chard, Fumé, Pinot, Cab Sauv, Cab Merl; Reserve range Chard, Pinot, Merl.
**BEST VINTAGES W** '86, '88, '90, '91 **R** '87, '88, '90, '91
**SUMMARY** The author's own winery, and therefore not rated; however, from 231 entries in 29 shows, Coldstream Hills has won 33 trophies, 63 gold medals, 45 silver medals and 67 bronze medals in Australian wine shows, with a medal success rate of over 75%, twice the national average.

## COOINDA VALE NR Est 1985 CD/ML $12.50 CD TAS
Bartonvale Road, Campania, Tas 7026 (002) 62 4227
**OPEN** By appointment **PRODUCTION** 150 cases
**WINEMAKER** Andrew Hood (Contract)
**PRINCIPAL WINES** Ries, Pinot.
**SUMMARY** Did not exhibit at the 1992 Tasmanial Regional Wine Show, but with Andrew Hood as contract winemaker, one is entitled to expect very competently made wines.

## COOLART VALLEY BA–BA Est 1981 LR/CD $11–15 CD
MORNINGTON P
Thomas Hill Road, Red Hill South, Vic 3937 (059) 89 2087
**OPEN** All w'ends Nov–Mar; first w'end month Apr–Oct
**PRODUCTION** 450 cases
**WINEMAKER** Peter Cumming (Contract)
**PRINCIPAL WINES** Sem, Chard, Ries, Cab Sauv, Cab Sauv Merl.
**SUMMARY** Made an outstanding Cabernet Sauvignon in 1989, with unusual weight and depth for the year, and perfect balance; a tangy, smoky 1990 Chardonnay rounded off an impressive debut. More recent samples not available at time of writing.

## COORINJA NR Est 1870 CD $8–10.50 CD PERTH HILLS
Toodyay Road, Toodyay, WA 6566 (096) 26 2280
**OPEN** Mon–Sat 8–5 **PRODUCTION** 3200
**WINEMAKER** Michael Wood
**PRINCIPAL WINES** Dry White, Claret, Burg, Port, Sherry, Muscat.
**SUMMARY** An evocative and historic winery nestling in a small gully which seems to be in a time-warp, begging to be used as a set for a film. A recent revamp of the packaging accompanied a more than respectable 1990 Hermitage, with lots of dark chocolate and sweet berry flavour, finishing with soft tannins.

## COPE WILLIAMS B–B Est 1977 LR/CD/ML $9.50–23 R
MACEDON
Glenfern Road, Romsey, Vic 3434 (054) 29 5428 fax (054) 29 5655
**OPEN** 7 days 10–5 **PRODUCTION** 6500 cases
**WINEMAKER** Michael Cope Williams
**PRINCIPAL WINES** Chard, Pinot, Cab Mer; Coat-of-Arms is second label, Ries, Chard and Cab Sauv; winery specialty sparkling wine, Macedon Brut.
**SUMMARY** One of the high country Macedon pioneers, specialising in

sparkling wines which are full flavoured, but also producing excellent Chardonnay and Pinot Noir table wines in the warmer vintages. A traditional 'English Green' type cricket ground is available for hire and booked out most days of the week from spring through till autumn.

## CORIOLE B–B Est 1969 NFR/CD/ML $10.50–15.50 R
STHN VALES

Chaffeys Road, McLaren Vale, SA 5171 (08) 323 8305 fax (08) 323 9136
**OPEN** Mon–Fri 9–5, w'ends 11–5 **PRODUCTION** 12 000 cases
**WINEMAKER** Stephen Hall
**PRINCIPAL WINES** Chard, Sem, Chenin, Sangiovese, Shir, Cab Shir, Cab Sauv.
**BEST VINTAGES W** '84, '89, '90, '91 **R** '80, '84, '88, '89
**SUMMARY** Blessed with some great old vineyards, Coriole has been a consistent producer of rich, full-flavoured red wines, often showing good use of oak. A rich, spice and plum 1989 Shiraz and luscious if oaky 1990 Chardonnay show the winery at its impressive best.

## COSHAM WINES NR Est 1989 PERTH HILLS
Lot 44 Union Road, Carmel via Kalamunda, WA 6076 (09) 291 6514
**OPEN** Not **PRODUCTION** 200 cases
**WINEMAKER** Anthony Sclanders
**SUMMARY** The newest of the Perth Hills ventures with a planned future production of 1000 cases, but no wines yet on the market.

## COWRA ESTATE, THE CB–CB Est 1973 NR/CD/ML/UK
(JBA) $10–18 R COWRA

Boorowa Road, Cowra, NSW 2794 (063) 421 136 fax (063) 42 4497
**OPEN** Tues–Sat 11–5, Sun 12–5 **PRODUCTION** 65 000 cases
**WINEMAKER** Simon Gilbert (Contract)
**PRINCIPAL WINES** Ries, Gewurtz, Sauv Bl, Directors Reserve Chard, Pinot, Cab Sauv.
**SUMMARY** A major producer with a strong export base, the wines of which I have tasted many times, but which for a variety of reasons do not seem to realise the full potential of the Cowra region for full-bodied white wines. It is not that they are bad wines; they are not, but they lack the style of the early Petaluma and the current Rothbury wines made from similar vintage sources.

## CRABTREE OF WATERVALE CB–B Est 1978
LR/CD/ML $9–11 CD CLARE V

North Terrace, Watervale, SA 5452 (088) 43 0069
**OPEN** 7 days 11–5 **PRODUCTION** 3500 cases
**WINEMAKER** Robert Crabtree
**PRINCIPAL WINES** Ries, Sem, Shir Cab Sauv, Muscat.
**BEST VINTAGES W** '82, '88, '89, '90 **R** '84, '86, '87, '89
**SUMMARY** The gently eccentric Robert Crabtree is one of the numerous great characters who inhabit the beautiful Clare Valley: the mixture of people, wine, history and beauty is a potent elixir, and you will not regret a visit to the winery, nor tasting the chewy, minty Shiraz Cabernet and full flavoured lime/toast Riesling.

## CRAIG AVON B–B Est 1986 LR/ML $19–23 R
MORNINGTON P

Craig Avon Lane, Merricks North, Vic 3926 (059) 89 7465
**OPEN** Not **PRODUCTION** 1000 cases
**WINEMAKER** Ken Lang
**PRINCIPAL WINES** Chard, Cab Sauv, Pinot.
**SUMMARY** The 1990 vintage produced pretty though typically light-bodied wines for this new winery: the Chardonnay, with the attractive

spicy oak which also made its appearance in a fresh Cabernet Sauvignon; the Pinot showed minty/spicy flavours which will appeal to some.

**CRAIGIE KNOWE** NR Est 1979 LR/ML $19.45–25 R TAS
Craigie Knowe, Cranbrook, Tas 7190 (vineyard only); postal 173 Macquarie Street, Hobart, Tas (002) 23 5620
**OPEN** Not **PRODUCTION** 350 cases
**WINEMAKER** Dr John Austwick
**PRINCIPAL WINES** Cab Sauv.
**SUMMARY** Makes a small quantity of full-flavoured, robust Cabernet Sauvignon in a tiny winery as a weekend relief from a busy metropolitan dental practice.

**CRAIGLEE** A–A Est 1976 NFR/CD/ML $13–15 CD
MACEDON
Sunbury Road, Sunbury, Vic 3429 (03) 744 1160
**OPEN** Sun–Mon, Wed–Fri 10–5 **PRODUCTION** 3000 cases
**WINEMAKER** Patrick Carmody
**PRINCIPAL WINES** Chard, Shir, Cab Sauv, Pinot.
**BEST VINTAGES** **W** '85, '86, '87, '90 **R** '85, '86, '88, '90
**SUMMARY** An historic winery with a proud nineteenth century record; after a prolonged hiatus once again producing wine of the highest quality, most notably a vibrantly peppery Shiraz (reaching a great height in 1990) and a smooth, deep-flavoured Cabernet Sauvignon.

**CRAIGMOOR** B–B Est 1858 LR/CD/ML $6.95–7.95 CD
MUDGEE
Craigmoor Road, Mudgee, NSW 2850 (063) 72 2208
**OPEN** 7 days 10–4 **PRODUCTION** NFP
**WINEMAKER** Robert Paul
**PRINCIPAL WINES** Sem Chard, Chard, Shir, Cab Sauv.
**SUMMARY** One of the oldest wineries in Australia to remain in continuous production, now subsumed into the Orlando/Wyndham group, with an inevitable loss of identity and individuality of wine-style, although the technical quality of the wines cannot be faulted.

**CRANEFORD** CB–B Est 1978 LR/CD/ML $10.50–14 CD
ADELAIDE HILLS
Main Street, Springton, SA 5235 (085) 68 2220
**OPEN** 7 days 11–5 **PRODUCTION** 1500 cases
**WINEMAKER** Colin Forbes
**PRINCIPAL WINES** Rh Ries, Chard, Shir, Cab Sauv.
**BEST VINTAGES** **W** '82, '86, '87, '90 **R** '85, '88, '89, '90
**SUMMARY** At times surprisingly mediocre Rhine Riesling, but some attractive red wines, most recently a vibrant, peppery spicy 1989 Shiraz following the very good minty 1988 Shiraz; Cabernet Sauvignon, too, has been good.

**CRANSWICK ESTATE** C–CB Est 1976 CD/UK
(Australian Wineries UK) $4.95–9.95 CD MIA
Walla Avenue, Griffith, NSW 2680 (069) 62 4133 fax (069) 62 2888
**OPEN** Mon–Fri 10–4.30
**PRODUCTION** 12 000 tonnes (750 000 case equivalent)
**WINEMAKER** Andrew Schulz
**PRINCIPAL WINES** Cranswick Est Chard, Sem Chard, Sem, Res Shir, Merl, Shir Merl; Redello, Barramundi red and white.
**SUMMARY** An interesting operation producing wines almost exclusively for export both in bottle and (largely) in bulk, but available cellar door. Wine quality is modest, there being an apparent similarity between the number of the brands and labels, reinforcing the impression

that this is a strictly marketing-driven operation.

## CRAWFORD RIVER  CA–B Est 1982 LR/CD/ML $12–15
CD  WESTERN VIC

Crawford via Condah, Vic 3303   (055) 78 2267

**OPEN** By appointment only  **PRODUCTION** 3000 cases

**WINEMAKER** John Thomson

**PRINCIPAL WINES** Ries, Sem Sauv Bl, Cab.

**BEST VINTAGES W** '84, '86, '88, '89 **R** '82, '86, '88

**SUMMARY** Some exemplary Rieslings, Botrytis Rieslings and Cabernet Sauvignons have been made by full-time grazier, part-time winemaker John Thomson who clearly has the winemaker's equivalent of the gardener's green thumb. Recent releases have not been up to the same standard, particularly the '90s.

## CULLEN WINES  A–A Est 1971 NFR/CD/ML $12.85–17.40
CD  MARGARET R

Caves Road, Willyabrup via Cowaramup, WA 6284   (097) 55 5277

**OPEN** 7 days 10–4  **PRODUCTION** 9000 cases

**WINEMAKER** Vanya Cullen

**PRINCIPAL WINES** Sauv Bl, Chard, Sem (oaked), Classic Dry White, Cab Merl, Pinot.

**BEST VINTAGES W** '86, '89, '90, '91 **R** '82, '86, '88, '89

**SUMMARY** One of the pioneers of Margaret River which has always produced long-lived wines of highly individual style. The cedary, red berry Cabernet Merlot, with fine grained tannins is invariably excellent, but at various times Sauvignon Blanc (in 1991 an opulently spicy oaked style), Chardonnay and Autumn Harvest Riesling have all shone.

## CURRENCY CREEK  B–B Est 1968 LR/CD/ML/UK
(Marcher Wines) $4.95–12.95 CD  LANGHORNE CREEK

Winery Road, Currency Creek, SA 5214   (085) 55 4069

**OPEN** 7 days 10–5  **PRODUCTION** 10 000 cases

**WINEMAKER** Phillip Tonkin

**PRINCIPAL WINES** Chard, Sauv Bl, Fumé, Ries, Pinot, Shir, Cab Sauv, fortifieds.

**BEST VINTAGES W** '84, '86, '89, '90 **R** '84, '85, '87, '89

**SUMMARY** Constant name changes (Santa Rosa, Tonkins have also been tried) do not help the quest for identity or recognition in the market place, but the winery has nonetheless produced some outstanding wood-matured whites and pleasant, soft reds selling at attractive prices. The '90 Chardonnay is a beautifully crafted wine, with piercing melon/grapefruit flavours, great length and subtle oak.

## DALFARRAS  B–B Est 1991 NFR $10.95–15.50 R
GOULBURN V

PO Box 123, Nagambie, Vic 3608 (057) 94 2637

**OPEN** Not  **PRODUCTION** 15 500 cases

**WINEMAKER** Alister Purbrick

**PRINCIPAL WINES** Chard, Sauv Bl, Marsanne, Shir, Cab Malb.

**SUMMARY** The personal project of Alister Purbrick and artist-wife Rosa Dalfarra, whose paintings adorn the labels of the wines. Alister, of course, is best known as winemaker at Chateau Tahbilk, the family winery and home, but this range of wines is intended (in Alister's words) to 'allow me to expand my winemaking horizons and mould wines in styles different to Chateau Tahbilk'. Quality is all one could expect, particularly the luscious '89 Marsanne.

## DALRYMPLE  NR Est 1987 LR/CD/ML $10–12 ML TAS

Heemskerk/Lebrina Road, Pipers Brook, Tas 7254 (vineyard only); postal

116 Frankland Street, Launceston, Tas 7250 (003) 82 7222
fax (003) 31 3179
**OPEN** By appointment **PRODUCTION** 1000 cases
**WINEMAKERS** Heemskerk (Contract for white wines), Andrew
Hood/Holm Oak (Contract for red wines)
**PRINCIPAL WINES** Chard, Pinot.
**SUMMARY** A partnership between Jill Mitchell and her sister and
brother-in-law, Anne and Bertel Sundstrup, inspired by father Bill
Mitchell's establishment of the Tamarway Vineyard in the late 1960s. In
1991 Tamarway reverted to the Sundstrup and Mitchell families, and it
too, will be producing wine in the future, probably under its own label
but sold ex the Dalrymple cellar door.

## DALWHINNIE A–A Est 1976 LR/CD/ML/UK
(Enotria, Gullin & Co) $16–18 R PYRENEES
Taltarni Road, Moonambel, Vic 3478 (054) 67 2388
**OPEN** 7 days 10–5 **PRODUCTION** 3000 cases
**WINEMAKER** David Jones
**PRINCIPAL WINES** Chard, Cab Sauv, Shir.
**BEST VINTAGES W** '86, '87, '88, '90 **R** 82, '86, '88, '89, '91
**SUMMARY** Hit a purple patch with its 1988 reds and 1990 Chardonnay,
confirming the latent promise of earlier vintages. The red wines are typical
of the Pyrenees, massive and chewy, but with fruit to burn; while the
Chardonnay is simply great, melon-accented, fine, elegant and long.

## DALYUP RIVER ESTATE NR Est 1987 LR/CD $9 CD
LWR GRT STHN
Murray's Road, Esperance, WA 6450 (090) 76 5027
**OPEN** W'ends 10–4 **PRODUCTION** 350 cases
**WINEMAKER** John Wade
**PRINCIPAL WINES** Ries, Chard, Shir.
**SUMMARY** Light but fresh 1990 vintage white wines were a quiet
debut, but with contract-making by John Wade at Plantagenet the future
seems assured.

## D'AQUINO'S NR Est 1952 LR/CD $4.99–6.99 R ORANGE
129-133 Bathurst Road, Orange, NSW 2800 (063) 62 7381
**OPEN** 7 days 9.30–8 **PRODUCTION** 3000 cases
**WINEMAKER** Rex D'Aquino
**PRINCIPAL WINES** Table, fortified, sparkl, flavoured wines.
**SUMMARY** An interesting outpost of the industry: Rex D'Aquino
graduated from Roseworthy in 1981 and makes wines from grapes
purchased in various parts of Australia, as well as operating a bonded-
spirit store and bottling plant and a large retail shop offering wines from
most well-known Australian wineries.

## D'ARENBERG B–BA Est 1928 NFR/CD/ML/UK (pending)
$6–15 CD STHN VALES
Osborn Road, McLaren Vale, SA 5171 (08) 323 8206
**OPEN** Mon–Sat/hols 9–5, Sun 12–4 **PRODUCTION** 57 000 cases
**WINEMAKER** Chester Osborn
**PRINCIPAL WINES** Chard, Ries, Wh Burg, Shir Cab Sauv, Shir, Burg.
**BEST VINTAGES W** '85, '87, '89, '90 **R** '86, '87, '88, '89
**SUMMARY** A rock of ages, yet showing some signs of moving with the
times, flirting with avant-garde packaging while continuing to make soft,
velvety McLaren Vale red wines which age with grace, and the occasional
startlingly good white wine. A sentimental favourite, I have to admit.

## DARLING ESTATE NR Est 1986 LR/CD/ML $9 CD
NE VIC

Whitfield/Myrtelford Road, Cheshunt, Vic 3678
phone and fax (057) 298 396
**OPEN** By appointment **PRODUCTION** 350 cases
**WINEMAKER** Guy Darling
**PRINCIPAL WINES** Chenin Bl, Pinot.
**SUMMARY** A long term grape grower in the King Valley, until 1991 a major supplier to Brown Bros, but with a parallel vineyard operation on the family tobacco farm.

## DARLING PARK  NR Est 1986 LR/CD/ML
MORNINGTON P
Lot 1 Browne Lane, Red Hill, Vic 3937   (059) 89 2732
**OPEN** W'ends 10–4  **PRODUCTION** 300 cases
**WINEMAKER** Kevin McCarthy
**PRINCIPAL WINES** Chard, Cab Merl.
**SUMMARY** First vintage in 1991, with cellar-door sales open from December 1991.

## DARLINGTON ESTATE  NR Est 1983 LR/CD/ML $9–15
CD  PERTH HILLS
Lot 39 Nelson Road, Glen Forrest, WA 6071   (09) 299 6268
**OPEN** Wed–Sat 12–5 Sun 10–5  **PRODUCTION** 2500 cases
**WINEMAKER** Balthazar van der Meer
**PRINCIPAL WINES** Chard, Sem Sauv Bl, Chenin, Colomb, Shir, Cab Sauv, Port.
**SUMMARY** In 1988 and 1989 Darlington showed just what the Perth Hills could achieve with Chardonnay, Semillon/Sauvignon Blanc and (in 1988) Cabernet Sauvignon — wines with great style, flavour and length. Subsequent vintages have disappointed except for a substantial, flavoursome 1989 Cabernet Sauvignon.

## DAVID TRAEGER WINES  B–B Est 1988 LR/ML
$11–14 R  GOULBURN V
399 High Street, Nagambie, Vic 3608  (057) 94 2318
**OPEN** Not  **PRODUCTION** 3000 cases
**WINEMAKER** David Traeger
**PRINCIPAL WINES** Verd, Shir, Cab.
**SUMMARY** David Traeger learnt much during his years as assistant winemaker at Mitchelton, and produced a quite delectable 1991 Verdelho, with the aroma and flavour of a white peach and just a touch of smoky oak.

## DAWSON ESTATE  CB–B Est 1980 NFR/CD/ML $9–12 CD
HUNTER V
Londons Road, Lovedale, NSW 2325   (049) 90 2904  fax (049) 91 1886
**OPEN** 7 days 9–5  **PRODUCTION** 5000 cases
**WINEMAKER** Ben Dawson
**PRINCIPAL WINES** Chard, Tram Ries.
**BEST VINTAGES  W** '80, '83, '86, '87, '91
**SUMMARY** A Chardonnay specialist producing wines of somewhat variable quality, but at their best showing all of the buttery, peachy richness one could hope for, and which repay cellaring.

## DE BORTOLI  CA–B Est 1928 NR/CD/ML/UK (Halewood)
$4–30 CD  GRIFFITH
De Bortoli Road, Bilbul, NSW 2680  (069) 63 5344  fax (069) 63 5382
**OPEN** Mon–Sat 8–5.30  **PRODUCTION** 1.6 million cases
**WINEMAKER** Darren De Bortoli
**PRINCIPAL WINES** Botrytis Sem, Chard, Ries, Sauv Bl, Chab, Shir, Pinot, Cab Sauv, Merl principally under Deen de Bortoli brand.
**BEST VINTAGES  W** '85, '87, '88, '90, '91 **R** '82, '86, '88, '91
**SUMMARY** Famous among the cognoscenti for its superb Botrytis

Semillon (the '87 is quite magnificent), which in fact accounts for only a minute part of its total production, this winery turns around low-priced varietal and generic wines which neither aspire to nor achieve any particular distinction. Financial and marketing acumen makes de Bortoli the fastest-growing large winery in Australia today.

**DE BORTOLI**   BA–A Est 1971 NFR/CD/ML/UK (Halewood) $10–16 R   YARRA V
Pinnacle Lane, Dixons Creek, Vic  3775   (059) 65 2271
**OPEN** Mon–Fri 9–5, w'ends 10–5.30 **PRODUCTION** 50 000 cases
**WINEMAKER** Steven Webber
**PRINCIPAL WINES** Chard, Ries, Shir, Pinot, Cab Sauv, Cab Shir; second label Windy Peak.
**BEST VINTAGES W** '89, '90, '91 **R** '88, '89, '90, '91
**SUMMARY** The former Chateau Yarrinya, now the quality arm of the bustling de Bortoli group, run by Leanne de Bortoli and husband Steven Webber, ex-Lindeman winemaker. Both the top label (de Bortoli) and the second label (Windy Peak) offer wines of consistently good quality and excellent value; the complex Chardonnay is often the pick of the crop, but the 1991 Windy Peak wines are utterly exceptional in their price bracket.

**DELACOLLINE ESTATE**   NR Est 1984 LR  $10–15 R
PORT LINCOLN
Whillas Road, Port Lincoln, SA 5606   (086) 82 5277
**OPEN** Not  **PRODUCTION** 2000 cases
**WINEMAKER** Tony Bassett
**PRINCIPAL WINES** Ries, Fumé Bl, Cab Sauv.
**SUMMARY** Joins Boston Bay as the second Port Lincoln producer; the white wines are made under contract by Tim Knappstein and the red wines by Neil Pike. The fragrant, toasty 1991 Rhine Riesling deservedly topped its class in the 1992 Winewise Small Winemakers competition.

**DELAMERE**   B–B Est 1983 LR/CD/ML $19 R  PIPERS BROOK
Bridport Road, Pipers Brook, Tas 7254   (003) 82 7190
**OPEN** 7 days 11–5  **PRODUCTION** 650 cases
**WINEMAKER** Richard H. Richardson
**PRINCIPAL WINES** Chard, Pinot.
**SUMMARY** Richie Richardson produces elegant, rather light-bodied wines which have a strong following. The Chardonnay has been most successful, particularly in 1991, with a textured, complex, malolactic-influenced wine with great, creamy feel in the mouth.

**DELATITE**   B–B Est 1982 NFR/CD/ML/UK (Anthony Byrne Wines) $10–16.50 CD   CENTRAL VIC
Stoneys Road, Mansfield, Vic 3722   (057) 75 2922  fax (057) 75 2911
**OPEN** 7 days 9–6  **PRODUCTION** 11 500 cases
**WINEMAKER** Rosalind Ritchie
**PRINCIPAL WINES** Sauv Bl, Ries, Gewurz, Chard, Malb, Shir, Pinot, sparkl.
**BEST VINTAGES W** '82, '86, '87, '90 **R** '82, '86, '88, '90
**SUMMARY** With its sweeping views across to the snow-clad Alps, this is uncompromising cool-climate viticulture, and the wines naturally reflect the climate. Light but intense Riesling and spicy Traminer flower with a year or two in bottle, and in years such as '88 and '90 the red wines achieve flavour and mouth-feel.

**DENNIS' DARINGA**   CB–B Est 1974 LR/CD/ML $14.40 R
STHN VALES
Kangarilla Road, McLaren Vale, SA 5171   (08) 323 8665  fax (08) 323 9121
**OPEN** 7 days 10–5  **PRODUCTION** NFP

**WINEMAKER** Peter Dennis
**PRINCIPAL WINES** Sauv Bl, Chard, Cab Sauv, Merl.
**SUMMARY** Low profile winery which has, from time to time, made some excellent wines, most notably typically full-blown, buttery/peachy Chardonnay.

### DEVIL'S LAIR NR Est 1981 LR/ML/UK $12.95–16.95 CD MARGARET R

Rocky Road, Forest Grove via Margaret River, WA 6285 (09) 386 2200; postal 80 Stirling Highway, Nedlands, WA 6099
**OPEN** via Captain Sterling Hotel, Nedlands, Sat 11–2
**PRODUCTION** 6500 cases
**WINEMAKER** John Wade (Contract)
**PRINCIPAL WINES** Chard, Sauv Bl, Sem, Pinot, Cab Sauv.
**SUMMARY** A new but very substantial operation, with just under 35 hectares of vineyard planted by the end of 1992. A 14 hectare lake, stocked with trout and yabbies, services the vineyard and adds to the beauty of the site. The project is a joint venture between former leading retailer John Jens, who trained at both Roseworthy College and the University of Santa Clara, California, and Phil Sexton, who started the Redback Brewery.

### DIAMOND VALLEY BA–A Est 1976 NFR/ML $9–17 CD YARRA V

Kinglake Road, St Andrews, Vic 3761 (03) 710 1484 fax (03) 710 1369
**OPEN** Not **PRODUCTION** 5000 cases
**WINEMAKER** David Lance
**PRINCIPAL WINES** Ries, Chard, Pinot, Cabernet (Bordeaux blend).
**BEST VINTAGES W** '84, '86, '89, '90 **R** '86, '88, '90, '91
**SUMMARY** One of the Yarra Valley's finest producers of Pinot Noir, and an early pace-setter for the variety, making wines of tremendous style and crystal clear varietal character. They are not Cabernet Sauvignon look-alikes, but true Pinot Noir, fragrant and intense, deceptively light in body, none better (or richer) than the glorious 1990 Estate Pinot Noir, a winner of seven trophies.

### DOMAINE CHANDON A–A Est 1986 NFR/CD/UK (Moet et Chandon UK) $19.50 R YARRA V

Greenpoint, Maroondah Highway, Coldstream, Vic 3770 (03) 739 1110 fax (03) 739 1095
**OPEN** 7 days 11–4.30 **PRODUCTION** 17 000 cases
**WINEMAKERS** Dr Tony Jordan and Wayne Donaldson
**PRINCIPAL WINES** Meth Champ only, under various numbered Cuvee labels (eg 89.1) with occasional regional and varietal releases (eg Yarra Valley Blanc de Noirs 88.3).
**SUMMARY** Wholly owned by Moet et Chandon, and by far the largest and most important wine facility in the Yarra Valley, superbly located with luxurious tasting facilities (a small tasting charge is levied). The wines are exemplary, thought by many to be the best produced by Moet et Chandon in any of its overseas subsidiary operations, a complex blend of French and Australian style.

### DONOLGA C–B Est 1979 CD/ML $5.75–7.80 CD STHN VALES

Main South Road, Aldinga, SA 5173 (085) 56 3179
**OPEN** 7 days 10–5 **PRODUCTION** 8500 cases
**WINEMAKER** Nick Girolamo
**PRINCIPAL WINES** Chard, Sauv Bl, Ries, Cab Sauv, Shir, Claret.
**BEST VINTAGES W** '86, '89, '90, '91 **R** '80, '85, '86, '90
**SUMMARY** Almost an anachronism in this day and age, selling entirely from cellar door to a local, largely ethnic clientele at prices which

compete with the supermarket specials.

**DONOVAN** CB–B Est 1977 LR/CD/ML $10–14.50 R
GRT WESTERN
Pomonal Road, Stawell, Vic 3380 (053) 58 2727
**OPEN** 7 days 10–4 **PRODUCTION** 2000 cases
**WINEMAKER** Chris Peters
**PRINCIPAL WINES** Ries, Dry Wh, Shir.
**BEST VINTAGES W** '89, '90 **R** '82, '85, '87, '88
**SUMMARY** Part-time winemaker and full-time school teacher Chris
Peters quietly makes some attractively fragrant Riesling (an excellent
crisp, toasty '91) and concentrated, powerful Shiraz for the Donovan
family, most of which is sold cellar door and by mail order.

**DOONKUNA ESTATE** BA–BA Est 1973 CD/ML $11–15
CD CANBERRA
Barton Highway, Murrumbateman, ACT 2582 (06) 227 5885
**OPEN** Mon–Fri 10–4 **PRODUCTION** 2000 cases
**WINEMAKER** Jan Murray
**PRINCIPAL WINES** Ries, Fumé, Chard, Pinot, Cab Sauv.
**BEST VINTAGES W** '87, '88, '89, '90 **R** '87, '88, '89, '90
**SUMMARY** With judicious help from consultants, Lady Janette Murray
will continue the work of the late Sir Brian Murray, former Victorian
Governor General, in making some of the best white wines in the
Canberra district, and forceful reds of somewhat lesser finesse, but turning
for the better with minty-flavoured '90s.

**DRAYTON'S** CA–BA Est 1853 LR/CD/ML $9.20–13.20 R
HUNTER V
Oakey Creek Rd, Cessnock, NSW 2321 (049) 98 7513 fax (049) 987 743
**OPEN** Mon–Sat 9–5, Sun 10–5 **PRODUCTION** NFP
**WINEMAKER** Trevor Drayton
**PRINCIPAL WINES** Sem, Wh Burg, Ries, Chard, Verd, Sauv Bl, Herm,
Cab Shir, Cab Merl; Oakey Creek is second label.
**BEST VINTAGES W** '86, '88, '89, '91 **R** '86, '88, '89, '91
**SUMMARY** 1991 Verdelho (full-bodied, lush and soft), 1991
Chardonnay Semillon (gentle peach and a touch of spice) and 1990
Hermitage Bin 5555 (very clean, sweet berry fruit with good weight)
show this traditional winery in the best possible light.

**DROMANA ESTATE** A–A Est 1982 NFR/CD/ML/UK
(Haughton Wines) $12–19 R MORNINGTON P
Cnr Harrison's Road and Bittern-Dromana Road, Dromana, Vic 3936
(059) 87 3275 fax (059) 81 0714
**OPEN** Wint: First w'end month 11–4, Sum: all hols then each w'end 11–4
**PRODUCTION** 12 000 cases
**WINEMAKER** Garry Crittenden
**PRINCIPAL WINES** Chard, Sauv Bl, Pinot, Cab Merl; second label
Schinus Molle; third (export) label The Briars.
**BEST VINTAGES W** '86, '88, '90, '91 **R** '86, '88, '90, '91
**SUMMARY** The highest-profile winery in the Peninsula which has had
outstanding success with its wines in the United Kingdom. The wines are
invariably well made, with positive varietal flavour and fruit supported by
judicious use of oak, while still attesting to their cool-climate origins.

**DUNCAN ESTATE** B–B Est 1968 LR/CD/ML $9–12 CD
CLARE V
Spring Gully Road, Clare, SA 5453 (088) 43 4335
**OPEN** 7 days 10–4 **PRODUCTION** 2200 cases
**WINEMAKER** Blair Duncan

**PRINCIPAL WINES** Ries, Tram Ries, Sauv Bl, Shir, Merl, Cab Sauv.
**BEST VINTAGES W** '85, '89, '90, '91 **R** 85, '88, '89, '90
**SUMMARY** A crisp, clean and delicate 1991 Rhine Riesling; a surprisingly good warm, cherry accented 1990 Pinot Noir, and (best of all), a cleverly made and spicily oaked 1990 Cabernet Shiraz Merlot all show what a useful winery this is.

**DYSON MASLIN BEACH** C–CB Est 1984 LR/CD/ML $8.50–12.50 R STHN VALES
Sherriff Road, Maslin Beach, SA 5170 (08) 386 1092
**OPEN** 7 days 10–5 **PRODUCTION** 1600 cases
**WINEMAKER** Allan Dyson
**PRINCIPAL WINES** Chard, Sauv Bl, Pinot, Cab Sauv, sparkling.
**SUMMARY** Typically of the district, Sauvignon Blanc has been one of the more consistent performers in the Maslin Beach portfolio, showing good varietal character and depth of flavour.

**EAGLE BAY ESTATE** NR Est 1982 LR/CD $12.50 CD MARGARET R
Eagle Bay Road, Eagle Bay, WA 6281 (097) 55 3346
**OPEN** 7 days 10–4 **PRODUCTION** 880 cases
**WINEMAKER** F. G. Ley (Consultant Dorham Mann)
**PRINCIPAL WINES** Sem, Sauv Bl, Shir.
**SUMMARY** Limited tastings of initial releases have not impressed, but were insufficient to form a reasonable judgement. Consultant winemaker Dorham Mann has vast experience, and the area is, of course, one of the finest in Australia.

**EAGLEHAWK ESTATE** B–BA Est 1865 NR/CD/ML $7.50 CD CLARE V
Main North Road, Watervale, SA 5452 (088) 43 0003
**OPEN** Mon–Fri 9–5, w'ends 12–4 **PRODUCTION** 100 000 cases
**WINEMAKER** Stephen John
**PRINCIPAL WINES** Ries, Fumé Bl, Shir Merl Cab.
**BEST VINTAGES W** '88, '89, '90 **R** '80, '88, '90
**SUMMARY** The Eaglehawk white wines have been a model of consistency, and an even more perfect model of economy; the full-flavoured lime accented Riesling and high-toned, tangy gooseberry/herbal 1991 Sauvignon Blanc are both strongly recommended at the price.

**EDEN SPRINGS WINE ESTATE** NR Est 1990 CD/ML $8.50–10 CD ADELAIDE HILLS
Boehm Springs Road, Springton, SA 5235 (085) 64 1056
**OPEN** 7 days 10–5 (see Eden Valley Wines)
**PRODUCTION** 2000 cases
**WINEMAKER** Peter Thompson
**PRINCIPAL WINES** Ries, Fumé Bl, Tawny Port.
**SUMMARY** The twin of Eden Valley Wines, but with its own address and label.

**EDEN VALLEY WINES** NR Est 1990 LR/CD/ML $8.50–10 CD ADELAIDE HILLS
Main Street, Eden Valley, SA 5235 (085) 64 1111 fax (085) 64 1011
**OPEN** 7 days 10–5 **PRODUCTION** 10 000 cases
**WINEMAKER** Peter Thompson
**PRINCIPAL WINES** Ries, Gewurz, Spat Fronti, Chard, Pinot, Shir Cab; under both Eden Valley Wines and Eden Springs Wine Estate labels.
**SUMMARY** Offers two restaurants, an arts and crafts shop, sales and tasting, and accommodation centred around the old stone winery built by Penfolds, owned by Hamiltons for many years, and now owned by Peter

and Karoline Thompson. Both the 1990 Shiraz (ripe, minty/berry sweet fruit flavours) and the 1990 Cabernet (a fraction over-ripe) are full flavoured, well made wines.

### ELAN VINEYARD   NR Est 1980 CD/ML $10 CD
MORNINGTON P
17 Turners Road, Bittern, Vic 3918   (059) 83 1858
**OPEN** First w'end month 11–5   **PRODUCTION** 100 cases
**WINEMAKER** Selma Lowther
**PRINCIPAL WINES** Chard, Shir, Cab Merl.
**SUMMARY** Selma Lowther, fresh from Charles Sturt University (as a mature age student) made an impressive debut with her spicy, fresh crisp 1990 Chardonnay. Production will increase rapidly from the tiny 1991 vintage; worth following.

### ELDERTON   B–B Est 1984 NR/CD/ML/UK
(Barton Brownsden & Saddler, Australian Wine Centre) $8.95–26.50 R
BAROSSA V
3 Tanunda Road, Nuriootpa, SA 5355   (085) 62 1058 fax (085) 62 2844
**OPEN** 7 days 10.30–5   **PRODUCTION** 32 000 cases
**WINEMAKER** Neil Ashmead
**PRINCIPAL WINES** Chab, Ries, sparkl, Pinot, Shir Cab, Cab Merl, Herm.
**BEST VINTAGES** **W** '84, '89, '90  **R** '82, '86, '87, '88
**SUMMARY** One of the more successful middle-sized wineries since its debut in 1984 (the vineyards have been owned by the Ashmead family for much longer) driven by the tireless marketing zeal of Neil Ashmead, who is winemaker in name only. Fleshy, clean, generous Hermitage is consistently good.

### ELGEE PARK   B–B Est 1972 LR/ML $10–19 ML
MORNINGTON P
Wallaces Road, Merricks North, Vic 3926   (059) 89 7338
**OPEN** Queen's B'day W'end Sun/Mon   **PRODUCTION** 1800 cases
**WINEMAKER** Tod Dexter (Contract)
**PRINCIPAL WINES** Chard, Ries, Viognier, Cab Merl.
**BEST VINTAGES** **W** '86, '88, '91  **R** '80, '85, '88, '90
**SUMMARY** The pioneer of the Mornington Peninsula in its twentieth-century rebirth, owned by Baillieu Myer and family; it is uncompromisingly dedicated to quality, with no expense spared. The stylish, tangy barrel-fermented 1990 Chardonnay won the Chardonnay class at the 1992 Winewise Small Winemakers Competition, a long overdue success.

### ELLENDALE ESTATE   NR Est 1978 CD $8 CD
SWAN V
Lot 109 Corona Way, Belhus, WA 6055   (09) 296 4581
**OPEN** By appointment only   **PRODUCTION** NFP
**WINEMAKER** John Barrett Lennard
**PRINCIPAL WINES** A range of varietal and generic table and fortified wines.
**SUMMARY** Ellendale is effectively in recess as it changes premises, with winemaking scheduled to recommence in 1993. The accent has always been on no-frills wine of commensurately modest quality and price.

### ELSEWHERE   B–B Est 1984 LR/CD $12–15 CD   STHN TAS
Glaziers Bay, Tas 7112   (002) 95 1509
**OPEN** By appointment only   **PRODUCTION** 3800 cases
**WINEMAKER** Andrew Hood (Contract)
**PRINCIPAL WINES** Chard, Ries, Cab Sauv, Pinot.
**SUMMARY** Eric and Lette Phillip's evocatively-named Elsewhere Vineyard is producing consistently good wines, with the fresh,

cherry/berry 1989 Cabernet Sauvignon, with its touch of spicy oak, the pick of the bunch, followed by a crisp, herbaceous 1991 Chardonnay looking more like an unoaked Sauvignon Blanc.

**ELTHAM VINEYARDS** NR Est 1990 ML $14.95–18.95 ML YARRA V
225 Shaws Roads, Arthurs Creek, Vic 3099  (03) 439 4688
fax (03) 439 5121
**OPEN** By appointment **PRODUCTION**  500 cases
**WINEMAKER** John Graves
**PRINCIPAL WINES** Chard, Pinot, Cab Sauv/Franc/Merl.
**SUMMARY**  Drawing upon vineyards at Arthurs Creek and Eltham, John Graves (brother of David Graves of the illustrious Californian Pinot producer Saintsbury) produces tiny quantities of quite stylish Chardonnay and Pinot Noir, the former showing nice barrel-ferment characters.

**EPPALOCK RIDGE** C–C Est 1979 LR/CD/ML $13.50–18 CD BENDIGO
Metcalfe Pool Road, Redesdale, Vic 3444  (054) 25 3135
**OPEN** 7 days 10–6  **PRODUCTION**  2800 cases
**WINEMAKER** Rod Hourigan
**PRINCIPAL WINES** Sem, Chard, Cab Sauv, Shir.
**BEST VINTAGES W** '85, '87, '89, '90 **R** '85, '88, '91
**SUMMARY**  Rather tannic and astringent wines from 1989 and 1990 have emanated from the former Romany Rye winery, which owns the original Flynn and Williams vineyard at Heathcote.

**ERINACEA** NR Est 1988 CD/ML $14 CD  MORNINGTON P
Devonport Drive, Rye, Vic 3941  (059) 88 6336
**OPEN** By appointment only **PRODUCTION**  350 cases
**WINEMAKER** Ron Glyn Jones
**PRINCIPAL WINES** Chard, Cab Sauv, Cab Franc.
**SUMMARY**  Medical practitioner Dr Ron Jones added a winemaking and viticulture degree to his qualifications in 1988, and as well as making tiny quantities of wine, acts as a consultant to others in the region. The 1990 Chardonnay was an uncertain start, appearing high in volatile acidity.

**ETTAMOGAH** NR Est 1978 CD/ML $4.50–10.50 CD  STHN NSW
Tabletop Road, Tabletop via Albury, NSW 2640  (060) 26 2366
**OPEN** Mon–Sat 9–5, Sun 9–4  **PRODUCTION**  3500 cases
**WINEMAKER** Brian Wilson
**PRINCIPAL WINES** Champ, Chard, Sem, Ries, Mos, Spat Lex, Cab Sauv, fortifieds.
**BEST VINTAGES W** '85, '88, '89, '90 **R** '85, '88, '89, '90
**SUMMARY**  Formerly called Coopers Tabletop, now under the care of former Griffith-based winemaker Brian Wilson, who brings with him a wealth of experience, and who is concentrating on fortified wines.

**EVANS FAMILY** A–A Est 1979 LR/CD/ML $15–17.50 R HUNTER V
Palmers Lane, Pokolbin, NSW 2321  (049) 98 7333
**OPEN** By invitation **PRODUCTION**  2900 cases
**WINEMAKER** Rothbury (Contract)
**PRINCIPAL WINES** Chard, sparkl, Gamay, Pinot.
**BEST VINTAGES W** '82, '84, '86, '87, '88, '91 **R** '91
**SUMMARY**  Sold chiefly through the extended Evans family and friends — who are invited to regular no-charge lunches with Len and Trish Evans, who (in Len's words) 'are aiming to create a gentle wine-

house feeling'. Given the great quality of the unctuous, buttery Chardonnay, the value rating should be AAA.

**EVANS & TATE** BA–BA Est 1972 NFR/CD/ML/UK (Charles Taylor Wines) $13.85–27.95 R SWAN V AND MARGARET R
Metricup Road, Willyabrup, WA 6284 (09) 296 4666 Gnangara Estate or (097) 55 6244 Redbrook Estate fax (09) 296 1148
**OPEN** Mon–Fri 9–5, w'ends 11–4.30 Gnangara or 7 days 10.30–4.30 Redbrook **PRODUCTION** 20 000 cases
**WINEMAKERS** Bill Crappsley and Krister Jonsson
**PRINCIPAL WINES** Sem Sauv Bl Chen Bl, Sem, Chard, Shir, Herm, Cab Sauv, Merl.
**BEST VINTAGES W** '84, '88, '89, '90, '91 **R** '83, '84, '87, '90
**SUMMARY** Single-handedly changed perceptions of the Swan Valley red wines in the '70s before opening its highly successful Margaret River operation, there excelling with highly stylised Semillon, Semillon blends and Chardonnay, winning much acclaim with the '91 vintage whites.

**FAIRFIELD** NR Est 1959 CD $6.50–12.50 CD NE VIC
Murray Valley Hwy, Browns Plains via Rutherglen, Vic 3685 (060) 32 9381
**OPEN** Mon–Sat 10–5, some Sun 12–5 **PRODUCTION** NFP
**WINEMAKER** Stephen Morris
**PRINCIPAL WINES** Wh Herm, Mos, Rosé, Shir, Cab Sauv, Durif, fortifieds.
**BEST VINTAGES R** '80, '82, '85, '86
**SUMMARY** Specialist in red and fortified wines made with nineteenth century wine equipment housed in the grounds of the historic Fairfield Mansion built by G. F. Morris. A tourist must.

**FELSBERG** NR Est 1983 CD/ML GRANITE BELT
Townsends Road, Glen Aplin, Qld 4381 (07) 300 1946
**OPEN** W'ends 9–4.30 **PRODUCTION** 500 cases
**WINEMAKER** Otto Haag
**PRINCIPAL WINES** Chard, Ries, Merl, Cab Merl, Shir.
**SUMMARY** After a prolonged gestation, opened for business in late 1991; a full range of the 1991 vintage wines tasted early in their life showed a variety of winemaking problems which needed to be addressed before the wines were bottled.

**FERGUSSON'S** CB–B Est 1968 LR/CD $7.50–18.50 CD YARRA V
Wills Road, Yarra Glen, Vic 3775 (059) 65 2237
**OPEN** 7 days 11–5 **PRODUCTION** 2800 cases
**WINEMAKER** Peter Fergusson
**PRINCIPAL WINES** Meth Champ, Ries, Chard, LH Lexia, Shir, Cab Sauv, Cab Merl, some from the Yarra Valley, some from elsewhere.
**BEST VINTAGES W** '86, '88, '90 **R** '82, '83, '86, '90
**SUMMARY** The combined restaurant-winery complex is one of the most frequently visited spots in the Yarra Valley, catering both for the general tourist and the wine lover. 1990 Benjamin Cabernet Sauvignon is a rich, chewy dark berry/briary mouthful of wine.

**FERMOY ESTATE** NR Est 1985 LR/CD/ML/UK (Boxford Wine Co) $13.50–14.90 CD MARGARET R
Metricup Road, Willyabrup, WA 6284 (097) 55 6285 fax (097) 55 6251
**OPEN** W'ends 10.30–4.30 **PRODUCTION** 5000 cases
**WINEMAKER** Michael Kelly
**PRINCIPAL WINES** Sem, Sauv Bl, Pinot, Cab Sauv.

**BEST VINTAGES W** '89, '90, '91 **R** '88, '89, '91
**SUMMARY** The wines have disappointed after a singularly auspicious debut with a gold medal winning Cabernet Sauvignon, light, elegant and with lovely fresh red berry fruit.

**FISHBURN & O'KEEFE** NR Est 1991 CD/ML/LR
$13.50–15 CD UPPER DERWENT, TAS
c/- Meadowbank Vineyard, Glenora, Tas 7140 (002) 86 1238
fax (002) 86 1168
**OPEN** 7 days Richmond Wine Centre, 27 Bridge St, Richmond
**PRODUCTION** 1500 cases
**WINEMAKER** Greg O'Keefe
**PRINCIPAL WINES** Ries, Chard, Pinot, Cab Sauv, sparkl.
**SUMMARY** Wine consultant and contract winemaker Greg O'Keefe, formerly winemaker at Normans, has joined forces with Hutchins schoolteacher Mike Fishburn to produce wines made from grapes purchased from various growers across Tasmania, but with an estate vineyard in the course of establishment. Both the sparkling wine and the 1991 Rhine Riesling are very well crafted, reflecting Greg O'Keefe's considerable winemaking experience.

**FLOWERDALE** CB–C Est 1976 CD/ML $13–16 CD
CENTRAL VIC
Yea Road, Flowerdale, Vic 3717 (03) 606 4612
**OPEN** Sat/Sun 10–5 **PRODUCTION** 500 cases
**WINEMAKER** Ros Ritchie (Contract)
**PRINCIPAL WINES** Chard, Chenin, Tram Ries, Pinot.
**BEST VINTAGES W** '87, '89, '90 **R** '86, '87, '88, '89
**SUMMARY** It seems that in all except the warmest years the climate at Yea is just too cool to allow the grapes to gain the level of flavour and weight we expect from classic varieties.

**FLYNN & WILLIAMS** BA–BA Est 1979 LR/ML $14 ML
MACEDON
Flynns Lane, Kyneton, Vic 3444 (054) 22 2228
**OPEN** Not **PRODUCTION** 600 cases
**WINEMAKERS** L. Williams, J. Flynn
**PRINCIPAL WINES** Cab Sauv.
**BEST VINTAGES R** '81, '82, '88, '90
**SUMMARY** Produces a sought-after, single wine made from 100% Cabernet Sauvignon grown at Kyneton, a sub district of Macedon able to produce wonderful red wines in warmer vintages, exemplified by the '88 and '91 vintages.

**FRANKLAND ESTATE** NR EST 1988 LR/ML/ $11.65 ML
LWR GRT STHN
RMB 705, Frankland, WA 6324 (098) 55 1555 fax (098) 55 1583
**OPEN** By appointment **PRODUCTION** 3300 cases
**WINEMAKER** Kim Hart (Contract)
**PRINCIPAL WINES** Ries, Chard, Sauv Bl, Cab Sauv/Franc/Merl.
**SUMMARY** The initial release of 1991 Rhine Riesling showed intense, perfumed, fragrant citrus fruit with considerable power and intensity on palate, and not surprisingly received a series of very favourable reviews.

**FRASER** C–C Est 1987 LR/CD/ML $10–12 CD HUNTER V
Lot 5 Wilderness Road, Rothbury, NSW 2321 (049) 30 7594
**OPEN** 7 days 10–5 **PRODUCTION** 2000 cases
**WINEMAKER** Peter Fraser
**PRINCIPAL WINES** Chenin, Sem, Sauv Bl, Chard, Shir.
**BEST VINTAGES W** '87, '90, '91 **R** '87, '90

**SUMMARY** The first wines released were excellent, but subsequent vintages have been disappointing, with erratic oak handling a problem.

**FREYCINET ESTATE**   CB–B Est 1978 LR/CD ML $10–16
MARGARET R
Lot 1 Gnarawary Road, Margaret River, WA 6285   (097) 57 6358
**OPEN** 7 days 10–4.30   **PRODUCTION** 3–4000 cases
**WINEMAKER** Peter Gherardi
**PRINCIPAL WINES** Chard, Chenin, Sem, Sauv Bl, Cab Sauv, Pinot.
**BEST VINTAGES** **W** '86, '88, '89, '90 **R** '86, '87, '88, '90
**SUMMARY** West Australian government viticulturist Peter Gherardi
has produced some excellent white wines ('89 Chenin Blanc, '90
Chardonnay) and a most impressive sappy/cherry 1990 Pinot Noir, but
was moving to sell Freycinet at the time of writing.

**FREYCINET**   BA–B Est 1980 LR/CD/ML/UK (Boxford Wine Co)
$14–23 R   EAST COASTAL TAS
Tasman Highway via Bicheno, Tas 7215   (002) 57 8384
**OPEN** 7 days 9–5.30   **PRODUCTION** 25 000 cases
**WINEMAKER** Geoff Bull
**PRINCIPAL WINES** Ries Muller, Chard, Sauv Bl, Pinot, Cab Sauv.
**SUMMARY** Freycinet has produced some superb wines in recent years
thanks in part to skilled consultancy advice in both vineyard and winery.

**GALAFREY**   B–B Est 1977 NFR/CD/ML $8.50–14 CD   LWR
GRT STHN
145 Lower Sterling Terrace, Albany, WA 6330   (098) 41 6533
**OPEN** Mon–Sat 10–5   **PRODUCTION** 3800 cases
**WINEMAKER** Ian Tyrer
**PRINCIPAL WINES** Chard, Ries, Muller, Shir, Cab Sauv, Port.
**BEST VINTAGES** **W** '84, '85, '88, '90 **R** '84, '85, '86, '90
**SUMMARY** Despite his unconventional winery (in a 100-year-old
converted woolstore) and his idiosyncratic sense of humour, Ian Tyrer is a
serious winemaker ever trying to improve quality within the constraints
of a modest budget. His 1990 white wines are proof of that success.

**GALAH**   B–A Est 1986 ML $7.50–9 ML   ADELAIDE HILLS
Box 231, Ashton, SA 5137   (08) 390 1243
**OPEN** Not   **PRODUCTION** 1000 cases
**WINEMAKER** Stephen George
**PRINCIPAL WINES** Meth Champ, Ries, Sem (wood matured), Chard,
Shir, Cab Merl, Cab Sauv, Cab Malb, Port.
**SUMMARY** A unique operation run by Stephen George, consultant
winemaker at Wendouree and winemaker at Ashton Hills; it has a one-off
licence allowing mail-list sales only, and the wines are selected as
cleanskins from other makers or made by Stephen George from vineyard
sources across South Australia. Some astonishing bargains appear on each
list, such as the 1990 Clare Valley Shiraz (a pure, powerful wine) and the
1989 Clare Valley Cabernet (redolent with spicy cassis and berry flavours).

**GARDEN GULLY**   B–B Est 1987 LR/CD/ML $8.30–14.90 CD
GRT WESTERN
Garden Gully, Great Western, Vic 3377   (053) 56 2400
**OPEN** Mon–Fri 12–5, w'ends 10–5   **PRODUCTION** 2500 cases
**WINEMAKER** Brian Fletcher
**PRINCIPAL WINES** Chard, Rh Ries, Shir, Meth Champ.
**BEST VINTAGES** **W** '88, '89, '90, '91 **R** '88, '89, '90, '91
**SUMMARY** Given the skills and local knowledge of the syndicate which
owns Garden Gully, it is not surprising the wines are consistently good
across the entire range: an attractive stone cellar-door sales area is an

additional reason to stop and pay a visit. The tangy/citric '91 Chardonnay is especially recommended.

**GATEWAY ESTATE** NR Est 1989 LR/CD HUNTER V
Cnr Broke & Branxton Rds, Pokolbin, NSW 2321 (049) 98 7844
**OPEN** 7 days 10.30–4 **PRODUCTION** 3000 cases
**WINEMAKER** Colin Peterson
**PRINCIPAL WINES** Chard, Sem, Wh Burg.
**SUMMARY** A new, principally cellar-door operation; the wines are made by Colin Peterson at Wollundry, but quality is unknown.

**GEHRIG BROS** C–CB Est 1858 LR/CD/ML $6–15 CD
NE VIC
Cnr Murray Valley Highway and Howlong Road, Barnawartha, Vic 3688
(060) 26 7296
**OPEN** Mon–Sat 9–5, Sun 10–5 **PRODUCTION** 5000 cases
**WINEMAKER** Brian Gehrig
**PRINCIPAL WINES** Chenin, Ries, Sauternes, Pinot, Shir, Cab Sauv, fortifieds.
**BEST VINTAGES W** '84, '86, '88, '90 **R** '83, '86, '88, '90
**SUMMARY** An extremely antiquated winery — even by the standards of north-eastern Victoria — which is being slowly modernised; the fortified wines are still a great deal better than the table wines.

**GEMBROOK HILL** NR Est 1983 LR/ML $18 R YARRA V
Launching Place Road, Gembrook, Vic (059) 68 1622
**OPEN** Not **PRODUCTION** NFP
**WINEMAKER** Fiona Purnell (Contract)
**PRINCIPAL WINES** Sauv Bl, Chard.
**SUMMARY** After a number of years of trial and error, Melbourne dentist Ian Marks' investment in Gembrook Hill paid off handsomely with the superb 1990 vintage, with the crisp, pungent, herbal/tobacco-accented 1990 Sauvignon Blanc winning both a trophy and gold medals, and the elegant 1990 Chardonnay, with pronounced spicy/clove oak overtones in much the same class. Tiny but worth searching out.

**GEOFF MERRILL** BA–B Est 1980 NFR/CD/ML/UK
(Atkinson & Baldwin) $19–23 R STHN VALES
Cnr Pimpala and Byards Road, Reynella, SA 5161 (08) 381 6877
**OPEN** Mon–Fri 10–4, Sun 12–4 **PRODUCTION** 3500 cases
**WINEMAKER** Geoff Merrill
**PRINCIPAL WINES** Sem Chard, Cab Sauv.
**BEST VINTAGES W** '81, '84, '87, '88, '91 **R** '80, '83, '85, '87, '90
**SUMMARY** The premium label of the three wines made by Merrill (Mount Hurtle and Stratmer being the other two); always given bottle age, the wines reflect the desire of this otherwise exuberant winemaker for elegance and subtlety.

**GIACONDA** BA–B Est 1985 LR/CD/ML/UK (Yapp) $23.95 CD
CENTRAL VIC
Cnr Wangaratta and McClay Roads, Beechworth, Vic 3747
(057) 27 0246
**OPEN** By appointment only **PRODUCTION** 1000 cases
**WINEMAKER** Rick Kinzbrunner
**PRINCIPAL WINES** Chard, Cab Mer Cab Franc, Pinot.
**BEST VINTAGES W** '86, '88, '89, '90 **R** '85, '86, '88, '90
**SUMMARY** Wines which have a super-cult status and which, given the tiny production, are extremely difficult to find. All have a cosmopolitan style befitting Rick Kinzbrunner's international winemaking experience; the Chardonnay succeeds most frequently, but the '89 and '90 Pinots are very good, showing sophisticated use of oak.

**GILBERTS** NR Est 1980 LR/CD/ML LWR GRT STHN
RMB 438 Albany Hwy, Kendenup via Mt Barker, WA 6323
(098) 51 4028
**OPEN** 7 days 9–5 while wine available   **PRODUCTION** 300 cases
**WINEMAKER** John Wade (Contract)
**PRINCIPAL WINES** Ries, Chard.
**SUMMARY** The now mature vineyard, coupled with contract
winemaking by John Wade at Plantagenet, has produced small quantities
of high quality Rhine Riesling and Chardonnay; the tiny production sells
out quickly each year, both wines showing strong varietal character allied
with the backbone which one comes to expect from the region.

**GLENARA** C–C Est 1971 LR/CD/ML $9.80–17.90 CD
ADELAIDE HILLS
126 Range Road, North Upper Hermitage, SA 5131
phone and fax (08) 380 5056
**OPEN** 7 days 10–5   **PRODUCTION** 3200 cases
**WINEMAKER** Trevor Jones
**PRINCIPAL WINES** Ries, Chard, Rosé, Shir, Cab Sauv, Ries
Beerenauslese.
**BEST VINTAGES W** '86, '89, '90 **R** '83, '84, '85
**SUMMARY** Glenara did not commence sales until 1988; its vineyards
were progressively established from 1971, and it was a contract grape
grower for many years.

**GLENAYR** NR Est 1975 LR/CD $12–16 CD TAS
Back Tea Tree Road, Richmond, Tas 7025 (vineyard only); postal   PO
Box 38, Richmond, Tas 7025   (002) 622 2388
**OPEN** Not   **PRODUCTION** 65 cases (frost reduced)
**WINEMAKER** Chris Harrington (at Stoney Domaione A)
**PRINCIPAL WINES** Ries, Pinot, Cab Sauv.
**SUMMARY** Produces the rich, full-bodied reds for which the Coal River
region of Tasmania seems destined to become known, the solid, plummy
and rich 1991 Pinot adding to some previously impressive Cabernets.

**GLENFINLASS** NR Est 1971 CD $7–12 CD   WELLINGTON
Elysian Farm, Parkes Road, Wellington, NSW 2820   (068) 45 2011 or
(068) 45 2221
**OPEN** Sat 9–5 or by appointment   **PRODUCTION** 500 cases
**WINEMAKER** Brian G. Holmes
**PRINCIPAL WINES** Sauv Bl, Shir, Cab Sauv.
**SUMMARY** The weekend and holiday hobby of Wellington solicitor Brian
Holmes, who has wisely decided to leave it at that. I have not tasted the
wines for many years, but the last wines I did taste were competently made.

**GLENGARRY VINEYARD** NR Est 1981 LR $8.50–9.50
R TAMAR V
Loop Road, Glengarry, Exeter, Tas 7275   (003) 318077 (Vineyard only)
**OPEN** Not   **PRODUCTION** 850 cases
**WINEMAKER** Don Buchanan (Contract)
**PRINCIPAL WINES** Pinot, Cab Sauv.
**SUMMARY** Glengarry has passed through several owners in recent
years, but the vineyard continues to produce relatively low yields of
intensely coloured and flavoured Pinot Noir and Cabernet Sauvignon.

**GNADENFREI ESTATE** NR Est 1979 CD/ML $7–12 CD
BAROSSA V
Seppeltsfield Road, Marananga via Tanunda, SA 5353   (085) 62 2522
**OPEN** 7 days 10–5.30   **PRODUCTION** 9000 cases
**WINEMAKER** Malcolm Seppelt

**PRINCIPAL WINES** Ries, Gewurtz, Frontignan, Shir, Cab Sauv, Pinot Herm, Port, sparkl.
**SUMMARY** A small and somewhat reclusive cellar-door operation, which increasingly relies on wines made at other wineries.

## GOLVINDA
NR Est 1971 CD $9–12 CD GIPPSLAND
RMB 4635 Lindenow Road, Lindenow South via Bairnsdale, Vic 3865
(051) 57 1480
**OPEN** 7 days 9–6 **PRODUCTION** NFP
**WINEMAKER** Robert Guy
**PRINCIPAL WINES** Ries, Chenin, Chard, Cab Sauv.
**BEST VINTAGES W** '82, '85, '86, '89 **R** '82, '86, '88
**SUMMARY** Robert Guy pioneered the Gippsland area, and produced some attractive wines in the late 70's, but the spark faded thereafter; by no means all of the wines now sold are of Gippsland origin.

## GOONAWARRA
NR Est 1863 LR/CD/ML/UK (Nicks Wine Intern'l) $15.50 R MACEDON
Sunbury Road, Sunbury, Vic 3429 (03) 744 7211 fax (03) 744 7648
**OPEN** W'ends 10–6 **PRODUCTION** 1600 cases
**WINEMAKER** John Barnier, John Ellis
**PRINCIPAL WINES** Chard, Sem, Cab Franc.
**BEST VINTAGES W** '86, '88, '89, '90 **R** '86, '88, '89, '90
**SUMMARY** An historic stone winery, established by a nineteenth century Victorian Premier, which also houses an excellent restaurant and tasting complex. Wine style (and quality) is still evolving, but improving.

## GOUNDREY
BA–A Est 1978 NFR/CD $8.95–18.90 R LWR GRT STHN
Muir Highway, Mount Barker, WA 6324 (098) 48 1525
fax (098) 48 1018
**OPEN** Mon–Sat 10–4, Sun 12–4 **PRODUCTION** 32 000 cases
**WINEMAKER** Steven Warne
**PRINCIPAL WINES** Ries, Sem, Sauv Bl, Chard, Shir, Cab Sauv; Langton is second label.
**BEST VINTAGES W** '88, '89, '90, '91 **R** '81, '85, '88, '90
**SUMMARY** Now the largest winery in the region, and set to become much larger again. In the corporate sense somewhat controversial, but in winemaking a consistent producer of fine, steely, long-lived Riesling, sophisticated Chardonnay (1991 outstanding) and Sauvignon Blanc using barrel-ferment techniques, and superbly structured, tart Cabernet Sauvignon.

## GRAND CRU ESTATE
B–A Est 1981 LR/CD/ML $8–10 CD ADELAIDE HILLS
Ross Dewell's Road, Springton, SA 5235 (085) 68 2378
**OPEN** 7 days 10–5 **PRODUCTION** 5000 cases
**WINEMAKER** K. J. Seppelt
**PRINCIPAL WINES** Ries, Chard, Cab Sauv, Herm, sparkl.
**BEST VINTAGES W** '85, '86, '88, '90 **R** '86, '87, '88, '90
**SUMMARY** Karl Seppelt successfully orchestrates his contract winemakers (Petaluma makes the white wines) but, despite his prior position as Seppelt marketing director, has been less successful in obtaining the recognition (and the distribution) these consistently good wines deserve.

## GRANITE CELLARS
NR Est 1991 CD $9–12 CD GRANITE BELT
Lot 9 New England Highway, Glen Aplin, Qld 4381 (076) 83 4324
**OPEN** 7 days 9–5 **PRODUCTION** 400 cases
**WINEMAKER** Robert Gray

PRINCIPAL WINES Sem, Shir, Cab Sauv.
SUMMARY A new venture of Rumbalara partner Bob Gray, with the first wines released end 1991; also incorporates a BYO restaurant.

## GRANT BURGE B–B Est 1988 NR/CD/ML $9.95–24 CD
BAROSSA V
Jacobs Creek, Tanunda, SA 5352 (085) 63 3700
OPEN 7 days 10–5 PRODUCTION 65 000 cases
WINEMAKER Grant Burge
PRINCIPAL WINES Chard, Ries, Sauv Bl, Sem, Fronti, Merl, Cab Sauv, Shir; Mesach is premium old-vine Shiraz.
SUMMARY As one might expect, this former Krondorf wunder-kind makes consistently good, full-flavoured and smooth wines chosen from the pick of the crop of his extensive vineyard holdings; the immaculately restored/rebuilt stone cellar-door sales buildings are another attraction.

## GREVILLEA ESTATE NR Est 1985 CD $8.50–12.80 CD
SOUTH COAST
Buckajo Road, Bega, NSW 2550 (064) 92 3006
OPEN 7 days 9–5 PRODUCTION 3000 cases
WINEMAKER Nicola Collins
PRINCIPAL WINES Chard, Gewurz, Tram Ries, Cab Sauv, Pinot.
SUMMARY A tourist-oriented winery which successfully sells all of its surprisingly large production through cellar door and to local restaurants; 1991 provided a palatable Chardonnay.

## GROSSET CA–B Est 1981 NFR/CD/ML $10.95–16.95
R CLARE V
King Street, Auburn, SA 5451 (088) 49 2175
OPEN Wed–Sun 10–5 PRODUCTION 5000 cases
WINEMAKER Jeffrey Grosset
PRINCIPAL WINES Ries, Sem, Chard, Cab Sauv, Gaia (Cab Merl blend).
BEST VINTAGES W '87, '89, '90, '91 R '82, '86, '89, '90
SUMMARY These are wines crafted with the utmost care from grapes grown to the most exacting standards; all need a certain amount of time in bottle to fill out and gain complexity, although a few show disconcerting yeast characters. The 1990 Chardonnay (a blend of Clare and Piccadilly fruit) and 1991 Polish Hill Rhine Riesling are particularly good.

## HAINAULT C–CB Est 1980 LR/CD/ML $10–24 CD PERTH
HILLS
Walnut Road, Bickley, WA 6076 (09) 293 8339
OPEN Thurs–Sun 10–5 PRODUCTION 2500 cases
WINEMAKER Peter Fimmel
PRINCIPAL WINES Gewurz, Sem, Chard, Cab Merl, Pinot.
SUMMARY Peter Fimmel has been the guiding force in the Perth Hills, and his commitment to wine is absolute. I simply wish I could be more enthusiastic about his wines or believe the Perth Hills is the right area for Pinot Noir, Fimmel's particular love.

## HALCYON DAZE CB–CB Est 1982 LR/ML $12–18 CD
YARRA V
Uplands Road, Lillydale, Vic 3140 (03) 726 7111
OPEN By appointment PRODUCTION 1500 cases
WINEMAKER Richard Rackley
PRINCIPAL WINES Ries, Chard, Cabernet.
SUMMARY One of the lower-profile wineries with small, predominantly estate-grown production and no external consultancy advice. Rhine Riesling ages with grace.

**HANGING ROCK** CA–B Est 1982 LR/CD/ML/UK (Nicks Wines Intern'l) $6–35 CD MACEDON
The Jim Jim, Jim Road, Newham, Vic 3442 (054) 27 0542
fax (054) 270 310
OPEN 7 days 10–5 PRODUCTION 19 000 cases
WINEMAKERS John Ellis, David Creed
PRINCIPAL WINES Chard, Sem Sauv Bl, Sem, Pinot , Shir, Cab Merl in Reserve, Jim Jim and Victoria Ranges; Picnic Wines is a successful second label.
BEST VINTAGES **W** '88, '90, '91 **R** '87, '88, '90, '91
SUMMARY The Macedon area has proved very marginal in spots, and the Hanging Rock vineyards, with their lovely vista towards the Rock, are no exception. Some of the best wines are sourced from elsewhere in Victoria, with a few rich, textured and concentrated reds from Bendigo at the top of the tree, together with a tangy 1991 Sauvignon Blanc.

**HAPP'S** B B Est 1978 NFR/CD/ML $10–15 CD MARGARET R
Commonage Road, Dunsborough, WA 6281 (097) 55 3300
fax (097) 55 3846
OPEN 7 days 10–5 PRODUCTION 7000 cases
WINEMAKER Erl Happ
PRINCIPAL WINES Chard, Verd, Shir, Merl, Cab Merl, Marg River Red, Port.
BEST VINTAGES **W** '88, '89, '90, '91 **R** '84, '86, '88, '91
SUMMARY Former schoolteacher turned potter and winemaker Erland Happ brings a highly intelligent mind to bear on all his endeavours, suffering fools not at all. A very good Chardonnay made its debut in 1990, but Merlot (and Cabernet Merlot) remains the winery specialty.

**HARCOURT VALLEY** NR Est 1976 LR/CD/ML $9.50–14.50 CD BENDIGO
118 km post, Calder Highway, Harcourt, Vic 3453 (054) 74 2223
OPEN 7 days 9–6 PRODUCTION 1000 cases
WINEMAKER John Livingstone
PRINCIPAL WINES Chard, Ries, Shir, Cab Sauv.
BEST VINTAGES **W** '85, '88, '90, '91 **R** '84, '86, '87, '90
SUMMARY Recent wine show tastings of the '89, '90 and '91 vintage wines have not impressed greatly, with some inconsistency among the judges' views of the 1989 Cabernet Sauvignon.

**HAY RIVER** NR Est 1974 LR $18 R LWR GRT STHN
Denmark Road, Mt Barker, WA 6324
OPEN Not PRODUCTION 1000 cases
WINEMAKER Goundrey Wines
PRINCIPAL WINES Cab Sauv.
SUMMARY Used to produce high quality Cabernet Sauvignon, deep in colour and with ever-present cassis/mint aroma and flavour, but the '88 and '89 vintages have not impressed. Sold almost entirely in Western Australia through retail outlets only.

**HAYWARD'S** NR Est 1975 CD $6.50–9 CD GOULBURN V
Lot 18A Hall Lane, Seymour, Vic 3660 (057) 92 3050
OPEN Mon–Sat 9–6, Sun 10–6 PRODUCTION Over 500 cases
WINEMAKER Sid Hayward
PRINCIPAL WINES Ries, Shir, Cab Sauv, Cab Shir.
BEST VINTAGES **W** '87, '88 **R** '86, '88, '90, '91
SUMMARY Haywards of Whiteheads Creek (to give it its full name) produces massive raw, tannic red wines which defy conventional evaluation and demand both tolerance and patience.

**HEATHCOTE** BA–B Est 1982 NFR/CD/ML $8–13.50 R
BENDIGO
183–185 High Street, Heathcote, Vic 3523 (054) 33 2595
fax (054) 33 3081
**OPEN** 7 days 10–6 **PRODUCTION** 5000 cases
**WINEMAKER** Stephen Reed
**PRINCIPAL WINES** Chard, Chenin, Gewurz, Pinot, Cab Sauv, Cab Shir.
**SUMMARY** Consistent producer of high quality white wines, most notably
a spicy Gewurztraminer and tangy barrel-fermented Chardonnay; the red
wines are clean and flavoursome, though not quite in the same league.

**HEEMSKERK** CA–CB Est 1967 LR/UK
(Maisons Marques et Domaines) $13.95–29.30 R PIPERS BROOK
Pipers Brook, Tas 7254 (003) 30 1900 fax (003) 82 7242
**OPEN** 7 days 9–5 **PRODUCTION** 10 000 cases
**WINEMAKER** Jean Baptiste Lecrallon
**PRINCIPAL WINES** Ries, Botrytis Ries, Chard, Pinot, Cab Sauv.
**BEST VINTAGES W** '86, '88, '90, '91 **R** '84, '88, '90, '91
**SUMMARY** Has disappointed more often than it has pleased, but came
out with a superb, sophisticated oak and cherry/strawberry/plum Pinot
Noir in 1990 which delivers the promise so long held out by the Pipers
Brook region.

**HEGGIES** BA–B Est 1971 NR/UK (H Fichel & Sons) $12–18.50 R
ADELAIDE HILLS
Cnr Heggies Range/Tanunda Ck Road, Adelaide Hills, SA
(Vineyard only) (085) 64 2423
**OPEN** Not **PRODUCTION** 15 000 cases
**WINEMAKER** Brian Walsh
**PRINCIPAL WINES** Ries, Botrytis Ries, Chard, Cabernets.
**BEST VINTAGES W** '89, '90, '91 **R** '86, '88, '90, '91
**SUMMARY** Particularly noted for its toasty/lime Rhine Rieslings and
rich Botrytis Riesling, but its zesty/citrusy/grapefruit 1990 Chardonnay is
a high quality wine with fruit rather than oak (as hitherto) doing the
work, and the 1991 Rhine Riesling showing why Yalumba moved to the
Hills for its premium Riesling.

**HELM'S** CB–CB Est 1974 LR/CD/ML $9–13 CD CANBERRA
Butt's Road, Murrumbateman, ACT 2582 (06) 227 5536
**OPEN** Thur–Mon 10–5 **PRODUCTION** 1500 cases
**WINEMAKER** Ken Helm
**PRINCIPAL WINES** Ries, Chard, Tram Ries, Muller, Cab Sauv, Cab
Merl, Merl.
**SUMMARY** One of the more commercially-oriented and energetic of the
Canberra district wineries; but not helped by inconsistent quality. The 1990
Rhine Riesling was very good, the 1991 not so, but the 1989 Merlot and
1990 Cabernet Merlot are both attractive, the latter with rich, ripe berry fruit.

**HENKE** CB–B Est 1970 LR/CD/ML $10 CD GOULBURN V
Lot 30A Henke Lane, Yarck, Vic 3719 (057) 97 6277
**OPEN** By appointment only **PRODUCTION** 440 cases
**WINEMAKER** Tim & Caroline Miller
**PRINCIPAL WINES** Shir, Shir Cab, Cab Sauv.
**SUMMARY** Produces tiny quantities of deep coloured full-flavoured,
minty red wines known only to a chosen few; in 1992 reds from the
1985–87 vintages were still available at cellar door.

**HENLEY PARK** CB–B Est 1935 LR/CD/ML $6.80–14.50 CD
SWAN V
Swan Street, West Swan, WA 6055 (09) 296 4328 fax (09) 296 1313

**OPEN** Mon–Sat 9–6, Sun 10–6 **PRODUCTION** 2500 cases
**WINEMAKER** Vincent Desplat
**PRINCIPAL WINES** Chenin, Chab, Fronti, Beaujolpif, Cab Sauv, fortified.
**BEST VINTAGES W** '88, '90, '91 **R** '80, '84, '87, '88
**SUMMARY** Beaujolpif is a French nickname for Beaujolais, so we are told; it does not take much imagination to think of an Australian nickname in similar vein, but the wine is in fact one of the best from the winery. It is owned by a Danish businessman (since 1987), has a French winemaker, and nestles in the heartland of the Yugoslavian wineries of the Swan Valley, indeed a tribute to multiculturalism.

**HENSCHKE** A–A Est 1868 NFR/CD/ML/UK
(Lay & Wheeler) $11–35 R ADELAIDE HILLS
Moculta Road, Keyneton, SA 5353 (085) 64 8223
**OPEN** Mon–Fri 9–4.30, Sat 9–12 **PRODUCTION** 35 000 cases
**WINEMAKER** Stephen Henschke
**PRINCIPAL WINES** Chard, Chenin, Gewurz, Ries, Sauv Bl, Sem, Cab Sauv. Hill of Grace, Mount Edelstone and Cyril Henschke are the great red wine labels; Lenswood (Adelaide Hills) the new addition.
**BEST VINTAGES W** '82, '85, '87, '89, '90 **R** '82, '84, '86, '88, '90
**SUMMARY** Unchallenged as one of the top half dozen wineries in Australia, and has gone from strength to strength over the past 13 years or so under the guidance of Stephen and Prue Henschke. The red wines fully capitalise on the very old, low-yielding, high quality vines, and are superbly made with sensitive but positive use of new small oak; the same skills are evident in the white wine making.

**HERCYNIA** NR Est 1985 LR/CD/ML $7–14 CD HILLTOPS
Prunevale Road, Kingsvale, NSW 2587 (063) 84 4243 fax (063) 84 4292
**OPEN** 7 days 10–5 **PRODUCTION** 650 cases
**WINEMAKER** Peter Robertson (Consultant)
**PRINCIPAL WINES** Ries, Chard, Sauv Bl, Pinot, Port, Muscat.
**BEST VINTAGES W** '85, '87, '88, '91 **R** '85, '87, '88, '90
**SUMMARY** Former Barwang owner Peter Robertson is keeping his hand in at Hercynia, making a pleasant ripe, red berry 1991 Shiraz.

**HERITAGE** BA–A Est 1984 LR/CD/ML $9.90–11.90 CD
BAROSSA V
Seppeltsfield Road, Marananga via Tanunda, SA 5352 (085) 62 2880
**OPEN** 7 days 11–5 **PRODUCTION** 4500 cases
**WINEMAKER** Stephen Hoff
**PRINCIPAL WINES** Ries, Chard, Shir, Cab Franc.
**BEST VINTAGES W** '86, '87, '90, '91 **R** '86, '88, '90, '91
**SUMMARY** A little-known winery which deserves a far wider audience, for Stephen Hoff is apt to produce some startlingly good wines. At various times the Chardonnay, Rhine Riesling (from Old Clare Valley vines) and Shiraz have all excelled.

**HERITAGE FARM** NR Est 1987 LR/CD/ML $3.50–8.50 CD
MURRAY R
RMB 1005 Murray Valley Highway, Cobram, Vic 3655 (058) 72 2376
**OPEN** 7 days 10–5 **PRODUCTION** 1600 cases
**WINEMAKER** Kevin Tyrrell
**PRINCIPAL WINES** Ries, Chard, generic whites and reds, fortifieds.
**SUMMARY** A recent arrival on the scene; I have not tasted any of the wines.

**HICKINBOTHAM** NR Est 1981 LR/CD/ML $19.80 R
MORNINGTON P
Cnr Wallaces Road and Nepean Highway, Dromana, Vic 3936
(059) 81 0355 fax (03) 397 2629

OPEN 1st Sun each mth 11–5 **PRODUCTION** 3200 cases
**WINEMAKER** Andrew Hickinbotham
**PRINCIPAL WINES** Chard, Sauv Bl, Cabernets from various regions.
**SUMMARY** After a peripatetic period, and a hiatus in winemaking, Hickinbotham has established a permanent vineyard and winery base at Dromana, but continues to make small parcels from grapes purchased across Southern Victoria. Wine quality has recently been extremely variable and often disappointing.

## HIGHBANK NR Est 1988 LR/ML $14 COONAWARRA
Coonawarra, SA 5263
OPEN Not **PRODUCTION** 300 cases
**WINEMAKER** Dennis Vice
**PRINCIPAL WINES** Chard.
**SUMMARY** Mount Gambier lecturer in viticulture Dennis Vice makes a tiny quantity of smooth, melon-accented Chardonnay of good quality which is sold through local restaurants and a small mailing list.

## HIGH WYCOMBE NR Est 1975 CD $7–14 CD
BAROSSA V
Bethany Road, Bethany via Tanunda, SA 5352 (085) 63 2776
OPEN 7 days 9–4.30 **PRODUCTION** 1000 cases
**WINEMAKER** Colin Davis
**PRINCIPAL WINES** Ries, Fronti, Mose, Shir, Cab Sauv, Muscat, Port.
**SUMMARY** Colin and Angela Davis run what they describe as the smallest winery in the Valley and a holiday cottage complex, selling all of their wine on-site.

## HILL SMITH ESTATE BA–A Est 1982 NR/UK (H. Sichel &
Sons) $13.20–13.80 R ADELAIDE HILLS
c/- Yalumba Winery, Angaston, SA 5353 (085) 64 2423 fax (085) 64 2549
OPEN Not **PRODUCTION** 10 000 cases
**WINEMAKER** Brian Walsh
**PRINCIPAL WINES** Chard, Sauv Bl, Cab Shir.
**BEST VINTAGES** '86, '88, '90, '91
**SUMMARY** A modestly priced range which has played a significant role in the Yalumba group's export success, but which has hit an absolute purple patch with its releases from 1988 (superb, structured red berry fruited Cabernet Shiraz) and 1990 (pungent gooseberry/herbal Sauvignon Blanc and sophisticated spicy, passionfruit/grapey Chardonnay).

## HJT BA–BA Est 1979 CD $9.90–13.50 CD NE VIC
Keenan Road, Glenrowan, Vic 3675 (057) 66 2252
OPEN Fri/Sat/hols 10–5 **PRODUCTION** 1200 cases
**WINEMAKER** Harry Tinson
**PRINCIPAL WINES** Ries, Chard, Chenin, Pinot, Cab Sauv, Merl Cab, Cab Pinot.
**BEST VINTAGES** W '84, '85, '87, '90 R '85, '86, '87, '90
**SUMMARY** Harry Tinson, ex-Bailey's winemaker and revered for his Muscats and Tokays, produced a legendary Chardonnay in 1984 and (to a degree) deservedly lives off the reputation of that wine; it and subsequent Chardonnays have been the pick of the crop.

## HOLLICK BA–BA Est 1983 NFR/CD/ML/UK (Various)
$11–15.20 R COONAWARRA
Racecourse Road, Coonawarra, SA 5263 (087) 37 2318 fax (087) 37 2952
OPEN 7 days 9–5 **PRODUCTION** 16 000 cases
**WINEMAKERS** Pat Tocaciu and Ian Hollick
**PRINCIPAL WINES** Chard, Ries, Meth Champ, Pinot, Cab Sauv, Cab Merl, Shir; Ravenswood is deluxe label.

**BEST VINTAGES W** '84, '88, '89, '90 **R** '84, '85, '88, '90
**SUMMARY** Hollick has, if it were possible, added to the reputation of
Coonawarra since it released its first wines in the mid '80s. Winner of
many trophies (including the most famous of all, the Jimmy Watson), its
wines shine in all categories: crisp, floral Riesling, elegant barrel-ferment
Chardonnay, smooth but full flavoured Shiraz, and fragrant berryish
Cabernet Merlot and Cabernet Sauvignon.

**HOLM OAK** NR Est 1983 LR/CD/ML $21.95 R TAMAR V
RSD 256 Rowella, West Tamar, Tas 7270 (003) 94 7577
**OPEN** By appointment only **PRODUCTION** NFP
**WINEMAKER** Nick Butler
**PRINCIPAL WINES** Pinot, Cab Sauv.
**SUMMARY** Produces massively coloured and flavoured Cabernet
Sauvignon, underlining once again the particular climate of the Tamar
Valley. Both the 1990 and 1991 Cabernet Sauvignon tasted ex-cask in
February 1992 showed great promise, with amazing depth and power.

**HOPPERS HILL** NR Est 1990 CD/ML $10–12 CD CENTRAL
TABLELANDS
Googodery Road, Cumnock, NSW 2867 (063) 677 270
**OPEN** W'ends 11–5 **PRODUCTION** NFP
**WINEMAKER** Robert Gilmore
**PRINCIPAL WINES** Chard, Sauv Bl, Dry White, Cab Franc/Merl, Cab
Sauv.
**SUMMARY** The Gilmores planted their vineyard in 1980, using organic
growing methods and using no preservatives or filtration in the winery which
was established in 1990. Not surprisingly, the wines cannot be judged or
assessed against normal standards, but may have appeal in a niche market.

**HORROCKS** CB–CB Est 1981 NFR/CD/ML $10–13 CD
CLARE V
Mintaro Road, Leasingham, SA 5452 (088) 43 0005 fax (088) 43 0150
**OPEN** 7 days 10–5 **PRODUCTION** 3500 cases
**WINEMAKER** Jeffrey Grosset
**PRINCIPAL WINES** Ries, Sem, Chard, Cab Merl, Cordon Cut Riesling.
**BEST VINTAGES W** '82, '85, '87, '90, '91 **R** '85, '87, '89, '90
**SUMMARY** I do not profess to understand why, but with the exception
of the Cordon Cut Riesling (a sweet, late-harvest wine of considerable
flavour) and the Semillon (good in both 1990 and 1991), the wines fail to
impress in blind tastings. It may be I am out of tune with Jeffrey
Grosset's yeast selection; certainly the quality of the Ackland family's
(Horrocks owners) grapes should not be the problem.

**HORSESHOE VALLEY** NR Est 1986 LR/ML $14–16 R
UPPER HUNTER V
Horseshoe Road, Horseshoe Valley via Denman, NSW 2328 (065) 47 3528
**OPEN** By appointment only **PRODUCTION** NFP
**WINEMAKER** John Hordern
**PRINCIPAL WINES** Sem, Sem Chard, Chard.
**SUMMARY** Seems to have fallen by the wayside after a wonderful start
in 1987.

**HOUGHTON** A–A Est 1836 NR/CD/ML/UK (John Fells)
$7.90–18 R SWAN V
Dale Road, Middle Swan, WA 6055 (09) 274 5100
**OPEN** Mon-Sat 10–5, Sun 11–4 **PRODUCTION** 200 000 cases
**WINEMAKER** Peter Dawson
**PRINCIPAL WINES** Wh Burg, Chab, Sem, Verd, Ries, Rosé, Cab Sauv,
Shir Malb under four ranges: Show Reserve, Gold Reserve, Houghtons

Standard and Wildflower Ridge.

**BEST VINTAGES W** '83, '86, '89, '90, '91 **R** '82, '86, '89, '90.
**SUMMARY** The A–A rating may seem extreme, but is very deliberate and is in no small measure justified by Houghton White Burgundy, on of Australia's largest selling white wines, almost entirely consumed within days of purchase, but which is superlative with seven or so years bottle-age. To borrow a phrase of the late Jack Mann, 'There are no bad wines here'. The 1991 Frankland River Rhine Riesling, redolent of lime and passionfruit, is a particular success.

**HOWARD PARK** A–B Est 1986 LR/ML/UK (Societe Paul Martin) $16–29 R  LWR GRT STHN
Lot 11, Little River Road, Denmark, WA 6333   (098) 48 1261
fax (098) 48 2064
**OPEN** Not  **PRODUCTION** 1350 cases
**WINEMAKER** John Wade
**PRINCIPAL WINES** Ries, Cab Sauv.
**BEST VINTAGES W** '86, '87, '89, '90, '91 **R** '86, '88, '89, '90
**SUMMARY** Just two wines, made with infinite care by the diminutive but vastly experienced and skilful John Wade, and which vie with each other for longevity: the classic, lightly citrus/lime accented Riesling needs at least five years, the almost startlingly aromatic, cassis flavoured and spice-tinged Cabernet Sauvignon a decade or more.

**HUGO** B–B Est 1982 LR/CD/ML/UK (Haughton Wines)
$10.50–14.90 R  STHN VALES
Elliott Road, McLaren Flat, SA 5171   (08) 383 0098
**OPEN** 7 days 10.30–5  **PRODUCTION** 5000 cases
**WINEMAKER** John Hugo
**PRINCIPAL WINES** Ries, Chard, Cab Sauv, Shir, Port, Muscat.
**BEST VINTAGES W** '84, '86, '87, '88 **R** '86, '87, '88, '90
**SUMMARY** A winery on the ascendant both in terms of production and quality, initially driven by a range of quite spectacular peaches-and-cream Chardonnay and powerful, modern Shiraz with lashings of clove/spice American oak. Most recent releases ('89 reds, '90 whites) have been less impressive.

**HUNGERFORD HILL** CB–B Est 1967 NR/CD $8.50–17 CD  HUNTER V
Cnr McDonalds and Broke Roads, Pokolbin, NSW 2321 (049) 98 7666
**OPEN** 7 days 9–5  **PRODUCTION** 19 500 cases
**WINEMAKER** Patrick Auld
**PRINCIPAL WINES** Sem, Sem Sauv Bl, Chard, Pinot, Shir, Cab Merl, under standard and Show Reserve labels.
**SUMMARY** No longer a functioning winery (that task is left to Tulloch and Lindemans, under common ownership by S. A. Brewing) and with a somewhat uncertain future, uncertainty exacerbated by the dreadful 1992 Hunter vintage.

**HUNTER ESTATE** CB–B Est 1972 NR/CD $7.40–10.70 R HUNTER V
Hermitage Road, Pokolbin, NSW 2321  (049) 98 7521
**OPEN** 7 days 9–5  **PRODUCTION** 20 000 cases
**WINEMAKER** Neil McGuigan
**PRINCIPAL WINES** Chard, Fumé, Sem, Sem Verd, Tram Ries, Wh Burg, Pinot, Shir, Cab Sauv.
**BEST VINTAGES W** '83, '87, '89, '91 **R** '85, '87, '89, '91
**SUMMARY** A minor offshoot of the Wyndham empire, producing a somewhat mixed bag of wines, but always showing strong fruit and no regional astringency.

**HUNTINGTON ESTATE** BA–A Est 1969 LR/CD/ML $6.50–9.50 CD MUDGEE
Cassilis Road, Mudgee, NSW 2850 (063) 73 3825 fax (063) 73 3730
**OPEN** Mon–Sat 9–5, Sun 11–3 **PRODUCTION** 20 000 cases
**WINEMAKER** Bob Roberts
**PRINCIPAL WINES** Sem, Chard, Pinot Rosé, Cab Sauv, Cab Merl, Shir, Pinot.
**BEST VINTAGES W** '82, '84, '88, '90 **R** '81, '84, '86, '89, '91
**SUMMARY** Bob Roberts is one of the nicest men in an industry which seems to attract nice people, but that does not necessarily flow through to wine quality. Happily, in the case of Huntington Estate it does: he makes textured, complex red wines which age with extreme grace.

**HUNTLEIGH** C–CB Est 1975 CD/ML $9–11 CD BENDIGO
Tunnecliffes Lane, Heathcote, Vic 3523 (054) 33 2795
**OPEN** 7 days 10–5.30 **PRODUCTION** 250 cases
**WINEMAKER** Leigh Hunt
**PRINCIPAL WINES** Tram Ries, Cab Sauv, Shir.
**SUMMARY** A retirement hobby, with robust, rather astringent red wines which need time in bottle to lose some of the rough edges.

**HUNT'S FOXHAVEN ESTATE** NR Est 1978 CD/ML $8–11 CD MARGARET R
Canal Rocks Road, Yallingup, WA 6282 (097) 55 2232
**OPEN** School hols 11–5 or by appointment **PRODUCTION** 550 cases
**WINEMAKER** David Hunt
**PRINCIPAL WINES** Ries, Sem Sauv Bl, Cab Sauv.
**SUMMARY** Has only just commenced commercial operations, and is still tiny. The only wines tasted suggest David Hunt is still learning the trade.

**IDYLL** CB–B Est 1966 LR/CD/ML/UK (Mayor Sworder) $10.75–15.65 R GEELONG
265 Ballan Road, Moorabool, Vic 3221 (052) 76 1280 fax (052) 76 1537
**OPEN** Tues–Sun 10–5 & pub hol Mon **PRODUCTION** 6000 cases
**WINEMAKER** Daryl Sefton
**PRINCIPAL WINES** Idyll Blush, Gewurz, Chard, Bone Idyll (light, unoaked Shir), oak-aged Shir, Cab Shir, Cab Sauv.
**BEST VINTAGES W** '84, '87, '88, '90 **R** '82, '85, '86, '90
**SUMMARY** A stalwart of the region, producing wines in an individual style (pungent, assertive Traminer, long-vatted reds) which are almost as well known and appreciated overseas as they are in Australia; purists may cavil at the lifted character of the reds stemming from a degree of volatile acidity.

**INGOLDBY** BA–A Est 1973 LR/CD/ML/UK (Milton Sandford) $10–16.50 CD STHN VALES
Ingoldby Road, McLaren Flat, SA 5171 (08) 383 0005
**OPEN** Mon–Fri 9–5, w'ends 11–5 **PRODUCTION** 16 000 cases
**WINEMAKER** W. Clappis
**PRINCIPAL WINES** Chard, Sauv Bl, Ries, Colomb, Cab, Shir.
**BEST VINTAGES W** '84, '86, '88, '90 **R** '85, '86, '87, '90, '91
**SUMMARY** Bill Clappis is a larger-than-life character who does not allow his irreverence to overshadow the serious business of successfully marketing wines which are consistently very good, with Chardonnay, Sauvignon Blanc and Cabernet Sauvignon at the forefront.

**INNISFAIL VINEYARDS** NR Est 1980 LR/ML/CD $12–16.80 R GEELONG
Cross Street, Batesford, Vic 3221 (052) 761 258
**OPEN** Sun 10–5 **PRODUCTION** 2000 cases

**WINEMAKER** Ron Griffiths

**PRINCIPAL WINES** Ries, Chard, Cab Sauv.

**SUMMARY** This 4-hectare vineyard released its first wines in 1988, made in a small but modern winery on-site with a chewy, complex Chardonnay from both 1989 and 1990 attesting to the quality of the vineyards.

## IRONBARK RIDGE VINEYARD NR Est 1984
LR/ML $14 ML IPSWICH

Middle Road Mail Service 825, Purga, Qld 4306 (007) 281 4440

**OPEN** By appointment **PRODUCTION** 300 cases

**WINEMAKER** Peter Scudamore-Smith

**PRINCIPAL WINES** Chard.

**SUMMARY** Ipswich is situated on the coastal side of the Great Dividing Range, and the high summer humidity and rainfall will inevitably provide challenges for viticulture here. The initial release of brassy-coloured 1990 Chardonnay was an uncertain start, but the 1991 is more conventional in colour and flavour.

## IRON POT BAY NR Est 1987 LR/CD/ML $10.85 Ml
TAMAR V

Rowella, Tas 7270 (003) 94 7320

**OPEN** By appointment **PRODUCTION** 800 cases

**WINEMAKER** Andrew Hood (Contract)

**PRINCIPAL WINES** Chard, Sem/Sauv Bl.

**SUMMARY** Iron Pot Bay has made a singularly impressive debut with its 1991 wines, with a fragrant, fresh passionfruit/melon/tropical Chardonnay and a grassy/herbal/tobacco accented Semillon Sauvignon Blanc, neither given any oak maturation, but with the style to score consistently high points in a number of show and other tastings.

## JACKSON'S HILL NR Est 1987 CD/ML $10–15
HUNTER V

Mount View Road, Mount View, NSW 2321 (049) 90 1273

**OPEN** W'ends 10–5 **PRODUCTION** 650 cases

**WINEMAKER** Mike Winborne

**PRINCIPAL WINES** Sem, Cab Franc, Botrytis Sem.

**SUMMARY** A new arrival on the spectacularly scenic Mount View Road: I have not yet tasted the wines.

## JADRAN NR Est 1967 LR/CD/ML $6–12 CD SWAN V
Reservoir Road, Orange Grove, WA 6109 (09) 459 1110

**OPEN** Mon–Sat 10–8, Sun 11–5 **PRODUCTION** NFP

**WINEMAKER** Steve Radojkovich

**PRINCIPAL WINES** Ries, Herm, generic white and red table, sparkl, fortified.

**SUMMARY** A quite substantial operation which basically services local clientele, occasionally producing wines of quite surprising quality from a variety of fruit sources. The 1990 Shiraz showed attractive scented cherry fruit with a touch of spice.

## JAMES HASELGROVE CB–CB Est 1980 LR/CD/ML
$9.10–19.50 CD STHN VALES AND COONAWARRA

Main Penola-Naracoorte Road, Coonawarra, SA 5263 (08) 323 8706 and Foggo Road, McLaren Vale, SA 5171 (08) 323 8706

**OPEN** 7 days 9–5 **PRODUCTION** 12 000 cases

**WINEMAKER** Nick Haselgrove

**PRINCIPAL WINES** Meth Champ, Chab, Chard, Ries, Gewurz, Cab Shir, Shir, Cab Sauv, Port; variously from Coonawarra and Southern Vales fruit.

**BEST VINTAGES** **W** '80, '82, '84, '90 **R** '80, '82, '84, '90

SUMMARY The business was sold by receivers appointed in 1991 to a syndicate of Adelaide businessmen; it seems that the Haselgrove family will continue to be involved in a winery which has obvious potential, particularly given its Coonawarra vineyards. Lack of expenditure on new oak shows in many of the current release wines.

## JANE BROOK ESTATE  CB–CB Est 1972 LR/CD/ML
$10.50–14.50 CD  SWAN V
Toodyay Road, Middle Swan, WA 6056  (09) 274 1432  fax (09) 274 1211
OPEN Mon–Sat 10–5, Sun 12–5  PRODUCTION 9500 cases
WINEMAKER David Atkinson
PRINCIPAL WINES Chenin, Chard, Sauv Bl, Ries, Fronti, Cab Merl, Cab Sauv, fortifieds.
BEST VINTAGES W '83, '88, '89, '90, '91 R '83, '85, '87, '88
SUMMARY An attractive winery which serves light alfresco lunches every day, and produces a range of wines from both Swan Valley and Mount Barker fruit which never offend but which seldom scale the heights.

## JASPER HILL  A–BA Est 1976 LR/CD/ML $13–21 R
BENDIGO
Drummonds Lane, Heathcote, Vic 3523  (054) 33 2528
OPEN W'ends 10–6  PRODUCTION 2500 cases
WINEMAKER Ron Laughton
PRINCIPAL WINES Ries, Shir, Shir Cab Franc.
BEST VINTAGES R '85, '86, '88, '90
SUMMARY Much admired survivor of the 1987 bushfires who makes red wines full of character and flavour, typically needing a decade or more in bottle to start showing their best; 1990 produced two outstanding red wines in this mould. The Riesling is often ignored, but can be every bit as good.

## JASPER VALLEY  NR Est 1976 LR/CD/ML $4–12 CD
SOUTH COAST
RMB 880 Croziers Road, Berry, NSW 2535  (044) 64 1596
OPEN Mon–Sat 9–5, Sun 10–5  PRODUCTION 4000 cases
WINEMAKER Contract
PRINCIPAL WINES Sem, Tram Ries, Ries, Mos, Cab Sauv, Cab Shir, Lambrusco.
SUMMARY A tourist-oriented winery, with most of its wine purchased as cleanskins from other makers.

## JEIR CREEK  CB–B Est 1984 LR/CD/ML $9–12 CD
CANBERRA
Gooda Creek Road, Murrumbateman, ACT 2582  (06) 227 5999
OPEN W'ends 10–5  PRODUCTION 1600 cases
WINEMAKER Rob Howell
PRINCIPAL WINES Ries, Sauv Bl, Chard, Shir, Cab Mer, Botrytis Sem.
SUMMARY Rob Howell came to part-time winemaking through a love of drinking fine wine, and is intent on improving both the quality and consistency of his wines; a 1988 Shiraz Cabernet showed what he can achieve with red wines, but there is still a way to go with the aromatic white wines.

## JENKE VINEYARDS  NR Est 1989 LR/CD/Ml $7.50–10.50
CD BAROSSA V
Barossa Valley Way, Rowland Flat, SA 5352 (085) 24 4154
OPEN Mon–Fr 10–4.30, w'ends 11–4.30  PRODUCTION 1200 cases
WINEMAKER Kym Jenke
PRINCIPAL WINES Ries, Sem, Chard, Shir, Cab Sauv.
SUMMARY The Jenke have been vignerons in the Barossa since 1854, and have over 25 hectares of vineyards; a small part of the production is

now made and marketed through a charming restored stone cottage cellar door. The wood-matured whites (Chardonnay and Semillon) show abundant flavour and are of good quality.

**JIM BARRY**   CA–BA Est 1974 NR/CD/ML/UK (Tanners) $7.90–40 CD   CLARE V
Main North Road, Clare, SA 5453   (088) 42 2261
**OPEN** Mon–Fri 9–5, w'ends 10–4   **PRODUCTION** 70 000 cases
**WINEMAKER** Mark Barry
**PRINCIPAL WINES** Ries, Chablis, Sauv Bl, Chard (unwooded), Cab Merl, Cab Sauv. The Armagh is a Grange pretender.
**BEST VINTAGES W** '86, '87, '88, '89 **R** '84, '87, '88, '89
**SUMMARY** A marketing furore which broke out in 1991 underlined the problems the winery has had in achieving satisfactory distribution at prices which the best wines deserve; a pity, because it has excellent vineyards and some recent consultancy has lifted wine quality to an impressive level. The Armargh justifies its high price, a red wine of spectacular opulence, while the 1991 Watervale Rhine Riesling is a classic, with intense lime toast.

**JINGALLA**   B–B Est 1979 LR/CD/ML $9–15.50 CD   LWR GRT STHN
RMB 114 Bolganup Dam Road, Porongurup, WA 6324
phone and fax (098) 53 1023
**OPEN** 7 days 10.30–5   **PRODUCTION** 1200 cases
**WINEMAKER** Goundrey Wines (Contract)
**PRINCIPAL WINES** Ries, Verd, Shir, Cab Sauv.
**BEST VINTAGES W** '84, '86, '89, '90 **R** '86, '87, '89
**SUMMARY** Once-modest quality has greatly improved, perhaps due to the hand of (recently appointed) contract winemaker Claudio Radenti; a wonderfully spicy/cherry 1989 Shiraz and fleshy/peachy Verdelhos in both 1990 and 1991 are especially good.

**JOHN GEHRIG**   C–B Est 1976 LR/CD/ML $6.50–18.90 CD NE VIC
On Oxley to Milawa Road, Oxley, Vic 3678   (057) 27 3395
**OPEN** Mon–Sat 9–5, Sun 10–6   **PRODUCTION** 3000 cases
**WINEMAKER** John Gehrig
**PRINCIPAL WINES** Ries, Chenin, Chard, sparkl, Verd, Pinot, Cab Merl, fortifieds.
**BEST VINTAGES W** '85, '87, '88, '90 **R** '82, '85, '88, '89
**SUMMARY** Honest, if seldom exciting, wines; the occasional Chardonnay, Pinot Noir and Cabernet Merlot have, however, risen above their station.

**JOLIMONT**   B–B Est 1986 LR/CD/ML $8.60–18 CD   NE VIC
Cnr Murray Valley Hwy and Corowa Rd, Rutherglen, Vic 3685
(060) 32 9922 fax (060) 32 9030
**OPEN** 7 days 9.30–5   **PRODUCTION** 10 000 cases
**WINEMAKER** Steven Warne (Previous)
**PRINCIPAL WINES** Sauv Bl Sem, Chard, Ries, Herm Bl, Pinot, Cab Sauv, Shir, fortifieds.
**SUMMARY** Housed in the historic former Seppelt winery, with a splendidly renovated tourist complex and restaurant, Jolimont is strongly recommended to all visitors to Rutherglen; well-made wines in a diverse range of styles.

**JONES**   CB–C Est 1864 LR/CD/ML   NE VIC
Chiltern Road, Rutherglen, Vic 3685   (060) 32 9496
**OPEN** 7 days 9.30–5   **PRODUCTION** NFP

**WINEMAKER** Les Jones
**PRINCIPAL WINES** Chab, Ries, Wh Burg, Light Red, Dry Red, Ports and other fortifieds.
**SUMMARY** An ultra-reclusive and ultra-traditional winery (despite the garish labels) making no-frills wines. Les Jones even regards details of his current wines and prices as 'my business only'.

**JUD'S HILL** B–B Est 1977 NFR $8.99–16.95 R CLARE V
Farrell Flat Road, Clare, SA 5343 (vineyard only)
**OPEN** Not **PRODUCTION** NFP
**WINEMAKER** Brian Barry
**PRINCIPAL WINES** Ries, Chab, Cab Sauv, Cab Merl.
**SUMMARY** In reality a vineyard-only operation, with a substantial part of the output sold as grapes to other wineries, and the wines made under contract at various wineries, albeit under Brian Barry's supervision. As one would expect, the quality is reliably good.

**KAESLER FARM** NR Est 1990 LR/CD/ML $7.50–13.70 CD
BAROSSA V
Barossa Valley Way, Nuriootpa, SA 5355 (085) 622 711 fax (085) 622 788
**OPEN** 7 days 10–5 **PRODUCTION** 3000 cases
**WINEMAKER** Roger Harbord (Contract)
**PRINCIPAL WINES** Prestige Sem, Rhine Ries, Old Vine Shir, Cab Sauv, fortified.
**SUMMARY** Toby and Treena Hueppauff purchased Kaesler Farm, with its 12 hectares of vines, in 1985, and since 1990 have had the wines made under contract by Roger Harboard at Basedows. Solid Semillon and dark cherry blackberry flavoured Old Vine Shiraz are the best wines.

**KAISER STUHL** CA–B Est 1931 NR/CD $4.30–11.80 R
BAROSSA V
Tanunda Road, Nuriootpa, SA 5355 (085) 62 0389
**OPEN** Mon–Sat 10–5, Sun 12–4 **PRODUCTION** NFP
**WINEMAKER** John Duval
**PRINCIPAL WINES** Black Forest, generic whites under Bin Nos (Bin 44, 55, 66, 77) Claret Bin 33 and Green Ribbon Ries, Red Ribbon Shir as premium releases; sparkl (Summer Wine).
**BEST VINTAGES W** '84, '86, '88, '90 **R** '86, '88, '90, '91
**SUMMARY** Where the future positioning of Kaiser Stuhl will be within the S. A. Brewing empire is presently unclear, although quite possibly there will be little change; the Ribbon wines have been under threat from time to time, not because of quality, but because of supply, and this should not necessarily be a problem in the future. Green Ribbon Rhine Riesling can be superb with five to ten years bottle age.

**KARA KARA** NR Est 1987 LR/CD/ML $12 CD PYRENEES
Sunraysia Highway via St Arnaud, Vic 3478 (054) 96 3294
**OPEN** W'ends, hols 1.30–6 **PRODUCTION** 1200 cases
**WINEMAKER** Mitchelton (Contract)
**PRINCIPAL WINES** Fumé Bl, Chard/Sem, Sauv Bl.
**SUMMARY** Hungarian-born Steve Zsigmond comes from a long line of vignerons, and sees Kara Kara as the eventual retirement occupation for himself and wife Marlene. The first step has been the decision to have their production contract made by Mitchelton (previously the grapes were sold) with a most attractive, cleverly oaked Fumé Blanc marking an auspicious start for the winery.

**KARINA** CA–B Est 1984 LR/CD/ML $10–14 CD
MORNINGTON P
Harrisons Road, Dromana, Vic 3936 phone and fax (059) 81 0137

OPEN W'ends 11–5, except vintage  PRODUCTION 1600 cases
WINEMAKER Graeme Pinney
PRINCIPAL WINES Ries, Sauv Bl, Cab Sauv.
BEST VINTAGES W '88, '89, '91 R '89, '90, '91
SUMMARY The white wines are characterisically light-bodied and elegant, the red wines much richer, led by the 1990 and 1991 Cabernet Sauvignons (with a little Merlot blended in) which have abundant cassis berry fruit and good structure.

## KARRELEA ESTATE B–BA Est 1982 LR/CD/ML $8–14 CD LWR GRT STHN

Duck Road, Mount Barker, WA 6324  (098) 51 1838
OPEN Fri–Sun/hols 10–5  PRODUCTION 200 cases
WINEMAKER John Wade
PRINCIPAL WINES Ries, Sauv Bl, Pinot, Cab Sauv Franc Merl, Pinot.
BEST VINTAGES W '87, '89, '90 R '87, '88
SUMMARY A consistent producer of excellent lime/passionfruit Rieslings which have won gold medals; the elegant Cabernet/Franc /Merlot blend can also be good, proving that the strictly organic grape-growing methods used are not a whimsical folly.

## KARRIVALE B–B Est 1979 LR/CD/ML $11.50 CD LWR GRT STHN

Woodlands, Porongurup, WA 6324  (098) 53 1009 fax (098) 53 1129
OPEN W'ends 10–5  PRODUCTION 500 cases
WINEMAKER John Wade
PRINCIPAL WINES Ries.
BEST VINTAGES W '87, '89, '90
SUMMARY A tiny Riesling specialist in the wilds of the Porongurups forced to change its name from Narang because Lindemans felt it could be confused with its Nyrang Hermitage brand; truly a strange world. The '91 Riesling is typical, showing firm lime/toast fruit, and the certainty of improving with age.

## KARRIVIEW NR Est 1986 CD/ML $11.50–$17.50 CD LWR GRT STHN

Scotsdale Road, Denmark, WA 6333  (098) 40 9381
OPEN 7 days 10–4  PRODUCTION 750 cases
WINEMAKER John Wade
PRINCIPAL WINES Ries, Chard, Pinot.
SUMMARY One of the newest arrivals which announced its presence in no uncertain fashion by winning two trophies at the 1990 Mount Barker show for its stylish, elegant, oaky 1990 Chardonnay, which has continued to develop. Headed for top rating if it keeps this pace up.

## KATNOOK ESTATE BA–B Est 1980 NFR/CD $12.60–22.25 CD COONAWARRA

Off main Penola-Naracoorte Road, Coonawarra, SA 5263  (087) 37 2394 fax (087) 37 2397
OPEN Mon–Fri 8–4.30, Sat 10–4  PRODUCTION 60 000 cases (including Riddoch label)
WINEMAKER Wayne Stehbens
PRINCIPAL WINES Ries, Sauv Bl, Chard, Pinot, Cab Sauv.
BEST VINTAGES W & R '86, '88, '90, '91
SUMMARY The prestige label of the vast Coonawarra Machinery Company empire, with access to the very best grapes from large vineyard holdings, and also to some high level consultancy advice. The wines are invariably full flavoured, with very strong varietal character; recent Chardonnays ('90 especially) and Sauvignon Blanc ('91) have impressed.

**KAY BROS AMERY**   DC–CB Est 1890 LR/CD/ML $8–10
CD STHN VALES
Kay Road, McLaren Vale, SA 5171   (08) 323 8211 fax (08) 323 9199
OPEN Mon–Fri 8–5, w'ends 12–5   PRODUCTION 5000 cases
WINEMAKER Colin Kay
PRINCIPAL WINES Ries, Sauv Bl, Cab Sauv, Shir, Pinot, Pinot Shir,
fortifieds.
BEST VINTAGES W '81, '86, '88, '90 R '85, '86, '88, '90
SUMMARY A traditional winery with a rich history and some priceless
old vines; the white wines are not recommended, but the Block 6 Shiraz
in particular offers good value for seekers of mainstream reds.

**KELLERMEISTER**   CB–B Est 1970 CD/ML $8–18.90 CD
BAROSSA V
Barossa Valley Highway, Lyndoch, SA 5351   (085) 24 4303
OPEN 7 days 9–6   PRODUCTION 6500 cases
WINEMAKER Trevor Jones
PRINCIPAL WINES Chard, Sauv Bl, Ries Gewurz, Sem Wh Burg, Shir,
Cab Sauv, fortifieds.
BEST VINTAGES W '86, '88, '89, '90 R '83, '85, '86, '90
SUMMARY Specialises in older vintage wines made in traditional
fashion, an extraordinary array of which are on offer at enticing prices,
including Rhine Rieslings back to 1984.

**KELLYBROOK**   CA–CB Est 1960 LR/CD/ML $8–17.50 CD
YARRA V
Fulford Road, Wonga Park, Vic 3115   (03) 722 1304
OPEN Mon–Sat 9–6, Sun 11–6   PRODUCTION 2800 cases
WINEMAKER Darren Kelly
PRINCIPAL WINES Meth Champ, Apple Brandy Liqueur Cider,
Sparkling Cider, Old Gold, Chard, Ries, Gewurz, Moselle, Colomb, Cab
Sauv.
SUMMARY A cider and apple-brandy maker turned winemaker; despite
some excellent 1988 red wines, the apple based ciders — still, sparkling
and distilled — are the most reliable, indeed excitingly good, products.

**KILLAWARRA**   CB–B Est 1975 NR/UK (Penfolds UK)
$6.30–11.50 R BAROSSA V
Tanunda Road, Nuriootpa, SA 5355 (085) 62 0389 fax (085) 62 1669
OPEN See Penfolds   PRODUCTION NFP
WINEMAKER John Duval
PRINCIPAL WINES Chab, Chard, Fumé Bl, Cab Sauv, Brut and
Premier Brut Sparkling.
SUMMARY Purely a brand name of the Penfolds group, but capable of
coming up with one or two surprisingly good wines from time to time,
particularly the Sparkling Premier Brut.

**KILLERBY LESCHENAULT**   BA–B Est 1973 LR/CD/ML
$9–15 R   MARGARET R
Minninup Road off Lakes Road, Gelorup, WA 6230   (097) 95 7222
fax (097) 95 7835
OPEN Mon–Fri 10–5, w'ends 10–6   PRODUCTION 7000 cases
WINEMAKER Matt Aldridge
PRINCIPAL WINES Chard, Sem, April White and April Red, Cab
Sauv, Pinot, Shir.
BEST VINTAGES W '82, '88, '89, '91 R '86, '87, '89, '91
SUMMARY With former Rosemount winemaker Matt Aldridge (married
to Anna Killerby) in charge, this winery swept all before it with the 1989
Cabernet Sauvignon (made by the late Dr Barry Killerby and blended by
Matt Aldridge) which won four trophies at the 1991 Perth Show. The 1991

April Red is another most attractive wine, not unlike a true Beaujolais.

**KINGS CREEK** BA–B Est 1981 LR/CD/ML $17 CD
MORNINGTON P
237 Myers Road, Bittern, Vic 3918 (059) 82 1715
**OPEN** Sun 11–5 **PRODUCTION** 800 cases
**WINEMAKERS** K. Quealy, K. McCarthy
**PRINCIPAL WINES** Chard, Pinot, Cab Sauv.
**SUMMARY** Has followed its trophy winning 1990 Pinot Noir with an
even better wine in 1991, marvellously stylish and Burgundian; the 1991
Chardonnay is also excellent.

**KINGSLEY** BA–B Est 1984 LR/CD $10–12 CD WEST VIC
50 Bancroft Street, Portland, Vic 3305 (055) 23 1864
**OPEN** 7 days 1–4 **PRODUCTION** 2000 cases
**WINEMAKER** Seppelt (Contract)
**PRINCIPAL WINES** Ries, Cab Sauv.
**SUMMARY** The Rhine Riesling, both dry and botrytised, can be
outstanding, attesting to Seppelt's competence and to the potential of the
very cool region in more favourable vintages. The '91 is very herbaceous,
almost Sauvignon Blanc-like, but very good.

**KNIGHT GRANITE HILLS** CA–B Est 1979 LR/CD/ML
$9–16 R MACEDON
Lancefield-Mia Mia Road, Baynton RSD 391, Kyneton, Vic 3444
(054) 23 7264
**OPEN** Mon–Sat 10–6, Sun 12–6 **PRODUCTION** 5500 cases
**WINEMAKER** Lew Knight
**PRINCIPAL WINES** Ries, Chard, Shir, Cab Sauv.
**BEST VINTAGES R** '86, '88, '90, '91
**SUMMARY** Introduced Australia to the spicy/peppery style of Shiraz
almost a decade ago; at their best, these wines are superb, as was the '91
Shiraz tasted ex-cask, but they are sometimes adversely affected by late
bottling.

**KNIGHTS VINES** NR Est 1986 CD/ML $8.50–10.50 CD
MUDGEE
Henry Lawson Drive, Mudgee, NSW 2850 (063) 73 3954
fax (063) 72 2399
**OPEN** Mon–Fri 10–4, w'ends 9–5 **PRODUCTION** NFP
**WINEMAKER** Peter Knights
**PRINCIPAL WINES** Sem, Chablis, Wh Burg, Claret and fortifieds.
**SUMMARY** A very small winery concentrating chiefly on generic table
and fortified wines, which has recently changed hands (and name — it
was formerly Caloola).

**KOMINOS** CB–B Est 1976 LR/CD/ML $8–11 CD
GRANITE BELT
New England Highway, Severnlea, Qld 4352 (076) 83 4311
**OPEN** 7 days 9–4.30 **PRODUCTION** NFP
**WINEMAKER** Tony Comino
**PRINCIPAL WINES** Chenin, Sem, Chard, Light Red, Shir, Cab Sauv.
**SUMMARY** Tony Comino is a dedicated viticulturist and winemaker; in
late 1991 wines to impress were a peachy/melon 1990 Chardonnay, a
lively herbal/berry 1990 Cabernet Sauvignon and a promising
concentrated 1991 Shiraz.

**KROEMER ESTATE** NR Est 1986 LR/CD/ML $9.50–15.50
CD BAROSSA V
Tanunda, SA 5352 (085) 63 3375 fax (085) 63 3758

**OPEN** Mon–Fri 10–4.30, w'ends 10–5 **PRODUCTION** 2000 cases
**WINEMAKER** Roger Harbord (Contract)
**PRINCIPAL WINES** Sylv, Ries, Sparkl, Shir, Cab Sauv.
**SUMMARY** Opened its doors on 30 June 1990 specialising — of all unlikely grapes — with Sylvaner; the '86 vintage (first) has matured surprisingly well, but subsequent attempts have been less convincing. On the other side of the ledger, an elegant, toasty 1990 Rhine Riesling showed Roger Harbord's skill.

### KRONDORF B–B Est 1978 NR/CD/UK (Lawlers) $7.40–19 R BAROSSA V

Krondorf Road, Tanunda, SA 5352 (085) 63 1245 fax (085) 62 3055
**OPEN** Mon–Sat 10–5, Sun 12–4 **PRODUCTION** NFP
**WINEMAKER** Nick Walker
**PRINCIPAL WINES** Ries, Chab, Chard, Chard Show Res, Tram Ries, Herm, Shir Cab, Cab Sauv, Cab Sauv Show Res.
**BEST VINTAGES W** '87, '88, '90, '91 **R** '80, '86, '88, '90, '91
**SUMMARY** Yet another winery which found itself as part of a larger group in 1991, this time under the aegis of Mildara. The brands seem reasonably strong, and little overt change has eventuated. The 1990 Show Reserve Chardonnay, incidentally, was (and is) an outstanding wine.

### KYEEMA ESTATE NR Est 1986 LR/ML $8–12 ML CANBERRA

PO Box 282, Belconnen, ACT 2616 (06) 254 7557 (AH)
**OPEN** Not **PRODUCTION** 400 cases
**WINEMAKER** Andrew McEwin
**PRINCIPAL WINES** Sem, Chard, Shir, Cab Sauv.
**SUMMARY** The very small scale of production makes winemaking very difficult, but the 1990 Semillón and 1989 Cabernet Sauvignon (the latter particularly) are both pleasant wines.

### LAANECOORIE NR Est 1982 LR/ML $16.95 R PYRENEES

RMB 1330 Dunolly, Vic 3472 (Vineyard only); postal Bendigo Road, Betley, Vic 3472
**OPEN** Not **PRODUCTION** 1000 cases
**WINEMAKER** John Ellis (Contract)
**PRINCIPAL WINES** A single Bordeaux-blend dry red of Cab Franc, Cab Sauv and Merlot in roughly equal proportions.
**SUMMARY** The release current in mid 1992 from the 1988 vintage, is an excellent wine: rich and full, with luscious minty/berryfruit and clean, soft tannins on the finish. The vineyard is in fact mid-way between the Bendigo and Pyrenees districts: it can claim membership of either. Laanecoorie, incidentally, means 'big kangaroo'.

### LADBROKE GROVE NR Est 1982 LR/CD/ML $9.50–11 CD COONAWARRA

Millicent Road, Penola, SA 5277 (087) 37 2997
**OPEN** 7 days 8.30–5 **PRODUCTION** 1500 cases
**WINEMAKER** Peter McDonald
**PRINCIPAL WINES** Ries, Shir.
**SUMMARY** Leads a somewhat shadowy existence outside the mainstream of Coonawarra wineries; wine quality has been variable. The wines are available through the Bushmans Inn Restaurant, Coonawarra Motor Lodge, and through Glenhuntly Cellars in Melbourne and Kellys in Brisbane.

### LAKE BREEZE NR Est 1987 CD/ML $8.50–13.90 CD LANGHORNE CREEK

Step Road, Langhorne Creek, SA 5255 (085) 37 3017

**OPEN** Wed/Fri/Sun 10–4.30 **PRODUCTION** 800 cases
**WINEMAKER** Greg Follett
**PRINCIPAL WINES** Chard, Cab Sauv, Cab Merl Shir, the last labelled Bernoota.
**SUMMARY** The Follett family have been farmers at Langhorne Creek since 1880, grape growers since the 1930's. Since 1987 a small proportion of their grapes has been made into wine, and a cellar-door sales facility was opened in early 1991. Wine quality is reputed to be very good.

## LAKE GEORGE CB–B Est 1971 LR $7.50–10 R
CANBERRA
Federal Highway, Collector, NSW 2581 (048) 48 0039
**OPEN** Not **PRODUCTION** 500 cases
**WINEMAKER** Dr Edgar F. Riek
**PRINCIPAL WINES** Chard, Sem, Pinot, Cab Sauv, Merl.
**BEST VINTAGES** W '86, '88, '90, '91 R '82, '86, '88, '91
**SUMMARY** Dr Edgar Rick is an inquisitive, iconoclastic winemaker who is not content with his role as Godfather and founder of the Canberra district, forever experimenting and innovating. His fortified wines, vintaged in North East Victoria but matured at Lake George, are very good.

## LAKE'S FOLLY A–A Est 1963 NFR/CD/ML/UK
(Lay and Wheeler) $16 CD HUNTER V
Broke Road, Pokolbin, NSW, 2321 (049) 98 7507 fax (049) 98 7322
**OPEN** Mon–Sat 10–4 **PRODUCTION** 4000 cases
**WINEMAKER** Stephen Lake
**PRINCIPAL WINES** Chard, Cab Sauv.
**BEST VINTAGES** W '81, '83, '86, '91 R '81, '87, '89, '91
**SUMMARY** The first of the weekend wineries to produce wines for commercial sale, long revered for its Cabernet Sauvignon and thereafter its Chardonnay. Not all of the wines have lived up to its reputation, but one cannot fault the '89s, made in the face of a difficult vintage, nor even less the '91s made in a great year — and showing it.

## LAMONT B–A Est 1978 CD $8–9 CD SWAN V
Bisdee Road, Millendon, WA 6056 (09) 296 4485
**OPEN** Wed–Sun 10–5 **PRODUCTION** 4000 cases
**WINEMAKER** Corin Lamont
**PRINCIPAL WINES** Wh Burg, Chard, Cab Rosé, Cab, Herm.
**BEST VINTAGES** W '81, '85, '89, '90 R '81, '83, '85, '89
**SUMMARY** Corin Lamont is the daughter of the late Jack Mann, and makes her wines in the image of those her father used to make, resplendent in their generosity. Lamont also boasts a superb restaurant.

## LANCEFIELD C–B Est 1985 LR/CD/ML $7.50–18 CD
MACEDON
Woodend Road, Lancefield, Vic 3435 (054) 29 1217
**OPEN** W'ends 12–6 **PRODUCTION** 1000 cases
**WINEMAKER** John Ellis (Contract)
**PRINCIPAL WINES** Gewurz, Colomb, Chard, Cab Sauv, sparkl.
**BEST VINTAGES** W '86, '88, '89, '91 R '86, '90, '91
**SUMMARY** Offers a mixture of wines sourced variously from Macedon and other regions relying in part upon the restaurant and live entertainment to draw custom. The wines are light but well enough made.

## LA PROVENCE NR Est 1956 LR/ML $12.50–21 CD
TAMAR V
Lalla, Tas 7267 (003) 95 1290
**OPEN** 7 days 10–6 **PRODUCTION** 600 cases
**WINEMAKER** Jean-Baptiste Lecaillon (Contract)

**PRINCIPAL WINES** Chard, Ries, Pinot.
**SUMMARY** Incorporates the pioneer vineyard of Frenchman Jean Miguet. The 1990 Pinot Noir, tasted in 1992, was disappointing; previous releases have shown weight and complexity.

**LARK HILL** B–B Est 1978 LR/CD/ML $9–15 CD
CANBERRA
RMB 281 Gundaroo Road, Bungendore, NSW 2621 (06) 238 1393
**OPEN** Wed–Sun 10–5 **PRODUCTION** 2500 cases
**WINEMAKERS** David & Sue Carpenter
**PRINCIPAL WINES** Ries, Sem, Chard, Light Red, Cab Merl, Ausl Ries.
**BEST VINTAGES** **W** '87, '88, '90, '91 **R** '86, '88, '90, '91
**SUMMARY** Once the most consistent all-round winemaker in the district, but recent releases have disappointed — with the honourable exception of the 1991 Auslese Riesling.

**LAURISTON** CB–B Est 1984 NR/CD/ML/UK
(Berri Renmano UK) $11.60–19.95 R ADELAIDE PLAINS
Heaslop Road, Angle Vale, SA 5117 (08) 284 7000 fax (085) 83 2224
**OPEN** Mon–Fri 9–5, Sat 11–5, Sun 1–5
**PRODUCTION** 3000 tonnes (190 000 case equivalent)
**WINEMAKER** Colin Glaetzer
**PRINCIPAL WINES** Meth Champ, Chard, Ries, Cab Sauv Shir, Port, Muscat.
**SUMMARY** The Lauriston wines are purchased either from other members of the Berri Renmano group or from external sources across Southern Australia; the wine styles vary accordingly.

**LAWSON HILL** NR Est 1985 LR/CD/ML $8.50–12 CD
MUDGEE
Henry Lawson Drive, Eurunderee, Mudgee, NSW 2850 (063) 73 3953
**OPEN** Thurs–Mon 9.30–4 **PRODUCTION** 1700 cases
**WINEMAKER** Jose Grace
**PRINCIPAL WINES** Sem Chard, Mos, Tram Ries, Cab Shir, Pinot.
**SUMMARY** The newest of the Mudgee wineries, the wines of which I have not tasted.

**LEASINGHAM** B–A Est 1893 NR/CD/UK
(Stevens Garnier Ltd) $6–11 R CLARE V
7 Dominic Street, Clare, SA 5453 (088) 42 2555 fax (088) 42 3293
**OPEN** 7 days 10–4.30 **PRODUCTION** 250 000 cases
**WINEMAKER** Chris Proud
**PRINCIPAL WINES** Hutt Creek Chab, Ries, Claret and Domaine Chard, Ries, Sem, Shir, and Cab Malb.
**BEST VINTAGES** **W** '86, '89, '90, '91 **R** '86, '88, '89, '90
**SUMMARY** A model of marketing discipline and clarity, unusual in this day and age; both the Hutt Creek and Domaine range are no less commendable for their consistency of quality and outstanding value for money, however little this may be recognised by the public.

**LECONFIELD** B–B Est 1974 NFR/CD/ML/UK
(Millex Pty Ltd) $11–20 R COONAWARRA
Main Penola-Naracoorte Road, Coonawarra, SA 5263 (087) 37 2326
fax (087) 37 2997
**OPEN** Mon–Fri 9–5, w'ends 10–4 **PRODUCTION** 38 000 cases
(including contract)
**WINEMAKER** Ralph Fowler
**PRINCIPAL WINES** Ries, Chard, Cab Sauv, Cab Mer.
**BEST VINTAGES** **W** '84, '86, '90, '91 **R** '80, '82, '88, '90, '91
**SUMMARY** Winemaker Ralph Fowler has made much progress in

restoring Leconfield to its former glory with an array of strongly flavoured '90 and '91 red wines and a honeyed, peachy '90 Chardonnay.

**LEEUWIN ESTATE** BA–B Est 1974 NFR/CD/UK (Domain Direct) $12.40–40 R MARGARET R

Gnarawary Road, Margaret River, WA 6285 (097) 57 6253

**OPEN** 7 days 10–4.30 **PRODUCTION** 25 000 cases

**WINEMAKER** Bob Cartwright

**PRINCIPAL WINES** Ries, Gewurz, Sauv Bl, Chard, Cab Sauv, Pinot; premium range Art Series, second label Prelude.

**BEST VINTAGES W** '82, '85, '87, '88 **R** '82, '85, '87, '88

**SUMMARY** The Horgan family retains both a shareholding and managerial role in Leeuwin Estate, and the restructured company has (happily) continued the long term marketing and promotional strategy set in easier times. The 1986 Chardonnay (fine, intense and tangy) and the superlative 1987 Cabernet Sauvignon are high-priced wines, but deserve to be, while the Prelude series offers a glimpse of the greatness at the top at equally fair prices.

**LEFROY BROOK** NR Est 1986 LR/ML $21.95 R LWR GRT STHN

Glauder Road, Pemberton, WA 6260 (09) 386 8385

**OPEN** Not **PRODUCTION** 300 cases

**WINEMAKER** Peter Fimmel

**PRINCIPAL WINES** Chard, Pinot.

**SUMMARY** One of the first Pemberton producers to come on-stream; the '89 and '90 vintages showed problems in the winery, perhaps due to the very small quantities, and give no real indication of the potential of the region.

**LELAND ESTATE** NR Est 1986 ML $11.75 ML ADELAIDE HILLS

PO Lenswood, SA 5240. No phone or fax

**OPEN** Not **PRODUCTION** 1600 cases

**WINEMAKER** Rob Cootes

**PRINCIPAL WINES** Sauv Bl, Pinot.

**SUMMARY** Former Yalumba senior winemaker Rob Cootes, with a Master of Science Degree, deliberately opted out of mainstream life when he established Leland Estate, living in a split-level, one roomed house built from timber salvaged from trees killed in the Ash Wednesday bush fires. The 1991 Sauvignon Blanc is as piercingly rich in gooseberry varietal flavour as any from the exciting Lenswood district in the Adelaide Hills. By the time of publication, the first Pinot Noir will have also been released.

**LENTON BRAE ESTATE** NR Est 1983 LR/CD $11–18 CD MARGARET R

Willyabrup Valley, Margaret River, WA (097) 55 6255

**OPEN** 7 days 10–6 **PRODUCTION** 4000 cases

**WINEMAKER** Dorham Mann (Consultant)

**PRINCIPAL WINES** Chard, Sauv Bl, Cab Sauv.

**SUMMARY** Former architect and town planner Bruce Tomlinson has built a strikingly beautiful winery, but will not stand for criticism of his wines.

**LEO BURING** BA–BA Est 1931 NR/CD/UK (Hatch Mansfield) $7.50–11.80 R BAROSSA V

Sturt Highway, Tanunda, SA 5352 (08) 563 2184 fax (085) 63 2804

**OPEN** Mon–Sat 10–4.30 **PRODUCTION** NFP

**WINEMAKERS** John Vickery, Rob Ruediger

**PRINCIPAL WINES** A range of varietally and regionally identified wines coming from Barossa and surrounds (predominantly Coonawarra and Padthaway), with emphasis on Ries, Chard and Cab Sauv. Deluxe wines are Reserve Bin Rieslings.

**BEST VINTAGES W** '72, '73, '75, '79, '84, '90 **R** '84, '86, '87, '90, '91
**SUMMARY** Generally acknowledged as Australia's greatest Riesling maker, thanks largely to the skills of John Vickery; these are wines which (at their best) age magnificently for 20 years or more. The wines in question are released under a changing Bin No. with the prefix (these days) of DW. The commercial wines are dependable, Premier Selection sometimes providing exceptional value for money. It is probable that under S. A. Brewing ownership, Leo Buring will concentrate primarily on Rhine Riesling from Eden, Clare and the Barossa Valley.

**LESNIK FAMILY** NR Est 1986 CD/ML HUNTER V
Branxton Road, Pokolbin, NSW 2321 (049) 98 7755 fax (049) 987 750
**OPEN** 7 days 9–5 **PRODUCTION** 3500 cases
**WINEMAKER** Josef Lesnik
**PRINCIPAL WINES** Sem, Ries, Chard, Tram Ries, LP Sem, Shir, Cab Sauv, fortifieds.
**SUMMARY** A no-holds-barred tourist-oriented cellar-door operation, offering wines from estate-grown grapes; quality has been variable but an outstanding, stylish 1991 barrel-fermented Chardonnay justifiably topped the Small Producers Class at the 1992 Royal Sydney Wine Show.

**LILLYDALE VINEYARDS** B–B Est 1976 LR/CD/ML
$9–17 R YARRA V
Lot 10 Davross Court, Seville, Vic 3139 (059) 64 2016
**OPEN** 7 days 10–5 **PRODUCTION** 9000 cases
**WINEMAKER** Alex White
**PRINCIPAL WINES** Ries, Sauv Bl, Gewurz, Chard, Pinot, Cab Sauv; second label is Yarra Range.
**BEST VINTAGES W** '82, '84, '86, '90 **R** '85, '86, '90, '91
**SUMMARY** One of the larger wineries in the Valley, and one of the old hands. The wines are deliberately made in a reserved style; Alex White is not one who believes in spending a great deal of money on new oak, preferring that the grapes (and the wine) should do the talking, helped by bottle-development. A tart, crisp, herbal 1991 Sauvignon Blanc is a very nice wine.

**LILLYPILLY ESTATE** CB–B Est 1982 CD/ML
$6.55–10.90 CD MIA
Lillypilly Road, Leeton, NSW 2705 (069) 53 4069 fax (069) 53 4980
**OPEN** Mon–Sat 10–5.30, Sun by appointment
**PRODUCTION** 9000 cases
**WINEMAKER** Robert Fiumara
**PRINCIPAL WINES** Ries, Chard, Tram Ries, Botrytis Noble Ries, Noble Muscat, Cab Sauv, Herm, Port.
**BEST VINTAGES W** '82, '84, '85, '89 **R** '84, '85, '89
**SUMMARY** The best wines by far are the botrytised white wines, with the Noble Muscat of Alexandria unique to the winery; these wines have both style and intensity of flavour, and can age well. Both the '87 and the '90 vintages were excellent in 1992.

**LINDEMANS** A–A Est 1908 NR/CD/UK (Percy Fox, Penfolds)
$9.80–19.50 COONAWARRA AND PADTHAWAY
Main Penola-Naracoorte Road, Coonawarra, SA 5263 (087) 36 3205
fax (087) 36 3250
**OPEN** 7 days 10–4 **PRODUCTION** NFP
**WINEMAKERS** Phillip John and Greg Clayfield
**PRINCIPAL WINES** Under the Lindeman label, Padthaway Ries, Chard, Sauv Bl, Pinot; Limestone Ridge Shir Cab, Pyrus and St George Cab Sauv; under the Rouge Homme label Chard, Pinot, Claret and Cab Sauv.

**BEST VINTAGES W & R** '76, '78, '82, '86, '88,' 90, '91
**SUMMARY** Despite the depredations of the brief period of ownership by
Penfolds, S. A. Brewing has continued to support and develop the
principal Lindeman and Rouge Homme brands. The Padthaway white
wines and Coonawarra reds are still widely recognised as some of the
finest examples of their type in Australia, with a formidable show record
to reinforce the point.

**LINDEMANS** CA–BA Est 1870 NR/CD/UK (Percy Fox)
$11.70–12.45 R HUNTER V
McDonalds Road, Pokolbin, NSW 2321 (049) 98 7501 fax (049) 98 7682
**OPEN** 7 days 9–5 **PRODUCTION** 60 000 cases
**WINEMAKERS** Phillip John and Patrick Auld
**PRINCIPAL WINES** Standard wines under annually changing Bin Nos
of Sem, Chab, Wh Burg, Sem Chard, Chard, Red Burg, Herm; deluxe
releases under Reserve Bin label and occasional older classic release label.
**BEST VINTAGES W** '68, '70, '79, '87, '91 **R** '65, '83, '86, '87, '91
**SUMMARY** Only time will tell where Lindemans Hunter Valley wines
are eventually positioned in the S. A. Brewing empire; certainly, the
vineyards which produced the great wines of the '50s and '60s are gone
forever, but the red wines in particular have shown a renaissance in recent
years. It may well be that the mid-market position of most of the wines
will be maintained under the new regime.

**LINDEMANS KARADOC** CB–A Est 1963 NR/CD
$4.60–7.60 R MURRAY R
Nangiloc Road, Karadoc via Mildura, Vic 3500 (050) 24 0303
fax (050) 24 0324
**OPEN** Mon–Sat 10–4.30 **PRODUCTION** 3.5 million cases
**WINEMAKER** Phillip John (Chief)
**PRINCIPAL WINES** Under Lindeman label Ben Ean Mos, Cawarra Chab,
Bin 23 Ries; under both Lindeman and Leo Buring Premier Selection label
Chab, Chard, Rh Ries, Sauv Bl, Sem Chard, Cab Shir, Cab Sauv; also special
export labels made in huge volume and not sold locally. Also winery-linked
Matthew Lang range Chab, Ries, Tram Ries, Wh Burg, Claret.
**SUMMARY** Now the production centre for all of the Lindeman and Leo
Buring wines, with the exception of special lines made in the Coonawarra
and Hunter wineries. The biggest and most modern single facility in
Australia allowing all important economies of scale, and the major
processing centre for the beverage wine sector (casks, flagons and low-
priced bottles) of the S. A. Brewing empire. Its achievment in making 4
million bottles of 1991 Bin 65 Chardonnay of show medal standard is of
great significance not only for Lindemans but for the cause of Australain
wine generally in overseas markets.

**LIRRALIRRA ESTATE** CB–CB Est 1981 CD/ML $8.50–15
YARRA V
Paynes Road, Lillydale, Vic 3140 (03) 735 0224
**OPEN** W'ends and hols 10–6 **PRODUCTION** 300 cases
**WINEMAKER** David Lloyd
**PRINCIPAL WINES** Sauv Bl Sem, Sem Sauv Bl Musc, Cab Merl, Cab
Sauv.
**SUMMARY** The '89 Cabernet Merlot and '90 Cabernet Sauvignon on
sale in 1992 are both pleasant wines, the latter with light but fresh
spicy/berry fruit. The white wines are less convincing.

**LITTLE RIVER** NR Est 1934 CD/ML $8–11 CD SWAN V
Cnr West Swan Road & Forest Roads, West Swan, WA 6055
(09) 296 4462
**OPEN** 7 days 10–5.30 **PRODUCTION** 5000 cases

**WINEMAKER** Peter Murfit
**PRINCIPAL WINES** Fronti, Ries, Verd, Chab, Cab Sauv, Shir, fortified.
**SUMMARY** Following several quick changes of ownership (and of consultant winemakers) the former Glenalwyn is going through a period of change, but is nonetheless aggressively marketing its wines ex cellar door, offering, amongst other things, the only 'Spatlese Sauterne' I have ever heard of.

**LITTLE'S** CB–CB Est 1983 LR/CD/ML $11–15 CD
HUNTER V
Lot 3 Palmers Lane, Pokolbin, NSW 2321   (049) 98 7626
**OPEN** 7 days 10–4.30   **PRODUCTION** 6000 cases
**WINEMAKER** Ian Little
**PRINCIPAL WINES** Sem, Chard, Sem Chard, Gewurz, Pinot Shir, Shir, Cab Sauv, port.
**BEST VINTAGES W** '86, '87, '88, '91 **R** '85, '86, '88, '91
**SUMMARY** A successful cellar-door operation with friendly service and friendly wines: aromatic, fresh and sometimes slightly sweet white wines and light, inoffensive red wines. The Vintage Port can be excellent, and the Semillon and Semillon Chardonnay greatly benefit from a few years in bottle.

**LOCHVIE** NR Est 1985 CD $9.50 CD   YARRA V
28 Lavender Park Road, Eltham, Vic 3095   (03) 439 9444
**OPEN** Sat 9–5   **PRODUCTION** 400 cases
**WINEMAKER** John Lewis
**PRINCIPAL WINES** Cab Merl.
**SUMMARY** A minute back-room winery, producing a wine with fresh fruit slightly marred by some astringency.

**LONG GULLY ESTATE** CB–B Est 1982 LR/CD/UK
(Elite Wines) $11.20–20 CD   YARRA V
Long Gully Road, Healesville, Vic 3777   (03) 807 4246 fax (03) 807 2213
**OPEN** W'ends 12–5   **PRODUCTION** 20 000 cases
**WINEMAKER** Peter Florance
**PRINCIPAL WINES** Chard, Sauv Bl, Sem, Ries, Merl, Pinot, Cab Sauv, Shir.
**BEST VINTAGES W** '88, '89, '90 **R** '88, '89, '90, '91
**SUMMARY** An aggressively expanding producer having success in both domestic and export markets with strongly flavoured, concentrated Chardonnay, Pinot Noir and Cabernet Sauvignon, which from time to time have enjoyed considerable show success. Quality can, however, be variable.

**LONGLEAT** C–B Est 1975 LR/ML/CD/UK (Nicks Wines Intn'l)
$7.95–15 CD   GOULBURN V
Old Weir Road, Murchison, Vic 3610   (058) 26 2294 fax (058) 26 2510
**OPEN** Mon–Sat 9–5, Sun 10–5   **PRODUCTION** 2000 cases
**WINEMAKER** Mark Schulz
**PRINCIPAL WINES** Ries, Sauv Bl, Chard, Sem, Cab Sauv, Shir, Cab Shir.
**SUMMARY** Very strongly flavoured and structured wines (made at Chateau Tahbilk) have a great deal of personality but not a great deal of finesse; the oaky but high flavoured '90 Chardonnay has had success in various forums.

**LOVEGROVE OF COTTLES BRIDGE** B–B Est 1988
LR/CD/ML $9.50–15 CD   YARRA V
1420 Heidelberg-Kinglake Road, Cottlesbridge, Vic 3099   (03) 718 1569
**OPEN** W'ends and hols 11.30–6.30
**PRODUCTION** 1000 cases approx
**WINEMAKER** Various contract
**PRINCIPAL WINES** Chard, Pinot, Cab Merl; Dunmoochin is second label.
**SUMMARY** A recently opened cellar door gives visitors to the pretty and distinctively different Diamond Valley sub-region a chance to taste some

very well made and full-flavoured wines, particularly the peachy, flavoursome '90 Chardonnay.

**LOWE FAMILY** B–B Est 1987 LR/ML $12.50 R MUDGEE
Ashbourne Vineyard, Tinja Lane, Mudgee, NSW 2850 (063) 72 1762
**OPEN** Not **PRODUCTION** 500 cases
**WINEMAKER** David Lowe
**PRINCIPAL WINES** Chard.
**SUMMARY** The family vineyard of former Rothbury winemaker David Lowe, making typically rich, full-bodied Chardonnay, albeit in tiny quantities.

**MCALISTER** NR Est 1975 LR/CD/ML $17 CD GIPPSLAND
Golden Beach Road, Longford, Vic 3851 (051) 49 7229
**OPEN** By appointment only **PRODUCTION** 600 cases
**WINEMAKER** Peter Edwards
**PRINCIPAL WINES** The McAlister, a Bordeaux-type blend of Cab Franc Merl.
**SUMMARY** Problems with cork mould in some vintages have marred the potential of what can be a wine of exceptional style and complexity.

**MCGUIGAN BROTHERS** NR Est 1992 NR/ML
$7.95–$11.95 R HUNTER V
PO Box 31, Branxton, NSW 2335 (049) 98 7782 fax (049) 91 2088
**OPEN** Not **PRODUCTION** 150 000 cases
**WINEMAKER** Neil McGuigan
**PRINCIPAL WINES** Wines released in three price ranges: Shareholders Reserve (Chard and Cab Merl), Bin Range (Chard and Herm) and Export Range (Graves Tram Ries and Black Shiraz).
**SUMMARY** After successfully raising funds through a public share issue at the end of 1991 McGuigan Wines Limited leapt out of the starting blocks like an Olympic sprinter, releasing its first wines in April 1992, but without having by then built or acquired a winery. These wines were from the 1989 vintage, and were necessarily purchased from another maker, presumably Brian and Neil McGuigan's former company, Wyndham Estate. It seems fair to assume that wine style will follow very much in the footsteps of the Wyndham wines, even though the wines will be sourced from vineyards in both South Australia and New South Wales.

**MCIVOR CREEK** C–CB Est 1974 LR/CD/ML $7.85–12.95 CD
BENDIGO
Costerfield Road, Heathcote, Vic 3523 (054) 33 3000 or (054) 33 2711
**OPEN** 7 days 10–5.30 **PRODUCTION** Over 1000 cases
**WINEMAKER** Peter Turley
**PRINCIPAL WINES** Ries, Ausl Ries, Sauv Bl, Shir, Cab Shir, Cab Sauv, fortifieds.
**BEST VINTAGES** W '86, '87, '89 R '87, '88, '89
**SUMMARY** The beautifully situated McIvor Creek winery is well worth a visit, and does offer wines in diverse styles of which the red wines are the most regional.

**MCMANUS** DC–CB Est 1970 CD/ML $2.50–8 CD MIA
Rogers Road, Yenda, NSW 2681 (069) 68 1064
**OPEN** Mon–Sat 9–5, Sun 12–5 **PRODUCTION** 700 cases
**WINEMAKER** Dr David McManus
**PRINCIPAL WINES** Chard, Dry White, Cab Sauv, Malb, Merl, Shir, Pinot Malb Shir.
**SUMMARY** An extremely idiosyncratic winery run by Griffith GP Dr David McManus, his sister and other family members. Natural winemaking methods lead to considerable variation in quality, but the prices are from another era.

**MCWILLIAMS HANWOOD** CB–A Est 1877 NR/CD/UK
(The Hanwood Group) $5.80–15.40 R MIA
Winery Road, Hanwood, NSW 2680 (069) 62 1333 fax (069) 63 0002
**OPEN** 7 days 9–5 **PRODUCTION** NFP
**WINEMAKER** James Brayne
**PRINCIPAL WINES** Under Inheritance label Chablis, Ries, Tram Ries,
Wh Burg, Shir, Cab; under Hanwood label Ries, Chard, Cab Sauv; also
limited volume premium regional releases from Coonawarra, Hilltops,
Eden Valley etc.
**BEST VINTAGES W** '87, '88, '90, '91 **R** '86, '88, '90, '91
**SUMMARY** The best wines to emanate from the Hanwood winery are in
fact those made from other regions, notably Hilltops in New South
Wales, Coonawarra and Eden Valley; it is a strategy which has been
successful and is likely to gain momentum.

**MCWILLIAMS MT PLEASANT** BA–BA Est 1880
NR/CD/UK (The Hanwood Group) $11–18.50 R HUNTER V
Marrowbone Road, Pokolbin, NSW 2321 (049) 98 7505
**OPEN** 7 days 9–5 **PRODUCTION** NFP
**WINEMAKER** Phillip Ryan
**PRINCIPAL WINES** An ever-expanding series of wines now appear
under various incarnations of the Mount Pleasant label; one needs a
doctorate in wine label interpretation to fathom whether these are simply
Mount Pleasant brands or whether they are indeed Hunter Valley sourced.
Price is the best guide.
**BEST VINTAGES W** '84, '86, '87, '91 **R** '65, '66, '86, '91
**SUMMARY** McWilliams Elizabeth (a pure Hunter wine) is now the only
mature Hunter Semillon generally commercially available, and is an
undervalued and underpriced treasure, with a consistently superb show
record. Under the skilled hand of Phillip Ryan, the small-run premium
Mount Pleasant wines are also flourishing, and worth the identification
effort; Chardonnay, in particular, has enjoyed outstanding show success in
recent years, but the small-volume Rosehill, OP & OH and similar
Hermitage releases can also be excellent.

**MADDENS LANE WINERY** NR Est 1989 CD/ML $15
CD YARRA V
Maddens Lane, Gruyere via Coldstream, Vic 3770 (059) 64 9279
**OPEN** By appointment **PRODUCTION** 150 cases
**WINEMAKER** Various Contract
**PRINCIPAL WINES** Sauv Bl/Sem, Chard.
**SUMMARY** A small and intermittent producer, selling its grapes in
some years, and in others having the wine vinified. It is the former
Prigorje Winery, now owned by Geoffrey and Felicity Norris.

**MADEW** BA–B Est 1984 LR/CD/ML $15 CD CANBERRA
Furlong Road, Queanbeyan, ACT 2620 (06) 299 2303
**OPEN** W'ends/pub hols 11–5 **PRODUCTION** 700 cases
**WINEMAKER** Greg Tilbrook
**PRINCIPAL WINES** Ries, Chard, Cab Mer.
**SUMMARY** The high rating marks a revolution in wine quality with the
1990 vintage; earlier vintages were very ordinary indeed, and in fact no
wines were released from '88 or '89. The appointment of Oenotec as
consultants did the trick; a superb '90 Chardonnay, with sophisticated
oak and full of peach and passionfruit, followed by a beautifully handled
crisp, toasty 1991 Rhine Riesling, show the potential of the winery.

**MAGLIERI** CA–B Est 1972 LR/CD/ML $2.50–9.50 CD STHN
VALES
Douglas Gully Road, McLaren Flat, SA 5171 (08) 383 0177

fax (08) 383 0136
**OPEN** Mon–Sat 9–4, Sun 12–4 **PRODUCTION** 1800 tonnes
**WINEMAKER** John Loxton
**PRINCIPAL WINES** Prolific Italian-accented range of generic and varietal table wines; Spumante, fortified and flavoured wines; also Ries, Sem Chard, Shirm Cab Sauv.
**SUMMARY** Maglieri has always described itself as the 'House of Lambrusco', and just to prove the point, produces a white Lambrusco which might surprise the Italians, but which adds another dimension to the conventional red Lambrusco. However, it can and does produce some very good table wines, such as its 1992 Sydney Show gold-medal winning 1990 Cabernet Sauvignon, a ripe, chewy wine crammed with flavour.

## MAIN RIDGE ESTATE  B–B Est 1975 LR/CD/ML
$18.50–20 R  MORNINGTON P
Lot 48 William Road, Red Hill, Vic 3937  (059) 89 2686
**OPEN** W'ends/hols 12–5 **PRODUCTION** 1500 cases
**WINEMAKER** Nat White
**PRINCIPAL WINES** Chard, Pinot, Cab Sauv.
**BEST VINTAGES W** '86, '88, '90, '91 **R** '80, '86, '88, '90, '91
**SUMMARY** Nat White gives meticulous attention to every aspect of his viticulture and winemaking, doing annual battle with one of the coolest sites on the Peninsula; fragrant Bordeaux-like Cabernet Sauvignons in 1989 and 1990 have impressed, as did the 1991 Pinot Noir.

## MAIR'S  B–B Est 1985 LR/CD/ML $15–17 CD  GIPPSLAND
Moe South Road, Moe South, Vic 3825  (051) 27 4229
**OPEN** By appointment only **PRODUCTION** 330 cases
**WINEMAKER** Stewart Mair
**PRINCIPAL WINES** Cab Sauv, labelled Coalville Red.
**BEST VINTAGES R** '84, '85, '87, '89, '90
**SUMMARY** Coalville Red can be very good, possessing an unusual combination of elegance and intensity, with tangy red berry flavours underpinned by a touch of mint and herbaceousness.

## MALCOLM CREEK  B–B Est 1980 LR $14 R
ADELAIDE HILLS
Bonython Road, Kersbrook, SA 5231  (08) 389 3235
**OPEN** Not **PRODUCTION** 250 cases
**WINEMAKER** Reg Tolley
**PRINCIPAL WINES** Chard, Cab Sauv.
**SUMMARY** The tiny hobby vineyard of Tolley's chief Reg Tolley, the vinous equivalent of a bus conductor's holiday; the wines are smooth, clean and somewhat simple, but are released with significant bottle age.

## MANNING PARK  NR Est 1979 CD/ML $9.50–12.50 CD
STHN VALES
Cnr Olivers Road and Chalkhill Road, McLaren Vale, SA 5171
(08) 323 8209
**OPEN** 7 days 9–5 **PRODUCTION** NFP
**WINEMAKER** Allan McLean
**PRINCIPAL WINES** Ries, Fumé, Wh Burg, Saut, Herm, Cab Sauv, Port, Muscat.
**SUMMARY** A low-key cellar-door operation which places special emphasis on old (and expensive) tawny ports.

## MARIENBERG  CB–B Est 1966 NR $7–9.60 R  STHN VALES
c/o Hill International Wines (02) 630 5429 fax (02) 583 2729
**OPEN** Not **PRODUCTION** 20 000 cases
**WINEMAKER** Nick Holmes

**PRINCIPAL WINES** Chab, Sauv Bl, Ries, Botrytis Ries, Pinot, Shir, Cab Sauv.

**SUMMARY** The Marienberg brand was purchased by the Hill group of companies in late 1991 following the retirement of Ursula Pridham. Releases under the new regime have been quite impressive.

## MARION'S VINEYARD NR Est 1980 LR/CD/ML $15–18 CD TAMAR V

Foreshore Drive, Deviot, Tas 7275  (003) 94 7434

**OPEN** 7 days 10–5  **PRODUCTION** 3500 cases

**WINEMAKER** Mark Semmens

**PRINCIPAL WINES** Chard, Muller, Pinot Gris, Pinot, Cab Sauv.

**SUMMARY** Produces the exceptionally strong flavoured and strongly structured reds for which the Tamar Valley is noted, and which are quite unlike any other Tasmanian wines; the lemony oak handling is sometimes assertive, but worked well in the '88 Cabernet and '89 Chardonnay.

## MARKEITA CELLARS NR Est 1974 CD/ML CENT WEST NSW

Mitchell Highway, Neura, NSW 2820  (068) 46 7277

**OPEN** 7 days 9–6  **PRODUCTION** 2000 cases

**WINEMAKER** K. Reinhard

**PRINCIPAL WINES** Fronti, Shir, Cab Sauv, numerous Ports.

**SUMMARY** Full-bodied red wines and fortifieds, some purchased elsewhere, are dispensed in containers of all shapes and sizes to both locals and passing tourists.

## MARKWOOD ESTATE NR Est 1971 CD $10–18 CD NE VIC

Morris Lane, Markwood, Vic 3678  (057) 27 0361

**OPEN** 7 days 9–5  **PRODUCTION** 900 cases

**WINEMAKER** Rick Morris

**PRINCIPAL WINES** Chard, Cab Sauv, Wh Port, Taw Port.

**SUMMARY** Rick Morris steadfastly refuses to submit samples; winery facilities are very limited and the last wines tasted were, well, rustic.

## MARRON CREEK NR Est 1988 LR/ML $12.50 LWR GRT STHN

Frankland-Rocky Gully Road, Frankland, WA 6396  (098) 55 2278

**OPEN** Not  **PRODUCTION** 400 cases

**WINEMAKER** Kim Hart

**PRINCIPAL WINES** Chard, Cab Sauv.

**SUMMARY** Marron Creek is the weekend and out-of-hours occupation for Alkoomi winemaker Kim Hart, and her husband. The fleshy, red berry 1989 Cabernet Sauvignon, with its sophisticated American oak, is an outstanding wine, the 1990 Chardonnay somewhat idiosyncratic but good.

## MARSH ESTATE B–B Est 1971 CD/ML $11–$14 CD HUNTER V

Deasey Road, Pokolbin, NSW 2321  (049) 98 7587

**OPEN** Mon–Fri 10–4.30, w'ends 10–5  **PRODUCTION** 5000 cases

**WINEMAKER** Peter Marsh

**PRINCIPAL WINES** Chard, Sem, Tram Ries, Champ, Saut, Herm, Cab Sauv, Port.

**BEST VINTAGES W** '85, '86, '87, '89  **R** '85, '86, '87, '89

**SUMMARY** Through sheer consistency, value-for-money and unrelenting hard work, the Marsh family (who purchased the former Quentin Estate in 1978) has built up a sufficiently loyal cellar door and mail-list clientele to allow all of the considerable production to be sold direct. Wine style is always direct, with oak playing a minimal role, and prolonged cellaring paying handsome dividends.

**MASSONI**  B–B Est 1984 LR/CD $22 R  MORNINGTON
Mornington-Flinders Road, Red Hill, Vic 3937   (059) 89 2060
fax (059) 892 348
**OPEN**  By appointment only  **PRODUCTION**  1500 cases
**WINEMAKER**  Daniel Green/Oenotec
**PRINCIPAL WINES**  Chard, Pinot, Cab Sauv.
**SUMMARY**  Chardonnay is the principal wine, strongly botrytis-
influenced in '88, rich and full in '89, rather light in '90, seemingly
needing time in bottle, outstanding in '91, with lush, peachy fruit.

**MAXWELL**  CB–B Est 1979 LR/CD/ML $6–12 CD  STHN VALES
26 Kangarilla Road, McLaren Vale, SA 5171   (08) 323 8200
**OPEN**  7 days 10–5  **PRODUCTION**  9500 cases
**WINEMAKER**  Mark Maxwell
**PRINCIPAL WINES**  Ries, Chard, Champ, Shir, Cab Merl, Cab Sauv,
Port, Mead.
**SUMMARY**  Full flavoured, rather traditional wines (and excellent mead)
are the order of the day, although Mark Maxwell is forever experimenting,
dropping some styles and introducing others.

**MEADOWBANK**  NR Est 1974 LR/CD/ML $14–15 CD
STHN TAS
Glenora, Derwent Valley, Tas 7410   (002) 86 1269  fax (002) 86 1133
**OPEN**  Mon–Fri 9–5  **PRODUCTION**  1800 cases
**WINEMAKER**  Greg O'Keefe
**PRINCIPAL WINES**  Chard, Ries, Cab Sauv, Shir.
**SUMMARY**  The Ellis family have been grape growers for many years,
originally selling to Hickinbotham Winemakers but now producing their
own wines, with former Normans winemaker Greg O'Keefe in charge —
and the full potential still to be realised.

**MERRICKS ESTATE**  B–B Est 1984 LR/CD/ML $19.95 R
MORNINGTON P
Thompsons Lane, Merricks, Vic 3916   (03) 612 7285  fax (03) 629 4035
**OPEN**  First w'end month 12–5  **PRODUCTION**  1600 cases
**WINEMAKER**  Alex White
**PRINCIPAL WINES**  Chard, Shir, Cab Sauv.
**SUMMARY**  The wonderfully spicy exotic Shiraz of earlier vintages
disappeared in '89 and '90, hopefully to reappear in future years. The other
wines have not had the same vibrant appeal, but both the '90 and '91
Chardonnay showed promise as young wines.

**MIDDLETON WINERY**  NR Est 1979 LR/CD $7.50–10
CD  STHN VALES
Flagstaff Hill Road, Middleton, SA 5213   (085) 55 4136
**OPEN**  Fri–Sun 10–5  **PRODUCTION**  3200 cases
**WINEMAKER**  Nigel Catt
**PRINCIPAL WINES**  Ries, Sem, Cab, Herm.
**SUMMARY**  Nigel Catt has demonstrated his winemaking skills at
Andrew Garrett and elsewhere, so wine quality should be good; despite its
decade of production, I have never seen or tasted its wines.

**MILDARA**  BA–A Est 1955 NR/CD/UK (Lawlers) $8–24 R
COONAWARRA
Main Penola-Naracoorte Road, Coonawarra, SA 5263   (087) 36 3380
fax (087) 36 3307
**OPEN**  Mon–Sat 10–4.30, Sun 12–4  **PRODUCTION**  NFP
**WINEMAKER**  Gavin Hogg
**PRINCIPAL WINES**  Jamieson's Run red is a volume brand leader,
Jamieson's Run Chardonnay is not.  Alexanders top of the range Bordeaux

blend; also varietal Herm and Cab Sauv.
**BEST VINTAGES R** '63, '64, '79, '82, '85, '86, '88, '90
**SUMMARY** In a space of four vintages Jamieson's Run red has been established as one of Australia's mid-price brand leaders, contributing handsomely to group profit, and picking up a Jimmy Watson Trophy along the way, attesting to the outstanding winemaking skills behind it. The other wines are fully representative of region and price.

**MILDARA** CB–BA Est 1888 NR/CD/UK (Lawlers) $7.40 R
MURRAY R
Wentworth Road, Merbein, Vic 3505   (050) 25 2303   fax (050) 25 3300
**OPEN** Mon–Fri 9–5, w'ends 12–4   **PRODUCTION** 1 million cases
**WINEMAKER** Alan Harris
**PRINCIPAL WINES** Church Hill Chard, Fumé Bl, Cab Merl; also makes fine Sherries (Chestnut Teal, George and Supreme) and superb Pot Still Brandy.
**SUMMARY** A somewhat antiquated Merbein facility remains the overall group production centre following its acquisition of Wolf Blass, although all of its premium wines are sourced from and made at Coonawarra. The Church Hill range is dependable, the sherries good.

**MILDURA VINEYARDS** NR Est 1974 CD/ML $3–6.70
CD  MURRAY R
Campbell Avenue, Irymple, Vic 3498   (050) 24 5843
**OPEN** Mon–Sat 10–4.30, Sun 1–4.30   **PRODUCTION** NFP
**WINEMAKER** Bruce Holm
**PRINCIPAL WINES** Chard, Ries, sparkl, Colomb, Cab Sauv, Shir Cab, Cab Merl, under Acacia Ridge, Victoria Gardens and Mildura Vineyards labels.
**SUMMARY** Offers wines of unknown quality at yesterday's prices.

**MILLINUP ESTATE** NR Est 1989 CD/ML $11–14.50 CD
LWR GRT STHN
RMB 1280 Porongurup Road, Porongurup, WA 6324   (098) 53 1105
**OPEN** Mon–Fri 10–4   **PRODUCTION** 220 cases
**WINEMAKER** John Wade (Contract)
**PRINCIPAL WINES** Ries, Cab Merl.
**SUMMARY** The Millinup Estate vineyard was planted in 1978, when it was called Point Creek. Owners Peter and Lesley Thorn purchased it in 1989, re-naming it and having the limited production vinified by John Wade at Plantagenet.

**MILNATHORT** NR Est 1983 CD/ML $9–10 CD TAS
Channel Highway, Birchs Bay, Tas 7162 (vineyard only); postal PO Box 4, Woodbridge, Tas 7162 (002) 67 4750
**OPEN** By appointment   **PRODUCTION** 130 cases
**WINEMAKER** Andrew Hood (Contract)
**PRINCIPAL WINES** Ries, Cab.
**SUMMARY** The tiny production of David and Anne Brock's vineyard has not prevented consultant winemaker Andrew Hood from producing a potent 1990 Cabernet Sauvignon, which, while quite herbaceous, has power and length; the 1991 Rhine Riesling is crisp and light, but again well made and could develop nicely in bottle.

**MINTARO WINES** CB–B Est 1986 LR/CD/ML $9–12 CD
CLARE V
Leasingham Road, Mintaro, SA 5415   (088) 43 9046
**OPEN** 7 days 9–5   **PRODUCTION** 2000 cases
**WINEMAKER** James Pearson
**PRINCIPAL WINES** Ries, Cab Sauv.

**SUMMARY** Has produced some very good Rhine Riesling over the years, developing well in bottle. The Cabernet Sauvignon, by contrast, has tended to dullness and/or bitterness.

**MINTON GROVE** C–C Est 1979 NR/CD/ML/UK (Knabsilenus Ltd) $8–9.95 R ADELAIDE PLAINS
Heaslip Road, Angle Vale, SA 5117 (08) 284 7700 fax (08) 284 7711
**OPEN** 7 days 10–5 **PRODUCTION** 16 000 cases
**WINEMAKER** Lindsay Stanley
**PRINCIPAL WINES** Sem/Chard, Sauv Bl/Colombard, Shir, Cab Sauv, Cab Mer.
**SUMMARY** It is business as usual for Minton Grove after its name change from Anglesey Wine Estate, producing moderately priced, inoffensive wines.

**MINYA, THE** NR Est 1974 LR/CD/ML $8–12.50 GEELONG
Minya Lane, Connewarre, Vic 3227 (052) 641 397
**OPEN** Hol w'ends, and by appointment **PRODUCTION** 1600 cases
**WINEMAKER** Geoff Dans
**PRINCIPAL WINES** Gewurtz, Grenache, Cab/Shir/Merl.
**SUMMARY** Geoff Dans first planted vines in 1974 on his family's dairy farm, followed by further plantings in 1982 and 1988. I have not tasted any of the wines.

**MIRAMAR** B–B Est 1977 LR/CD/ML $10–13 R MUDGEE
Henry Lawson Drive, Mudgee, NSW 2850 (063) 73 3874
**OPEN** 7 days 9–5 **PRODUCTION** 9000 cases
**WINEMAKER** Ian MacRae
**PRINCIPAL WINES** Sem, Sem Chard, Chard, Sauv Bl, Ries, Tram Ries, Rosé, Pinot, Shir, Cab Sauv, Port.
**BEST VINTAGES W** '81, '84, '88, '91 **R** '84, '85, '86, '88
**SUMMARY** Has achieved fame for highly concentrated, tangy, complex Chardonnay which ages superbly; the '81 was a gold medal and trophy winner in 1990, and the '88 is headed down the same track. Overall, the white wines are better than the reds, but the latter do benefit from cellaring.

**MIRANDA** CA–BA Est 1939 NR/CD/UK (Pacific Wines) $2.95–$14.90 CD MIA
57 Jondaryan Avenue, Griffith, NSW 2680 (069) 62 4033
fax (069) 62 6944
**OPEN** 7 days 9–5
**PRODUCTION** 20 000 tonnes (1 300 000 case equivalent)
**WINEMAKER** Shayne Cunningham
**PRINCIPAL WINES** Under premium Wyangan label Chard, Sem, Ries, Sauv Bl, Cab Merl, Sauterne, Herm; numerous other table and fortified wines under Miranda and Mirrool Creek labels.
**SUMMARY** Miranda is enjoying a boom, triggered in part by its astute purchasing of quality fruit from the Clare and Barossa Valleys in 1991 and its acquisition of the Rovalley Winery. The 1991 Rhine Riesling won several gold medals in national shows thanks to its classic toasty/lime aroma and flavour.

**MISTY VALLEY WINES** NR Est 1986 LR/ML $12–15 ML YARRA V
Lot 1 Greenwood Lane, Steel's Creek, Vic 3775 (059) 625 083
fax (03) 853 5929
**OPEN** Not **PRODUCTION** 400 cases
**WINEMAKER** John Ellis (Contract)
**PRINCIPAL WINES** Gewurz, Chard, Pinot.
**SUMMARY** Both the Gewurztraminer and the Chardonnay from 1990 leave no doubt about the potential of this small but beautiful vineyard; the

wines are principally sold through the mailing list, the address being PO Box 240, Healesville, Vic 3777.

## MITCHELL CELLARS B–B Est 1975 NFR/CD/ML $10–14 CD CLARE V

Hughes Park Road, Skillogalee Valley, Sevenhill via Clare, SA 5453 (088) 43 4258

**OPEN** 7 days 10–4 **PRODUCTION** 12 000 cases
**WINEMAKER** Neil Pike
**PRINCIPAL WINES** Ries, Sem (wood aged), Shir, Cab Sauv; Mount Oakden is second label.
**BEST VINTAGES W** '80, '82, '86, '90 **R** '80, '82, '86, '88, '90
**SUMMARY** Has been one of the foremost producers of Rhine Riesling (witness its now glorious though still fresh '80 Rhine Riesling), and these remain the winery strengths. The '88 Cabernet Sauvignon is a first class wine, Bordeaux-like in its silky structure, but the Semillon and Shiraz seem excessively oaky.

## MITCHELTON CA–BA Est 1974 NR/CD/ML/UK $4.95–22.95 CD GOULBURN

Mitchellstown via Nagambie, Vic 3608 (057) 94 2710 fax (057) 94 2615
**OPEN** Mon–Sat 9–5, Sun/hols 10–5
**PRODUCTION** 1500 tonnes (95 000 case equivalent)
**WINEMAKER** Don Lewis
**PRINCIPAL WINES** Ries, Sauv Bl, Marsanne, Chard, Cab Sauv, Shir, Pinot, sparkl.
**BEST VINTAGES W** '80, '81, '86, '90 **R** '82, '86, '87, '90
**SUMMARY** A diverse range of labels from Classic Release at the top through to Thomas Mitchell at the bottom provide wines from young to fully mature, from modest to very good, fairly to very well priced. Oak flavours are often pronounced, but the oak handling is skilled, particularly in the winery specialty Marsanne.

## MONBULK DC–C Est 1984 LR/CD/ML $8.50–13.90 CD YARRA V

Macclesfield Road, Monbulk, Vic 3793 (03) 756 6965
**OPEN** W'ends 12–5 **PRODUCTION** 1000 cases
**WINEMAKER** Paul Jabornik
**PRINCIPAL WINES** Chard, Ries, Pinot, Cab Sauv, Shir; also Kiwi fruit wines.
**BEST VINTAGES W** '88, '90 **R** '89, '90
**SUMMARY** Originally concentrated on Kiwi fruit wines, but now extending to table wines; the very cool Monbulk sub-region should be capable of producing wines of distinctive style, but the table wines are (unfortunately) not of the same standard as the Kiwi fruit wines.

## MONICHINO CB–BA Est 1968 LR/CD/ML $5–10.50 CD NTII GOULBURN R

Berrys Road, Katunga, Vic 3640 (058) 64 6452
**OPEN** 7 days 9–6 **PRODUCTION** 8000 cases
**WINEMAKER** Carlo Monichino
**PRINCIPAL WINES** Chard, Sauv Bl, Chab, Cab Sauv, Cab Shir, Cab Mal, Shir.
**SUMMARY** An altogether surprising winery which quietly makes very clean, fresh wines in which the fruit character has been carefully preserved.

## MONTARA B–B Est 1970 LR/CD/ML $9.20–14.50 CD GRT WESTERN

Chalambar Road, Ararat, Vic 3377 (053) 52 3868 fax (053) 52 4968
**OPEN** Mon–Sat 9.30–5, Sun 12–4 **PRODUCTION** 8000 cases

**WINEMAKER** Mike McRae
**PRINCIPAL WINES** Chard, Ries, Ondenc, Chasselas, Pinot, Shir, Cab Sauv, Port.
**BEST VINTAGES W** '84, '85, '88, '90 **R** '86, '87, '89, '91
**SUMMARY** Reliable maker of full-flavoured, soft and generous wines which anomalously produces Pinot Noir of, at times, exceptional style and varietal character. The '89 was another success, although increasing competition from southern Victoria with this variety may prove difficult to overcome in the future.

## MONTROSE B–A Est 1973 NR/CD/UK (Australian Wineries)
$6.95–9.95 R MUDGEE
Henry Lawson Drive, Mudgee, NSW 2850 (063) 73 3853
**OPEN** 7 days 9–4 **PRODUCTION** 50 000 cases
**WINEMAKER** Robert Paul
**PRINCIPAL WINES** Chard, Chab, Wh Burg, Sem, Poet's Corner Dry White, Saut, Shir, Poet's Corner Dry Red, Cab Sauv.
**BEST VINTAGES W** '86, '88, '89, '91 **R** '82, '86, '89, '91
**SUMMARY** A small piece of the Orlando/Wyndham empire, acting partly as a grape and bulk wine source for that empire, and partly as a quality producer in its own right, making typically full-flavoured whites and deep coloured reds; Poets Corner impresses for its value, the '91 white wines for their quality.

## MOONDAH BROOK ESTATE B–B Est 1968 NR/UK
(Whiclar & Gordon) $10.10–18 R SWAN V
Gin Gin (Vineyard only)
**OPEN** Not **PRODUCTION** 1000 tonnes (65 000 case equivalent)
**WINEMAKER** Peter Dawson
**PRINCIPAL WINES** Chard, Chenin, Verdelho, Cab Sauv.
**SUMMARY** Consistently smooth, generously flavoured white wines which can age very well, as the 1985 Show Reserve Chenin handsomely demonstrates.

## MOOREBANK ESTATE NR Est 1987 CD/ML
$13.50–16.50 CD HUNTER V
Palmers Lane, Pokolbin, NSW 2321 (049) 98 7610
**OPEN** Wed–Sun 10–4 **PRODUCTION** 1300 cases
**WINEMAKER** Iain Riggs (Contract)
**PRINCIPAL WINES** Chard Sem, Gewurz, Merlot.
**BEST VINTAGES W** '87, '88, '89, '91
**SUMMARY** A newly opened winery; contract winemaking by Iain Riggs of Brokenwood and a 100% show record suggest quality is good.

## MOORILLA ESTATE B–B Est 1958 NFR/CD/ML
$13.50–19.50 CD STHN TAS
655 Main Road, Berriedale, Tas 7011 (002) 49 2949
**OPEN** 7 days 10–5 **PRODUCTION** 15 000 cases
**WINEMAKER** Julian Alcorso
**PRINCIPAL WINES** Ries, Chard, Gewurz, Cab Sauv, Pinot.
**BEST VINTAGES W** '87, '89, '90, '91 **R** '84, '88, '89, '91
**SUMMARY** While an avowed Pinot Noir specialist, the white wines of recent vintages have impressed most, showing elegant but intense fruit and skilled winemaking. The restaurant and wine tasting centre are outstanding, and simply must be visited.

## MOOROODUC ESTATE A–BA Est 1984 LR/CD/ML $20 R
MORNINGTON P
Derril Road, Moorooduc, Vic 3936 (03) 696 4130 (059) 78 8585
**OPEN** First w'end each month **PRODUCTION** 1500 cases

**WINEMAKER** Dr Richard McIntyre
**PRINCIPAL WINES** Chard, Pinot, Cab Sauv.
**BEST VINTAGES W & R** '86, '88, '90, '91
**SUMMARY** Dr Richard McIntyre, with help from consultant Nat White, produces one of the richest and most complex Chardonnays in the region, with grapefruit/peach fruit set against sumptuous spicy oak; the '88, '89 and '90 Chardonnays are all of the highest quality. The 1990 Cabernet Sauvignon, too, was an excellent wine for the year, but surpassed as a young wine by the great 1991 Cabernet Sauvignon with its lush, perfectly ripened cassis-accented fruit.

## MORNINGTON VINEYARDS B–B Est 1988 ML $16 R
MORNINGTON P
Moorooduc Road, Mornington, Vic 3931  (03) 817 3156  fax (03) 416 1084
**OPEN** Not  **PRODUCTION** 800 cases
**WINEMAKER** Tod Dexter (Contract)
**PRINCIPAL WINES** Chard, Pinot.
**SUMMARY** Came on-stream with its 1990 Chardonnay, made by Tod Dexter at Stoniers Merricks; immaculate viticulture and competent contract winemaking produced a crisp Chardonnay with melon and grapefruit flavours first up; as the vines mature flavour and weight will increase; the '91s were better still, with a perfumed, spicy, plum and cherry Pinot Noir to the fore.

## MORNINGSIDE NR Est 1980 LR/ML $10–12.50 ML STHN TAS
Middle Tea Tree Road, Tea Tree, Tas 7017  (002) 68 1748
**OPEN** Not  **PRODUCTION** 120 cases
**WINEMAKER** Peter Bosworth
**PRINCIPAL WINES** Ries, Pinot, Cab Sauv.
**SUMMARY** The name Morningside was given to the old property on which the vineyard stands because it gets the morning sun earliest. The property on the other side of the valley was known as 'Eveningside', and, consistently with the observation of the early settlers, the Morningside grapes achieve full maturity with good colour and varietal flavour. Production is, as yet, tiny but will increase as the 1.5 hectare vineyard matures.

## MORRIS A–A Est 1859 NR/CD $8–36 CD  NE VIC
Mia Mia Road, Rutherglen, Vic 3685  (060) 26 7303  fax (060) 26 7445
**OPEN** Mon–Sat 9–5, Sun 10–5  **PRODUCTION** 32 000 cases
**WINEMAKER** Mick Morris
**PRINCIPAL WINES** Sem, Chard, Ries, Cab Sauv, Shir, Pinot, Muscat, Tokay, Port.
**SUMMARY** One of the greatest of the fortified wine makers, some would say the greatest. If you wish to test that view, try the Old Premium Muscat and Old Premium Tokay which, at $36 a bottle, are absolute bargains given their age and quality. The table wines are dependable, the white wines all being made by owner Orlando.

## MOSS BROTHERS NR Est 1984 LR/CD/ML $11.80–15.50
CD  MARGARET R
Caves Road, Willyabrup, WA 6280  (097) 55 6270  fax (097) 55 6298
**OPEN** 7 days 10–6  **PRODUCTION** 5000 cases
**WINEMAKERS** Jane & David Moss
**PRINCIPAL WINES** Chard, Sem, Sauv Bl, Cab, Moses Rock White/Red.
**SUMMARY** A lovely '89 Chardonnay and a classy '90 Semillon have been the best wines so far; it is too early to make a proper judgement on quality. The Moss brothers do exist, incidentally.

## MOSS WOOD BA–BA Est 1969 NFR/CD/ML/UK
(Peter Diplock) $14–21 CD  MARGARET R
Metricup Road, Willyabrup via Cowaramup, WA 6284  (097) 55 6266

OPEN By appointment  PRODUCTION 5000 cases
WINEMAKER Keith Mugford
PRINCIPAL WINES Sem (Wood Mat), Sem, Chard, Cab Sauv, Pinot.
BEST VINTAGES W '83, '85, '88, '90 R '83, '85, '87, '90
SUMMARY Widely regarded as one of the best wineries in the region, capable of producing glorious Semillon (the best outside the Hunter Valley) in both oaked and unoaked forms, unctuous Chardonnay and elegant, gently herbaceous, superfine Cabernet Sauvignon which lives for many years. Regrettably, not all of the recent releases have lived up to this exalted reputation.

## MOUNTADAM  BA–B Est 1970 NFR/CD/ML/UK (Haughton Fine Wines) $15–30 R  ADELAIDE HILLS

High Eden Road, High Eden Ridge, SA 5235 (08) 362 8804
fax (08) 362 8942
OPEN Mon–Fri 10–3, w'ends 11–4  PRODUCTION 16 000 cases
WINEMAKER Adam Wynn
PRINCIPAL WINES Ries, Chard, Pinot, Cab Sauv.
BEST VINTAGES W '84, '87, '89, '90 R '84, '88, '90, '91
SUMMARY Lauded to the skies by Robert Parker and other leading international judges, who clearly appreciate the complexity of the wines. I've been of the same opinion since the 1989 vintage, and especially the '90 Chardonnay, a wine of tremendous length and subtle, complex melon/grapefruit flavour.

## MOUNT ALEXANDER  NR Est 1984 LR/CD/ML $6–14 CD  BENDIGO

Calder Highway, North Harcourt, Vic 3453  (054) 74 2262
OPEN 7 days 10–5.30  PRODUCTION 5000 cases
WINEMAKER Keith Walkden
PRINCIPAL WINES Chard, Ries, Sauv Bl, Sem, Cab Merl, Shir, Pinot, Cider.
SUMMARY A substantial operation with large vineyards planted to all the right varieties. It is several years since I have tasted the wines.

## MOUNT ANAKIE  CB–B Est 1969 LR/CD $10–18 R GEELONG

Staughton Vale Road, Anakie, Vic 3221  (052) 84 1452
OPEN Tues–Sun 10.30–5  PRODUCTION 10 000 cases
WINEMAKER Otto Zambelli
PRINCIPAL WINES Ries, Chard, Sem, Grenache, Cab, Shir.
BEST VINTAGES W '81, '87, '88, '90 R '84, '86, '87, '88
SUMMARY Also known as Zambelli Estate, and has produced some excellent wines (under its various ownerships and winemakers), all distinguished by their depth and intensity of flavour. Recent vintages have been unconvincing.

## MOUNTAIN CREEK  NR EST 1973 CD/ML $12.50 PYRENEES

Mountain Creek Road, Moonambel, Vic 3478
OPEN W'ends by appointment  PRODUCTION 1600 cases
WINEMAKER Taltarni (Contract)
PRINCIPAL WINES Sauv Bl, Cab Sauv.
SUMMARY Brian Cherry acquired the Mountain Creek Vineyard in 1975 and has slowly extended it. The first wine was made in 1987, all or part of the grapes before and in some years since then sold to other Pyrenees wineries. The wine is made under contract, and shows all of the substance and weight for which the district is renowned. The 1990 Sauvignon Blanc and '88 Cabernet Sauvignon are both commendable wines.

**MOUNT AVOCA**  B–B Est 1978 NFR/CD/ML/UK
(McKinley Vintners) $9.50–14.60 CD  PYRENEES
Moates Lane, Avoca, Vic 3467  (054) 65 3282
**OPEN**  Mon–Sat 10–5, Sun 12–5  **PRODUCTION**  11 000 cases
**WINEMAKERS**  John Barry and Rodney Morrish
**PRINCIPAL WINES**  Dry Wh, Sauv Bl, Chard, Sem, Cab Sauv, Shir.
**BEST VINTAGES  W** '87, '88, '89, '90  **R** '86, '87, '88, '91
**SUMMARY**  Produces solidly flavoured and structured wines which have
a widespread audience; the white wines are particularly reliable, while the
'91 Cabernet Sauvignon promises to be the best red yet from this winery.

**MOUNT CHALAMBAR**  B–B Est 1978 NFR $10.50–14.50
R GRT WESTERN
Off Tatyoon Road, Ararat, Vic 3377  (053) 54 3207
**OPEN**  Not  **PRODUCTION**  1600 cases
**WINEMAKER**  Trevor Mast
**PRINCIPAL WINES**  Ries, Chard.
**SUMMARY**  Sparkling wine making has, it seems, gone into recess,
leaving the focus of attention on full-flavoured, lime-accented Rhine
Riesling and barrel-fermented Chardonnay.

**MOUNT DUNEED**  CB–CB Est 1970 LR/CD/ML $17–15 CD
GEELONG
Feehan's Road, Mount Duneed, Vic 3216  (052) 64 1281
**OPEN**  Sat 9–5, Sun 12–5  **PRODUCTION**  1000 cases
**WINEMAKER**  Ken Campbell
**PRINCIPAL WINES**  Sem Sauv Bl, Ries, Botrytis Sem, Cab Malb, Cab
Sauv.
**SUMMARY**  Rather idiosyncratic wines are the order of the day, some of
which can develop surprisingly well in bottle; the Botrytis Noble Rot
Semillon has, from time to time, been of very high quality.

**MOUNT HELEN**  Est 1979 CB–CB NFR/ML/UK
(Mt Helen UK) $9.65–20.90 R CENTRAL GOULBURN
Strathbogie Ranges (vineyard only)  (054) 821 911
**OPEN**  See Tisdall  **PRODUCTION**  NFP
**WINEMAKER**  Jeff Clarke
**PRINCIPAL WINES**  Chard, Fumé Bl, Ries, Cab Merl, Merl, Pinot;
top-of-the-range released under Winemakers Reserve label.
**BEST VINTAGES  W & R** '82, '84, '88, '90
**SUMMARY**  Mount Helen has always promised a great deal, and
occasionally delivers it. For reasons I do not profess to understand, wine
quality is not always what it should be, with some extreme winemaker
interpretations appearing on the one hand, and vineyard problems on the
other. Mount Helen, incidentally, is a separate vineyard and brand owned
by Tisdall.

**MOUNT HURTLE**  BA–BA Est 1897 NFR/CD/ML/UK
(Atkinson & Baldwin) $8–14 CD  STHN VALES
Cnr Pimpala and Byards Road, Reynella, SA 5161  (08) 381 6877
fax (08) 322 2244
**OPEN**  Mon–Fri 10–4, Sun 10–4
**PRODUCTION**  28 000 cases (total group production)
**WINEMAKER**  Geoff Merrill
**PRINCIPAL WINES**  Sem Sauv Bl, Cab Sauv.
**BEST VINTAGES  W** '86, '87, '89, '90  **R** '84, '85, '86, '88, '90
**SUMMARY**  Once seen, the stridently flamboyant label of Mount Hurtle is
not easily forgotten, which is no doubt precisely what Geoff Merrill intended.
The style of the wine in the bottle is altogether more restrained and elegant,
with the accent on freshness and varietal clarity. The name is that of the

beautiful century-old stone winery at which all the Merrill brands are made.

## MOUNT IDA  NR Est 1978 LR $10–15 R  BENDIGO
Northern Highway, Heathcote, Vic 3523  (054) 821 911
**OPEN** At Tisdall  **PRODUCTION** NFP
**WINEMAKER** Jeff Clarke
**PRINCIPAL WINES** Chard, Ries, Cab Franc, Mer, Shir.
**BEST VINTAGES** '82, '85, '90, '91
**SUMMARY** Established by the famous artist Leonard French and Dr James Munro, but purchased by Tisdall after the 1987 bushfires. Up to the time of the fires, wonderfully smooth, rich red wines with almost voluptous sweet, minty fruit were the hallmark. Has now been turned into a brand with the addition of two white wines and a new red blend, all sourced elsewhere.

## MOUNT LANGI GHIRAN  A–A Est 1970 NFR/CD/ML $9.50–16.50 R GRT WESTERN
Vine Road, Buangor, Vic 3375  (053) 54 3207
**OPEN** Mon–Fri 9–5, w'ends 12–5  **PRODUCTION** 11 000 cases
**WINEMAKER** Trevor Mast
**PRINCIPAL WINES** Chard, Ries, Cab Sauv, Shir, Circa (a regional blend).
**BEST VINTAGES W** '84, '85, '87, '91 **R** '83, '85, '86, '89, '90, '91
**SUMMARY** A maker of outstanding cool-climate peppery Shiraz, crammed with flavour and vinosity, and very good Cabernet Sauvignon. The Shiraz points the way for cool-climate examples of the variety, for weight, texture and fruit richness all accompany the vibrant pepper-spice aroma and flavour. Both the '89 and '90 Shiraz are quite wonderful wines.

## MOUNT MAGNUS  NR Est 1933 CD/ML $4.95–9.50 CD GRANITE BELT
Donnellys Castle Road, Pozieres, Qld 4352  (076) 85 3313
**OPEN** 7 days 9–5  **PRODUCTION** NFP
**WINEMAKER** Andrew Braithweight
**PRINCIPAL WINES** Sem Chard, Ries, Gewurz Tram, LP Sem, Cab Sauv.
**SUMMARY** One of the oldest vineyards in the district, which has had a chequered history and numerous changes of ownership and winemakers. I have not tasted the wines for several years.

## MOUNT MARTHA VINEYARD  NR Est 1986 ML $12–16 ML MORNINGTON P
Range Road, Mount Martha, Vic 3934 (059) 74 2700 fax (059) 74 4007
**OPEN** Not  **PRODUCTION** 500 cases
**WINEMAKER** Kevin McCarthy (Contract)
**PRINCIPAL WINES** Chard, Sauv Bl, Cab Sauv.
**SUMMARY** The small Mount Martha Vineyard is owned by the Matson and Scalley families, overlooking Port Phillip Bay on undulating loam. Competent contract winemaking should ensure the quality of the wines.

## MOUNT MARY  A–B Est 1971 LR/ML $20–24 ML  YARRA V
Coldstream West Road, Lillydale, Vic 3140  (03) 739 1761
**OPEN** Not  **PRODUCTION** NFP
**WINEMAKER** Dr John Middleton
**PRINCIPAL WINES** Chard, Sauv Bl Sem Muscad, Pinot, Cab (Bordeaux blends).
**SUMMARY** Superbly refined, elegant and intense Cabernets, and usually outstanding and long lived Pinot Noirs, fully justify Mount Mary's exalted reputation; the white Bordeaux blend of Semillon, Muscadelle and Sauvignon Blanc is good, though not in the same class. The '88 Cabernets and '89 Pinot Noir are both excellent wines.

**MOUNT PRIOR** NR Est 1860 CD/ML $6.50–13.50 CD  NE VIC
Cnr River Road & Popes Lane, Rutherglen, Vic 3685   (060) 26 5591
fax (060) 26 7456
**OPEN** 7 days 10–5   **PRODUCTION** 9000 cases
**WINEMAKER** Garry Wall
**PRINCIPAL WINES** Chard, Chenin, Wh Burg, Durif, Carignan, Cab
Sauv, Shir.
**SUMMARY** Re-established in 1989 after a disastrous foray into exports
to the United States; the experience of Garry Wall should ensure quality,
although a somewhat jammy 1991 Carignan is more of academic interest
than anything else.

**MOUNT VIEW ESTATE** C–CB Est 1971 CD/ML $10–14
CD  HUNTER V
Mount View Road, Mount View, NSW 2325   (049) 90 3307
**OPEN** Fri–Mon 9–5, Tues–Thur 10–4   **PRODUCTION** 2000 cases
**WINEMAKER** H. W. Tulloch
**PRINCIPAL WINES** Chard, Sauv Bl, Verd, Herm, Cab Merl, fortifieds.
**BEST VINTAGES** W '83, '86, '87, '91 R '83, '86, '87, '91
**SUMMARY** Some new oak would help the table wines immeasurably;
the range of fortified wines are rather better.

**MOUNT VINCENT** DB–C Est 1980 LR/CD/ML $12–15 CD
MUDGEE
Common Road, Mudgee, NSW 2850   (063) 72 3184
**OPEN** Mon–Sat 10–5, Sun 10–4   **PRODUCTION** 2000 cases
**WINEMAKER** Jane Nevell
**PRINCIPAL WINES** Ries, Cab Sauv, Liqueur Muscat, Meads, Mead Ale.
**SUMMARY** The table wines are made without preservatives, and simply
show how difficult it is to make wine this way. The meads are very good,
also the mead ale.

**MOUNTILFORD** NR Est 1981 CD/ML $8–9.50 CD  MUDGEE
Vincent Road, Ilford, NSW 2850   (063) 58 8544
**OPEN** 7 days 10–4   **PRODUCTION** 1900 cases
**WINEMAKER** Don Cumming
**PRINCIPAL WINES** Chard, Syl Tram, Ries, Pinot, Shir Cab, Port.
**SUMMARY** A quiet cellar-door operation; the '90 Shiraz is by far the
best of a distinctly mixed bunch.

**MOUNTVIEW WINES** NR Est 1991 CD/ML $7–9 CD
GRANITE BELT
Mount Sterling Road, Glen Aplin, Qld 4381   (076) 834 316
**OPEN** W'ends/hols 9–5   **PRODUCTION** 450 cases
**WINEMAKER** David Price
**PRINCIPAL WINES** Sem/Sauv Bl, Light Red, Shir.
**SUMMARY** David and Linda Price are refugees from the Sydney rat-
race who opened a tiny red cedar barn-style winery, and proceeded to
make an attractive sweet berry Shiraz in 1990.

**MUDGEE WINES** NR Est 1963 CD/ML $7.50–9 CD  MUDGEE
Henry Lawson Drive, Mudgee, NSW 2850   (063) 72 2258
**OPEN** Mon–Sat 10–5, Sun 12–5   **PRODUCTION** 1000 cases
**WINEMAKER** Jennifer Meek
**PRINCIPAL WINES** Chard, Gewurz, Crouchen, Ries, Rosé, Shir, Pinot,
Cab Sauv.
**SUMMARY** All of the wines are naturally fermented with wild yeasts
and made without the addition of any chemicals or substances including
sulphur dioxide, a very demanding route, particularly with white wines.
For some consumers, any shortcoming in quality will be quite acceptable.

**MURRAY ROBSON** B–B Est 1970 LR/CD/ML $13–19 CD
HUNTER V
Halls Road, Pokolbin, NSW 2321   (049) 98 7539
**OPEN** 7 days 9–5   **PRODUCTION** 12 800 cases
**WINEMAKER** Murray Robson
**PRINCIPAL WINES** A range of evocative labels including Pepper Tree
Vineyard, Frost Hollow, Mulberry Row (for blended wines) and traditional
varietals including Chard, Pinot, Shir and Cab Sauv.
**SUMMARY** The Murray Robson saga of the past five years has not dimmed
his enthusiasm nor the faith (and financial strength) of partner James Fairfax.
The new generation wines are basically sound and clean, with fresh fruit; '91
Pepper Tree Semillon and '88 Pepper Tree Hermitage were among the best.

**MURRINDINDI** CB–B Est 1979 LR/CD/ML $11.60–13.30 CD
STHN VIC
RMB 6070 Cummins Lane, Murrindindi, Vic 3717   (057) 97 8217
**OPEN** By appointment only   **PRODUCTION** 1400 cases
**WINEMAKER** Alan Cuthbertson
**PRINCIPAL WINES** Chard, Cab Merl.
**SUMMARY** Something of an orphan, not quite in the Yarra Valley nor
in Macedon, but (like Flowerdale) in a climate so cool it is marginal for
table wine making, and perhaps better suited to sparkling wine overall.
The warmest years have produced some very elegant Cabernet Merlots,
'91 a smiliarly elegant Chardonnay.

**NICHOLSON RIVER** A–BA Est 1978 LR/CD/ML/UK
(John Armit Wines) $9–22 CD   GIPPSLAND
Liddells Road, Nicholson, Vic 3882   (051) 56 8241
**OPEN** 7 days 10–5 preferably by appointment   **PRODUCTION** 700 cases
**WINEMAKER** Ken Eckersley
**PRINCIPAL WINES** Sem, Chard, Ries, Pinot, Cabernets; second label is
Mountview.
**BEST VINTAGES** **W** '86, '87, '88, '91 **R** '87, '89, '90, '91
**SUMMARY** The fierce commitment to quality in the face of the
temperamental Gippsland climate and frustratingly small production has
been handsomely repaid by some stupendous Chardonnays, none better
than the Montrachet-like '88.

**NIOKA RIDGE** DB–C Est 1979 LR/CD/ML $6.50–12.50 CD
HILLTOPS
Barwang Road, Young, NSW 2594   (063) 82 2903
**OPEN** 7 days 9–6   **PRODUCTION** 2200 cases
**WINEMAKER** Phil Price
**PRINCIPAL WINES** Chard, Ries, Cab Shir, Cab Malb, fortifieds.
**SUMMARY** A winery which struggles hard to overcome the difficulties
of isolation, not always succeeding.

**NOON'S** NR Est 1976 CD/ML $10–12.50 CD STHN VALES
Rifle Range Road, McLaren Vale, SA 5171 (08) 270 4253
**OPEN** 7 days 10–5   **PRODUCTION** 2000 cases
**WINEMAKER** David Noon
**PRINCIPAL WINES** Rosé, Cab Sauv, Burg, Dry Red, Shir Cab.
**SUMMARY** Massive wines which I once greatly admired; either they
have changed or I have, for I now find them excessively extractive and
astringent. I wish it were otherwise.

**NORMANS** BA–BA Est 1851 NR/CD/ML/UK (Ehrmanns)
$7.30–23 R STHN VALES
Grants Gully Road, Clarendon, SA 5157   (08) 383 6138
**OPEN** 7 days 10–5   **PRODUCTION** 150 000 cases

**WINEMAKER** Brian Light
**PRINCIPAL WINES** Ries, Chard, Fumé, Chenin, Chablis, Pinot, Herm, Cab Sauv, fortifieds, under the Chandlers Hill, Clarendon and top-of-the-range Chais Clarendon labels.
**BEST VINTAGES W** '82, '85, '87, '90 **R** '88, '89, '90
**SUMMARY** Consistent producers of wines which, within their price categories, have considerable appeal. Always smooth and well crafted, they can reach great heights under the Chais Clarendon label, and offer exceptional value under the Chandlers Hill label, exemplified by the '91 Merlot Cabernet, a lively, fresh wine with unexpectedly good varietal character.

**NOTLEY GORGE** NR Est 1983 LR/CD/ML $15 ML TAS
Loop Road, Glengarry, Tas 7275 (vineyard only)  (003) 961 166
**OPEN** By appointment  **PRODUCTION** 1400 cases
**WINEMAKER** Various contract
**PRINCIPAL WINES** Sauv Bl, Chard, Pinot, Cab Sauv (light red).
**SUMMARY** Marine engineer Doug Bowen (no relation to the Doug Bowen of Coonawarra) spreads his favours around, having his Sauvignon Blanc processed at Domaine A, Chardonnay at Rochecombe, and Pinot Noir crushed at Notley Gorge, pressed at Holm Oak and then returned to Notley Gorge for maturation in the former apple orchard cool store, a building which just happened to be on the property and which precipitated him into wine production. The 1991 Chardonnay is a well made, attractive, if very herbaceous, wine.

**OAKRIDGE ESTATE** BA–B Est 1982 LR/CD/ML/UK
(Reid Wines) $14–25 CD  YARRA V
Aitken Road, Seville, Vic 3139  (059) 64 3379  fax (059) 64 4524
**OPEN** W'ends 10–5  **PRODUCTION** 1100 cases
**WINEMAKER** Michael Zitzlaff
**PRINCIPAL WINES** Cab Sauv under Quercus and Reserve labels.
**BEST VINTAGES R** '84, '85, '86, '90
**SUMMARY** Has provided some of the greatest Yarra Valley Cabernets; the vintage rating reflects some young vine influence between 1986 and 1990. In the future this winery is concentrating on the Reserve Cabernet Sauvignon, the 1990 vintage being one of the best (and most complex) Cabernets to come from the Yarra Valley to date.

**OAKVALE** CB–B Est 1893 LR/CD/ML/UK (Heyman Bros)
$11–16 CD  HUNTER V
Broke Road, Pokolbin, NSW 2321  (049) 98 7520  fax (049) 987 7747
**OPEN** 7 days 9–5  **PRODUCTION** 5000 cases
**WINEMAKER** Barry Shields
**PRINCIPAL WINES** Sem, Sem Chard, Chard, Shir, Cab Sauv.
**BEST VINTAGES W** '88, '89, '91 **R** '88, '89, '90, '91
**SUMMARY** The emphasis is on Semillon, Chardonnay and a blend of the two, in both oaked and unoaked versions. A few errant aromas appear from time to time; bottle age does help, as the toasty/honeyed 1989 Semillon Chardonnay handsomely demonstrated in 1992.

**OLD BARN** NR Est 1861 CD/ML $4.80–12 CD BAROSSA V
Langmeil Road, Tanunda, SA 5352  (085) 630 111
**OPEN** Mon–Fri 9–5, w'ends, hols 11–4  **PRODUCTION** NFP
**WINEMAKER** Various contract
**PRINCIPAL WINES** Ries, Dry White, Light Dry Red, Quaffing Red, Cab Shir, Cab Mal, fortifieds.
**SUMMARY** Owned by a partnership of Barry and Elizabeth Chinner and Janet Hatch, with an honorary establishment date of 1861, being the date of construction of the old stone barn from which the wines are exclusively sold. The wines themselves are either made elsewhere or

purchased from other makers for the Old Barn label.

**OLD CAVES WINERY** NR Est 1980 CD/ML $6–10.50 CD
GRANITE BELT
New England Highway, Stanthorpe, Qld 4380 (076) 81 1494
**OPEN** 7 days 9–5 **PRODUCTION** 2500 cases
**WINEMAKER** David Zanatta
**PRINCIPAL WINES** Chard, Shir, Cab Sauv and a range of generic
wines in both bottle and flagon, including fortified.
**SUMMARY** A range of wines tasted from the 1990 and '91 vintages
showed significant winemaking problems, but over the years Old Caves
has produced some pleasant wines.

**OLIVE FARM** CB–B Est 1829 LR/CD/ML $8.80–12 CD SWAN V
77 Great Eastern Highway, South Guildford, WA 6055 (09) 277 2989
fax (09) 279 4372
**OPEN** Mon–Fri 10–5, Sat 9–3 **PRODUCTION** 9500 cases
**WINEMAKER** Ian Yurisich
**PRINCIPAL WINES** Verd, Chenin, Chab, Sem, Chard, Gewurtz, Cab
Shir, Herm, Cab Sauv, Cab/Shir/Mer, Sherry, Port, sparkl.
**SUMMARY** The oldest winery in Australia in use today, and arguably
the least communicative. The ultra-low profile tends to disguise the fact
that wine quality is by and large good.

**OLIVERHILL** NR Est 1973 CD/ML $3.50–11 CD STHN
VALES
Seaview Road, McLaren Vale, SA 5171 (08) 323 8922
**OPEN** 7 days 10–5 **PRODUCTION** 1300 cases
**WINEMAKER** Vincenzo Berlingieri
**PRINCIPAL WINES** Great Outdoors white and red, Chard, Shir Cab,
Port and Muscat.
**SUMMARY** Vincenzo Berlingieri's towering presence once extended to
Sydney promotional trips; these days he is content to run Oliverhill
without fanfare and, with his wife Kiawngo, run a unique Italian-Chinese
restaurant. Open 7 days for lunch and dinner by appointment.

**ORLANDO** A–A Est 1847 NR/CD/UK (Caxton Tower) $6–29 R
BAROSSA V
Sturt Highway, Rowland Flat, SA 5350 (085) 24 4500 fax (085) 21 3100
**OPEN** Mon–Fri 9.30–5, w'ends 10–4 **PRODUCTION** NFP
**WINEMAKER** Robin Day
**PRINCIPAL WINES** A plethora of brands (in ascending order)
including Coolabah casks and flagons, Jacobs Creek, RF, Gramps (the last
three covering all styles), St Hugo Cab Sauv, St Hilary Chard, St Helga
Ries, Flaxmans Gewurz, Lawsons Shir, Steingarten Ries and Jacaranda
Ridge Cab Sauv. All of the major grape varieties are represented.
**BEST VINTAGES W** '82, '88, '90, '91 **R** '66, '71, '82, '86, '88, '90, '91
**SUMMARY** With the Wyndham group under its belt, Orlando is now the
second largest producer in Australia, although well behind the massive S. A.
Brewing agglomerate. As befits a group of this size, and given Australian
technology, you basically get what you pay for, with full value for money always
guaranteed in a highly (some would say indecently) competitive market.

**PADTHAWAY ESTATE, THE** NR Est 1980 LR/CD/ML
$15–18.50 R PADTHAWAY
Keith-Naracoorte Road, Padthaway, SA 5271 (087) 65 5039
fax (087) 65 5097
**OPEN** 7 days 10–4 **PRODUCTION** 6000 cases
**WINEMAKER** Leigh Clarnette
**PRINCIPAL WINES** Chard, sparkling, Pinot.

SUMMARY The only functioning winery in Padthaway, set in the superb grounds of the Estate in a large and gracious old stone woolshed; the homestead is in the Relais et Chateaux mould, offering luxurious accommodation and fine food. The focus is on elegantly packaged Méthode Champenoise, with style still to be finally determined.

**PALMARA** NR Est 1985 ML $12 COAL RIVER, TAS
Main Road, Richmond, Tas 7025 (002) 622 462; postal PO Box 75, Rosny Park, Tas 7018
OPEN Not PRODUCTION 100 cases
WINEMAKER Andrew Hood
PRINCIPAL WINES Chard, Pinot, Cab Sauv.
SUMMARY Allan Bird has the Palmara wines made for him by Andrew Hood, all in tiny quantities. By far the best tasted to date has been a potent, cherry/plum 1990 Pinot Noir, with strong charred oak flavours running through it, and years in front of it. Barrel samples of the 1991 wines could not be properly assessed, and judgement must be suspended.

**PANKHURST WINES** NR Est 1986 ML $12 CANBERRA
Old Woodgrove, Woodgrove Road, Hall, NSW 2618 (06) 230 2592
fax (06) 273 1936
OPEN Not PRODUCTION 900 cases
WINEMAKER Dr Roger Harris (Contract)
PRINCIPAL WINES Chard, Sem, Pinot, Cab Merl.
SUMMARY Agricultural scientist and consultant Allan Pankhurst and wife Christine (with a degree in pharmaceutical science) have established a three hectare, split vineyard. The strongly flavoured, chewy 1990 Cabernet Merlot, redolent with sweet berry fruit, augurs well for the future.

**PANORAMA** CB–CB Est 1975 LR $10–13 R HUON V
193 Waterworks Road, Dynnyrne, Tas 7005 (002) 23 1948
OPEN Not PRODUCTION 900 cases
WINEMAKER Steve Ferencz
PRINCIPAL WINES Chard, Muller, Pinot.
SUMMARY The quality of the underlying fruit, paticularly with the red wines, is not in doubt: these have great colour and startling richness of flavour in years such as 1990 and 1991. The full potential has sometimes been held back by problems with indifferent oak, but not so in the case of the superb 1990 Cabernet Sauvignon, with its luscious, red berry/cassis fruit, a worthy gold medal winner at the 1992 Tasmanian Regional Wines Show.

**PARINGA ESTATE** CA–BA Est 1985 LR/CD/ML $13.50–18
CD MORNINGTON P
44 Paringa Road, Red Hill South, Vic 3937 (059) 89 2669
OPEN W'ends 11–5, 7 days sum hols PRODUCTION 1000 cases
WINEMAKER Lindsay McCall
PRINCIPAL WINES Chard, Cab Sauv, Shir.
SUMMARY The Shiraz is consistently outstanding, often picked in June yet showing vibrant spice/pepper flavours and ageing beautifully in the short term. The other wines have also begun to regularly win show medals.

**PARKER WINES** NR Est 1968 LR/CD/ML $11.70–13.80 R
HUNTER V
McDonalds Road, Pokolbin, NSW 2321 phone and fax (049) 987 585
OPEN 7 days 9.30–4.30 PRODUCTION 12 000 cases
WINEMAKER David Lowe
PRINCIPAL WINES Sem, Chard, Pinot, Shir.
SUMMARY Established as Tamburlaine, this seemingly ill-starred winery then became Tamalee, then Sobels and now Parker — after its owner Stan Parker. With ex-Rothbury chief winemaker David Lowe in

charge, it is reasonable to hope — and indeed expect — that the fortunes of what is now Parker Wines will take a turn for the better.

## PARKER COONAWARRA ESTATE NR Est 1975
NFR/UK (Corney & Barrow) $16.99–29.95 R COONAWARRA
Penola Road, Coonawarra, SA
**OPEN** Not **PRODUCTION** 1000 cases
**WINEMAKER** Ralph Fowler (Contract)
**PRINCIPAL WINES** Cab Sauv under two labels, Parker Estate and Parker Estate Terra Rosa First Growth.
**SUMMARY** Parker Coonawarra Estate is a joint venture between the Parker, Fowler and Balnaves families: John Parker, former chairman of Hungerford Hill; Doug Balnaves, long-term viticulturist in Coonawarra; and Ralph Fowler, winemaker at Leconfield and contract maker for Parker Coonawarra Estate. The partnership grows 400 tonnes of fruit a year, and selects the best 16–20 tonnes for the Parker label. Not surprisingly, the first release of 1988 Terra Rosa First Growth has been a prolific show winner, with its opulent, seductive berry fruit and beautifully judged American oak. The '89 and '90 vintages waiting in the wings are also very good wines.

## PARKLANE WINES NR Est 1986 CD/ML $9–12 CD
CANBERRA
Brooklands Road, via Hall, ACT 2618 phone and fax (06) 230 2263
**OPEN** W'ends 11–5 **PRODUCTION** 2500 cases
**WINEMAKER** Alwyn Lane
**PRINCIPAL WINES** Ries, Fumé Bl, Chard, Pinot, Cabernets.
**SUMMARY** Alwyn and Margaret Lane run the 8 hectare vineyard and winery as a full-time occupation, making only estate-grown wines, and with plans to increase production to 4500 cases by 1996. The first vintage was 1989, and a very pretty cherry/plum flavoured Pinot from 1990 promised much for the future.

## PASSING CLOUDS B–B Est 1974 LR/CD/ML $12.50–19.95
CD BENDIGO
Kurting Road, Kingower, Vic 3517 (054) 38 8257
**OPEN** 7 days 9–6 by appointment **PRODUCTION** 2500 cases
**WINEMAKER** Graeme Leith
**PRINCIPAL WINES** Shir/Cab, Pinot, Cab/Cab Fr/Mer.
**BEST VINTAGES R** '82, '84, '86, '90
**SUMMARY** Graeme Leith is one of the great personalities of the industry, with a superb sense of humour, and makes lovely regional reds, with cassis, berry and mint fruit.

## PATRITTI DC–B Est 1926 LR/CD/ML $2.50–6.50 CD
ADELAIDE PLAINS
13-23 Clacton Road, Dover Gardens, SA 5048 (08) 296 8261
fax (08) 296 5088
**OPEN** Mon–Sat 9–6 **PRODUCTION** 65 000 cases
**WINEMAKERS** G. & J. Patritti
**PRINCIPAL WINES** A kaleidoscopic array of table, sparkling, fortified and flavoured wines (and spirits) offered in bottle and flagon.
**SUMMARY** One of the old-style winemaker-cum-merchant offering wines and spirits at old-style prices.

## PATTERSONS B–B Est 1982 ML $14–18 ML LWR GRT STHN
28 Montem Street, Mount Barker, WA 6324 (098) 511 629 (AH)
**OPEN** By appointment **PRODUCTION** 900 cases
**WINEMAKER** John Wade
**PRINCIPAL WINES** Chard, Shir, Pinot.
**BEST VINTAGES** '86, '89, '90, '91

**SUMMARY** Schoolteachers Sue and Arthur Patterson have grown Chardonnay and grazed cattle as a weekend relaxation for a decade; a vertical tasting of their Chardonnay (made by various contract makers) since 1986 showed the worth of relaxation — the wines had real style and flavour. The 1992 debut of the '90 Shiraz, with crisp, fragrant pepper spice, was no less impressive.

**PAUL CONTI** CB–B Est 1968 LR/CD $10.70–17.70 R SW COASTAL
529 Wanneroo Road, Wanneroo, WA 6065 (09) 409 9160
**OPEN** Mon–Sat 9.30–5.30 **PRODUCTION** 9500 cases
**WINEMAKER** Paul Conti
**PRINCIPAL WINES** Chard, Chab, Chenin, Fronti, Herm, Port.
**BEST VINTAGES W** '85, '89, '90 **R** '82, '87, '89
**SUMMARY** A low-key operation which consistently makes clean, smooth dry white wines intensely fruity and slightly sweet Frontignac and fresh cherry/berry flavoured Hermitage.

**PAULETT** CB–B Est 1983 LR/CD/ML $9.50–11.50 CD CLARE V
Polish Hill Road, Polish Hill River, SA 5453 (088) 43 4328
fax (088) 43 4202
**OPEN** 7 days 10–4.30 **PRODUCTION** 4800 cases
**WINEMAKER** Neil Paulett
**PRINCIPAL WINES** Sauv Bl, Ries, Chard, Shir, Cab Merl, sparkl.
**BEST VINTAGES W** 86, '88, '90, '91 **R** '84, '86, '89, '90, '91
**SUMMARY** Neil Paulett has had a lifetime of experience in the industry, starting at Penfolds Wybong in the Upper Hunter Valley in the '60s. Oak problems marred some of the '89 reds, but a spicy, barrel-fermented '91 Chardonnay impressed.

**PAUL OSICKA** BA–A Est 1955 LR/CD $11–14 CD GOULBURN V
Graytown, Vic 3608 (057) 94 9235
**OPEN** Mon–Sat 10–5, Sun 12–5 **PRODUCTION** NFP
**WINEMAKER** Paul Osicka
**PRINCIPAL WINES** Chard, Ries, Cab Sauv, Herm, Port.
**BEST VINTAGES W** '89, '90 **R** '86, '87, '89, '90
**SUMMARY** Produces red wines which are never less than good, and are sometimes outstanding; for example the '89 Shiraz is wonderfully rich, minty and spicy.

**PEACOCK HILL** B–B Est 1986 LR/CD $13.50–16.50 R HUNTER V
Cnr Palmers Lane and Branxton Road, Pokolbin, NSW 2325
(049) 98 7557
**OPEN** Through Pokolbin Estate **PRODUCTION** 250 cases
**WINEMAKER** Rothbury Estate (Contract)
**PRINCIPAL WINES** Chard, Shir, Cab Sauv.
**SUMMARY** Established when a syndicate purchased part of the Rothbury Estate Herlstone vineyard and used Rothbury as contract winemaker, initially concentrating on the export market. Wine quality has been consistently good.

**PEEL ESTATE** C–C Est 1974 LR/CD/ML/UK (Peel Estate UK) $13–16 R SW COASTAL
Fletcher Road, Baldivis, WA 6210 (09) 524 1221
**OPEN** 7 days 10–5 **PRODUCTION** 5000 cases
**WINEMAKER** Will Nairn
**PRINCIPAL WINES** Chard, Chenin (Wood Mat), Verd, Shir, Cab Sauv, Zinfan.

SUMMARY· Will Nairn has concentrated on wood-matured Chenin Blanc and light but elegant reds, with some success; recent oak handling has not been convincing, but the underlying wine quality is good.

## PENDARVES ESTATE NR Est 1986 LR/CD/ML $13–16 ML HUNTER V

Lot 10 Old North Road, Belford, NSW 2335  (02) 974 5794 or (02) 913 1088

**OPEN** W'ends 12–5  **PRODUCTION** 1500 cases
**WINEMAKER** Mark Davidson and Greg Silkman (Contract)
**PRINCIPAL WINES** Chard, Verdel, Pinot/Chambourcin, Cab/Merl/Mal.
**SUMMARY** The perpetual motion general practitioner and founder of the Australian Medical Friends of Wine, Dr Philip Norrie, is a born communicator and marketer, as well as a wine historian and author of note; given wines of the richness of the 1991 Chardonnay and Verdelho, Pendarves is bound to flourish.

## PENFOLDS A–A Est 1844 NR/CD/UK (Penfolds Wines) $6–70 R BAROSSA V

Tanunda Road, Nuriootpa, SA 5355  (085) 62 0389  fax (085) 62 1669
**OPEN** Mon–Sat 10–5, Sun 12–4  **PRODUCTION** NFP
**WINEMAKER** John Duval
**PRINCIPAL WINES** As with the other majors, emphasis is on brands, allied with long-established Bin number products. Bin 28 Kalimna, 128 Coonawarra Claret, 389 Cab Shir, 707 Cab Sauv; brands include Koonunga Hill Claret, Magill Estate, Clare Estate, St Henri Claret and Grange Herm. Has fairly recently moved into Chard and Sem Chard.
**BEST VINTAGES R** '55, '62, '66, '71, '76, '82, '83, '86, '88, '90
**SUMMARY** Makes what has often been described as Australia's only first growth claret — Grange Hermitage — a wine which can age with exceptional grace for over 30 years. Strongly flavoured, complex, oak influenced wines have always been its forte; Bin 707 Cabernet Sauvignon has comprehensively replaced St Henri Claret as the second wine in the line-up, while Koonunga Hill is regarded as one of the best budget-priced reds available throughout the year. Minchinbury sparkling wine is a brand leader in its category.

## PENINSULA ESTATE NR Est 1985 LR/CD/ML $12–20 R MORNINGTON P

Red Hill Road, Red Hill, Vic 3937  (059) 89 2866
**OPEN** 1st w'end each month  **PRODUCTION** 2500 cases
**WINEMAKER** Kevin McCarthy
**PRINCIPAL WINES** Ries, Chard, Sem/Sauv Bl, Cab, Cab Merl, Pinot.
**SUMMARY** Yet another newcomer to the Peninsula, with light crisp Chardonnays and a fresh, simple Pinot Noir from the 1990 vintage.

## PENLEY ESTATE BA–B Est 1988 NFR/CD/ML/UK (Lay & Wheeler, Australian Wine Centre) $14–30 R COONAWARRA

McLeans Road, Coonawarra, SA 5263  (08) 366 4106  fax (08) 231 0589
**OPEN** 7 days 10–5  **PRODUCTION** Over 6500 cases
**WINEMAKER** Kym Tolley
**PRINCIPAL WINES** Chard, Shir Cab, Cab Sauv, Meth Champ.
**SUMMARY** An ultra-ambitious and potentially high-profile winery, sparing no expense in its quest for quality and having success right from the outset; production will ultimately be estate-grown, the early wines having been made from purchased grapes. The 1989 Cabernet Sauvignon won two trophies and six gold medals, thanks in part to positive oak handling; the '90 Chardonnay was another pungently flavoured and oaked wine which had much show success.

**PENOWARRA** NR Est 1978 CD/ML $8–10 CD
COONAWARRA
Main Penola-Naracoorte Road, Penola, SA 5277 (087) 37 2458
OPEN Most Sat/Sun 9–5 PRODUCTION 500 cases
WINEMAKER Ken Ward
PRINCIPAL WINES Ries, Shir, Cab Sauv, Wh Port.
SUMMARY A low-profile cellar door operation making no frills wine:
those last tasted were adequate but not exciting.

**PENWORTHAM WINE CELLARS** NR Est 1990
CD/ML $7.50–9.50 CD CLARE V
Government Road, Penwortham, SA (088) 43 4345
OPEN Sat 10–5, Sun 10–4 PRODUCTION 800 cases
WINEMAKER R. Hughes
PRINCIPAL WINES Ries, Burg, Muscat Fronti, Port.
SUMMARY A new arrival on the Clare Valley scene; I have not tasted
any of the wines.

**PEPPERS CREEK** CB–B Est 1986 LR/CD/ML $15–17.50 CD
HUNTER V
Broke Road, Pokolbin, NSW 2321 (049) 98 7532
OPEN Wed–Sun 10–5 PRODUCTION 800 cases
WINEMAKER Peter Ireland
PRINCIPAL WINES Sem, Chard, Shir, Merl.
BEST VINTAGES W '87, '88, '90 R '87, '88, '89
SUMMARY Has made a series of full-flavoured, attractive red wines; the
white wines are rather less convincing.

**PETALUMA** A–A Est 1979 NFR/CD/UK (Geoffrey Roberts)
$14–28 R ADELAIDE HILLS
Spring Gully Road, Piccadilly, SA 5151 (08) 339 4122
fax (08) 339 5253
OPEN Mon–Fri 9.30–5, w'ends 10–5 (At Bridgewater Mill)
PRODUCTION 35 000 cases
WINEMAKER Brian Croser
PRINCIPAL WINES Ries, Chard, Coonawarra (a Cabernet blend),
Croser (sparkling).
BEST VINTAGES W '80, '87, '90, '91 R '87, '88, '90, '91
SUMMARY Most would agree Petaluma is Australia's leading small (or
not so small) winery, making beautifully crafted wines. The quality of the
1988 and 1990 Coonawarra red wines is outstanding, in front of anything
previously achieved; the 1990 Rhine Riesling (from Clare) is likewise
outstanding.

**PETER LEHMANN** B–BA Est 1979 NR/CD/ML/UK
(Eurobrands Ltd) $9.90–18.50 R BAROSSA V
Samuel Road off Para Road, Tanunda, SA 5352 (085) 63 2500
OPEN Mon–Fri 9.30–5, w'ends 11–4.30 PRODUCTION NFP
WINEMAKER Peter Lehmann
PRINCIPAL WINES Chard, Chenin, Fumé, Ries, Sem, Sem Chard, Shir,
Pinot, Cab Sauv. Cellar Collection is top label; Clancy's Gold Preference
the leading blended red wine.
BEST VINTAGES W '82, '86, '90 R '80, '82, '88, '90
SUMMARY The stalwart of the Barossa Valley, which he knows better
and loves more than anyone else. The substantial production reflects
grower loyalty and very competent winemaking: these honest wines
always give you extra value for money. The '89 Clancy's is a perfectly
made, spicy, elegant yet seductive red, the '90 and '91 white wines of
superior quality across the range.

**PETERSONS** B–B Est 1971 LR/CD/ML $9.50–15 CD
HUNTER V
Mount View Road, Mount View, NSW 2325   (049) 90 1704
**OPEN** 7 days 9–5   **PRODUCTION** 5000 cases
**WINEMAKER** Gary Reed
**PRINCIPAL WINES** Sem, Chard, Gewurz, Pinot, Shir, Cab Sauv.
**SUMMARY** Petersons may have slipped from the high pedestal on which
it once sat but retains its market-place image. The '91 white wines did
not impress in the 1992 Sydney Show, exhibiting aggressive unintegrated
oak, but may settle down with time in bottle.

**PEWSEY VALE** BA–B Est 1961 NFR/UK (Geoffrey Roberts)
$11–14 R   ADELAIDE HILLS
Browne's Road, Pewsey Vale, Adelaide Hills, SA  (vineyard only)
**OPEN** Not (see Yalumba)   **PRODUCTION** 25 000 cases
**WINEMAKER** Alan Hoey
**PRINCIPAL WINES** Ries, Botrytis Ries, Cab Sauv.
**BEST VINTAGES W** '86, '88, '90, '91  **R** '86, '88, '89, '90
**SUMMARY** Followed on its good '90 Riesling with an even better '91,
crisp, toasty and classically structured, with a lively, long palate. An
extraordinary ripe, essency '89 Cabernet Sauvignon will win some, lose
some.

**PFEIFFER** CB–B Est 1880 CD/ML $7.80–12 CD  NE VIC
Distillery Road, Wahgunyah, Vic 3687   (060) 33 3158
fax (060) 333 158
**OPEN** Mon–Sat 9–5, Sun 11–4   **PRODUCTION** 6500 cases
**WINEMAKER** Christopher Pfeiffer
**PRINCIPAL WINES** Sauv Bl, Chard, Ries, Spat Fronti, Gamay, Pinot,
Shir Cab, fortifieds.
**SUMMARY** Ex-Lindeman fortified wine maker Chris Pfeiffer occupies
one of the historic wineries which abound in the north-east, and which is
worth a visit on this score alone. The fortified wines are good, and the
table wines have improved considerably over recent vintages.

**PHILLIPS** C–C Est 1908 LR/CD $5.95–8.95 CD  NTH
GOULBURN R
52 Vaughan Street, Shepparton, Vic 3630  (058) 21 2051
**OPEN** Mon–Sat 9–6,  **PRODUCTION** Nil
**WINEMAKER** Don Phillips
**PRINCIPAL WINES** Shir (from '83 and '89 vintages).
**SUMMARY** Phillips is a sporadic producer of wine, with Shiraz the
mainstay.

**PICCADILLY FIELDS** B–B Est 1989 LR/ML $14.90–19.45
R  ADELAIDE HILLS
Udy's Road, Piccadilly, SA 5151  (08) 272 2239
**OPEN** Not **PRODUCTION** 1000 cases
**WINEMAKER** Sam Virgara
**PRINCIPAL WINES** Chard, Merl/Cab Franc.
**SUMMARY** A tiny winery which takes its names from that part of the
Adelaide Hills made famous by Petaluma. The 1991 Merlot Cabernet
Franc (due for release end 1992) tasted from cask has massive flavour and
tannins; if tamed before bottling, it could add a new dimension to the
wines of the region.

**PIERRO** A–B Est 1980 LR/CD/ML/UK (Milton Sandford Wines)
$16–30 R  MARGARET R
Caves Road, Willyabrup via Cowaramup, WA 6285  (097) 55 6220
**OPEN** 7 days 10–5  **PRODUCTION** 3000 cases

**WINEMAKER** Michael Peterkin
**PRINCIPAL WINES** Chard, Les Trois Cuvee (Sem Sauv Bl Chard), Pinot.
**BEST VINTAGES W** '86, '87, '90, '91 **R** '80, '82, '87, '90
**SUMMARY** Dr Michael Peterkin has gone from strength to strength with his exceptionally complex Chardonnays, made using the full gamut of 'dirty French' techniques, and exemplified by the tangy, challenging '90 Chardonnay. The rich, soft '91 Semillon Sauvignon Blanc is decidedly less controversial.

**PIESSE BROOK** NR Est 1974 LR/CD/ML $5.50–18 CD
PERTH HILLS
Lot 731 Aldersyde Road, Bickley, WA 6076 (09) 293 3309
**OPEN** W'ends 10–5 **PRODUCTION** 300 cases
**WINEMAKER** Brian P. Murphy
**PRINCIPAL WINES** Sem, Cab Shir, Shir, Cabernet.
**SUMMARY** Surprisingly good red wines made in tiny quantities.

**PIETER VAN GENT** NR Est 1979 LR/CD $6–12 CD
MUDGEE
Black Springs Road, Mudgee, NSW 2850 (063) 73 3807
**OPEN** Mon–Sat 9–5, Sun 12–4 **PRODUCTION** 5000 cases
**WINEMAKER** Pieter Van Gent
**PRINCIPAL WINES** Chard, Shir, Muller, Cab Sauv, Pipeclay Port and other fortifieds.
**SUMMARY** Reclusive maker whose fortified wines, in particular, have a loyal following.

**PIKES** B–B Est 1985 NFR/CD/ML/UK (Haughton Fine Wines)
$9–13 CD CLARE V
Polish Hill River Road, Sevenhill, SA 5453 (088) 43 4370
**OPEN** W'ends 10–5 **PRODUCTION** 9000 cases
**WINEMAKER** Neil Pike
**PRINCIPAL WINES** Ries, Sauv Bl, Chard, Shir, Cab Sauv.
**BEST VINTAGES W** '86, '87, '89, '90 **R** '86, '87, '88, '90
**SUMMARY** Strongly flavoured and structured wines are increasingly the order of the day. This will appeal to those who look for total impact rather than finesse or subtlety.

**PIPERS BROOK** BA–B Est 1973 NFR/CD/ML/UK
(Pol Roger Ltd) $13.95–45 R NTHN TAS ·
Bridport Road, Pipers Brook, Tas 7254 (003) 82 7197 fax (003) 82 7226
**OPEN** 7 days Dec–Mar, Mon–Fri Apr–Nov 10–5
**PRODUCTION** 14 000 cases
**WINEMAKER** Andrew Pirie
**PRINCIPAL WINES** Chard, Ries, Sem, Tram Ries, Pinot, Cab Sauv; Summit Chardonnay is deluxe release.
**BEST VINTAGES W** '84, '86, '88, '91 **R** '82, '84, '86, '90
**SUMMARY** Dr Andrew Pirie founded the Pipers Brook region; an immensely knowledgeable and skilled viticulturist and winemaker, he heads a progressive and ever-growing company, producing some of the most beautifully packaged of all Australian wines. After a series of light vintages, Pipers Brook bounced back with stunning '91 white wines, full of richness and complexity.

**PIRRAMIMMA** C–C Est 1892 NFR/CD/ML/UK (Crestview Ltd)
$9.40–14.50 CD STHN VALES
Johnston Road, McLaren Vale, SA 5171 (08) 323 8205 fax (08) 323 9224
**OPEN** Mon–Sat 10–5, Sun/hols 12–4
**PRODUCTION** 41 000 cases
**WINEMAKER** Geoff Johnston

**PRINCIPAL WINES** Chard, Sauv Bl, Chab, Ries, Cab Sauv, Cab Merl, Shir.
**SUMMARY** Once a firm favourite of mine, recent releases (from the mid '80s onwards) have been disappointing.

## PLANTAGENET BA–BA Est 1968 NFR/CD/ML/UK
(Whittaker Wines) $8.50–18 CD LWR GRT STHN
Albany Highway, Mount Barker, WA 6324 (098) 51 1150
fax (098) 51 1839
**OPEN** Mon–Fri 9–5, w'ends 10–4 **PRODUCTION** 12 000 cases
**WINEMAKER** John Wade
**PRINCIPAL WINES** Chard, Ries, Chenin, Sauv Bl, Fronti, Fleur, Shir, Cab.
**BEST VINTAGES W** '85, '86, '88, '90 **R** '83, '85, '86, '88, '91
**SUMMARY** A consistent producer of very good to outstanding wines; pungent, lime Riesling, firm, complex grapefruit-tinged Chardonnay, spicy Shiraz and suave, long-lived Cabernet Sauvignon.

## PLATT'S C–C Est 1983 LR/CD/ML $9–12 CD MUDGEE
Mudgee Road, Gulgong, NSW 2852 (063) 74 1700
**OPEN** 7 days 9–5 **PRODUCTION** 4000 cases
**WINEMAKER** Barry Platt
**PRINCIPAL WINES** Chard, Sem, Gewurz, Cab Sauv.
**SUMMARY** Inconsistent and often rather unhappy use of oak prevents many of the wines realising their potential.

## PLUNKETTS WHITEGATE NR Est 1980 LR/CD/ML
$7–17 CD CENT GOULBURN V
Whitegate, Upton Road, Avenell, Vic 3664 (057) 96 2275
fax (057) 96 2118
**OPEN** 7 days 10–5 **PRODUCTION** 2800 cases
**WINEMAKERS** Alan and Mathew Plunkett (Consultant David Traeger)
**PRINCIPAL WINES** Chard, Cab Merl.
**SUMMARY** The Plunketts produce 350 tonnes of grapes a year from their extensive vineyard planted in 1980, selling most and making a small portion into wine. The initial releases offered were solid, if unexciting.

## POKOLBIN ESTATE NR Est 1980 LR/CD/ML $13–17 CD
HUNTER V
MacDonalds Road, Pokolbin, NSW 2321 (049) 98 7524
**OPEN** 7 days 10–6 **PRODUCTION** 4000 cases
**WINEMAKER** Trevor Drayton
**PRINCIPAL WINES** Wh Burg, Chard, Tram Ries, Sem, Shir, Cab Sauv.
**SUMMARY** An unusual outlet, offering its own-label wines made under contract by Trevor Drayton, together with the wines of Lakes Folly, Peacock Hill and Pothana, and with cheap varietal 'cleanskins'. Wine quality under the Pokolbin Creek label is very modest.

## PORT PHILLIP ESTATE NR Est 1987 CD/ML
MORNINGTON P
261 Red Hill Road, Red Hill, Vic 3937 (059) 89 2708
**OPEN** First w'end each month **PRODUCTION** 2000 cases
**WINEMAKER** Alex White (Contract)
**PRINCIPAL WINES** Chard, Pinot, Cabernets, Shir.
**SUMMARY** The vineyard of leading Melbourne Queen's Counsel Jeffrey Sher; it is not planned to market any wine prior to 1993, and cellar door sales will not be open until some time in that year.

## POTHANA NR Est 1983 LR/CD/ML $9–12 ML HUNTER V
Carramar, Belford, NSW 2335 (065) 74 7164
**OPEN** Through Pokolbin Estate **PRODUCTION** 3200 cases

**WINEMAKER** David Hook
**PRINCIPAL WINES** Chard, Sem, Pinot.
**SUMMARY** Principally sold through Pokolbin Estate (see above) and by mailing list; the '91 Chardonnay is a soft, buttery/toasty wine in mainstream Hunter Valley style.

**POWERCOURT** NR Est 1972 LR/CD/ML $15 ML TAMAR V
McEwans Road, Legana, Tas 7277 (003) 30 1225
**OPEN** By appointment only **PRODUCTION** 830 cases
**WINEMAKER** Ralph Power
**PRINCIPAL WINES** Cab Sauv, Pinot, Beaujolais.
**SUMMARY** A small specialist red winemaker; the 1990 Cabernet Sauvignon was awarded a highly commended (silver medal equivalent) at that year's Hobart Wine Show.

**PRIMO ESTATE** BA–A Est 1979 NFR/CD/ML/UK (Australian Wine Centre) $9–19 CD ADELAIDE PLAINS
Old Port Wakefield Road, Virginia, SA 5120 (08) 380 9442
**OPEN** Mon–Fri 9–5, Sat/hols 10–4.30, closed 1 Jan to 31 May each year
**PRODUCTION** 12 000 cases
**WINEMAKER** Joseph Grilli
**PRINCIPAL WINES** Ries, Colomb, Sauv Bl, Chard, Botrytis Ries, Shir, Cab Sauv, Joseph Cab Merl.
**BEST VINTAGES W** '82, '86, '87, '90 **R** '81, '85, '86, '90
**SUMMARY** Roseworthy dux Joe Grilli has risen way above the constraints of the hot Adelaide Plains to produce an innovative and always excellent range of wines from a tangy Sauvignon-like Colombard through to the classic proportions of the Joseph Cabernet Merlot.

**PRINCE ALBERT** CB–B Est 1975 LR/CD/ML $12 CD GEELONG
100 Lemins Road, Waurn Ponds, Vic 3221 phone and fax (052) 41 8091
**OPEN** Sun 10–5 **PRODUCTION** 900 cases
**WINEMAKER** Bruce Hyett
**PRINCIPAL WINES** Pinot.
**BEST VINTAGES R** '83, '86, '87, '89, '91
**SUMMARY** Australia's true Pinot Noir specialist (it has only ever made the one wine) which also made much of the early running with the variety: the wines always show good varietal character, although some are a fraction simple.

**QUEEN ADELAIDE** CB–B Est 1858 NR/UK (Australian Wine Centre) $7 R BAROSSA V
181 Flinders Street, Adelaide, SA 5000 (08) 236 3400 fax (08) 224 0964
**OPEN** Not **PRODUCTION** NFP
**WINEMAKER** Penfolds Group winemakers
**PRINCIPAL WINES** Chab, Chard, Ries, Sauv Bl, Spat Lexia, Wh Burg, Pinot, Claret, sparkl.
**SUMMARY** The famous brand established by Woodley Wines, and some years ago subsumed into the Seppelt and now Penfolds Wine Group. It is a pure brand, without any particular home, either in terms of winemaking or fruit sources, but ironically quality has increased since its acquisition by Seppelt.

**READS** NR Est 1972 LR/CD/ML $7.50–13 CD NE VIC
Evans Lane, Oxley, Vic 3678 (057) 27 3386 fax (057) 27 3559
**OPEN** Mon–Sat 9–5, Sun 10–6 **PRODUCTION** 1900 cases
**WINEMAKER** Kenneth Read
**PRINCIPAL WINES** Ries, Chard, Sauv Bl, Crouchen, Cab Shir, Cab Sauv, Port.

**SUMMARY** Limited tastings have not impressed, but there may be a jewel lurking somewhere, such as the medal-winning 1990 Sauvignon Blanc.

**REDBANK** A–B Est 1973 NFR/CD/ML/UK
(Charles Taylor Wines) $5.90–39 CD PYRENEES
Sunraysia Highway, Redbank, Vic 3467 (054) 67 7255
**OPEN** Mon–Sat 9–5, Sun 10–5 **PRODUCTION** 5100 cases
**WINEMAKER** Neill Robb
**PRINCIPAL WINES** Chard, Sallys Paddock, Cab Sauv, Shir, Herm, Port.
**BEST VINTAGES R** '81, '86, '88, '89
**SUMMARY** Sallys Paddock has established a formidable but justified reputation; it is the quintessence of Central Victorian red wine style, smooth but long-lived, of invariably excellent quality, with pronounced cherry/red berry fruit underlain by a touch of mint. The '90 continues the excellent form of the '89, with even better things promised by the '91.

**REDGATE** CB–CB Est 1977 LR/CD/ML $11–16 CD
MARGARET R
Boodjidup Road, Margaret River, WA 6285 (097) 57 6208
fax (097) 576 308
**OPEN** 7 days 10–5 **PRODUCTION** 6500 cases
**WINEMAKERS** P. R. Ullinger and V. Willock
**PRINCIPAL WINES** Chenin, Sauv Bl Sem, Sem, Cab Shir, Cab Sauv.
**BEST VINTAGES W** '86, '88, '89, '90 **R** '85, '86, '87, '88
**SUMMARY** The wines on sale through 1990 and 1991 were rather plain, a newly-introduced Reserve Sauvignon Blanc (from 1990) being the best; Redgate has done better in the past, and will no doubt do so again.

**REDHILL WINES** NR Est 1986 LR/CD $12.15 CD
MORNINGTON P
Shoreham Road, Red Hill South, Vic 3937 (059) 89 8660
**OPEN** 7 days 9–5 mid 1992 **PRODUCTION** 3500 cases
**WINEMAKER** Contract
**PRINCIPAL WINES** Chard, Pinot, Cab Sauv.
**SUMMARY** With almost 20 hectares of vines coming into production, and Yellowglen founder Ian Home as managing director, Redhill is poised to join Dromana Estate and Stoniers Merricks as one of the major players in the district. A complex, structured 1990 Chardonnay with apparent malolactic influence was a confident start.

**REDMAN** CB–CB Est 1966 NR/CD $7.90–14.90 R
COONAWARRA
Main Penola-Naracoorte Road, Coonawarra, SA 5253 (087) 36 3331
**OPEN** Mon–Sat 9–5, Sun 10–4 **PRODUCTION** 17 000 cases
**WINEMAKER** Bruce Redman
**PRINCIPAL WINES** Claret, Cab Sauv.
**BEST VINTAGES R** '84, '86, '88, '90
**SUMMARY** The Redman wines are not bad, but they should be among the best of Coonawarra — which they are not. A lack of interest (or investment) in new oak is one problem, off-taints and lack of fruit intensity another. The potential is there, however; a flicker shows in the '89 Cabernet Sauvignon.

**RENMANO** B–A Est 1914 NR/CD/ML/UK
(Berri Renmano Europe) $9–13 R RIVERLANDS
Sturt Highway, Renmark, SA 5341 (085) 86 6771
**OPEN** Mon–Sat 9–5 **PRODUCTION** 20 000 tonnes (14 000 000 litres)
**WINEMAKER** David Hayman
**PRINCIPAL WINES** Chairmans Selection Chard, Sauv Bl, Ries, Cab Sauv, Herm.

**BEST VINTAGES W** '84, '88, '90, '91 **R** '84, '85, '88, '90
**SUMMARY** The unctuous, buttery Chardonnay (foremost) and Cabernet Sauvignon lead the Chairmans Selection range, which is remarkable both for its consistency of quality and for its exceptional value for money.

## REYNOLDS YARRAMAN  B–B Est 1967 LR/CD/ML $14–17 CD  UPPER HUNTER V
Yarraman Road, Wybong, Muswellbrook, NSW 2333   (065) 47 8127 fax (065) 478 127
**OPEN** Mon–Sat 10–4, Sun 11–4  **PRODUCTION** 5000 cases
**WINEMAKER** Jon Reynolds
**PRINCIPAL WINES** Chard, Sem, Cab Sauv, Cab Merl.
**SUMMARY** Formerly Horderns Wybong Estate, now owned by talented ex-Houghton and Wyndham winemaker Jon Reynolds and wife Jane; the high-toned, pungently flavoured wines are full of character.

## RIBBON VALE ESTATE  B–B Est 1977 LR/CD $10–15 CD MARGARET R
Lot 5 Caves Road, Willyabrup via Cowaramup, WA 6284   (097) 55 6272
**OPEN** W'ends 10–5  **PRODUCTION** 3200 cases
**WINEMAKER** Mike Davies
**PRINCIPAL WINES** Sem, Sauv Bl, Sem Sauv Bl, Cab Merl, Cab Sauv, Merlot.
**BEST VINTAGES W** '82, '85, '88, '90 **R** '87, '88, '89, '91
**SUMMARY** Makes crisp, herbaceous Semillon and Sauvignon Blanc (and blends), ideal seafood wines, and classically austere, fine-tuned Cabernets (witness the '88), all in mainstream regional style.

## RICHARD HAMILTON  B–B Est 1972 NFR/CD $7.50–17.70 R  STHN VALES
Willunga Vineyards, Main South Road, Willunga, SA 5172
(085) 56 2288 fax (085) 56 2868
**OPEN** Mon–Fri 9–4, w'ends 10–4  **PRODUCTION** NFP
**WINEMAKER** Ralph Fowler
**PRINCIPAL WINES** Chard, Sem Sauv Bl, Cab Sauv, Shir, Pinot, Port.
**BEST VINTAGES W** '86, '88, '90, '91 **R** '86, '88, '90, '91
**SUMMARY** With the arrival of Ralph Fowler as winemaker and Brian Miller as marketing manager the quality, the consistency and profile of Richard Hamilton wines are on the rise; peachy sweet Chardonnay and a striking peppery/herbaceous 1990 Shiraz (from 100 year old vines) are signs of things to come.

## RICHMOND GROVE  B–B Est 1977 NR/CD $6.95–9.95 R HUNTER V
Hermitage Road, Pokolbin, NSW 2321  (049) 98 7792 fax (049) 98 7783
**OPEN** 7 days 9.30–4.30  **PRODUCTION** 64 000 cases
**WINEMAKER** John Baruzzi
**PRINCIPAL WINES** Chab, Chard, Dry White, Tram/Ries, Wh Burg, Herm, Merl, Cab Sauv.
**SUMMARY** At one time appearing like a loose cannon within the Wyndham group, which has produced a string of consistently good wines from the '90 and '91 vintages.

## RIDGE WINES, THE  C–C Est 1984 CD/ML $9.20–12.50 CD COONAWARRA
Naracoorte Road, Coonawarra, SA 5263   (087) 36 5071
**OPEN** 7 days 9–5  **PRODUCTION** 2000 cases
**WINEMAKER** Sid Kidman
**PRINCIPAL WINES** Ries, Cab Sauv, Shir.
**BEST VINTAGES W** '84, '87, '88, '89 **R** '84, '86, '87, '88

SUMMARY Quite simply, the quality should be better given the area and Sid Kidman's viticultural expertise.

## RIVERINA WINES NR Est 1971 CD MIA
Farm 1, 305 Hillston Road, Tharbogang, NSW 2680 (069) 62 4122
OPEN Mon–Sat 9–6, Sun 10–3 PRODUCTION 9 million litres
WINEMAKER John Casella
PRINCIPAL WINES 15 varieties are processed, the overwhelming proportion of which is sold in bulk; bottled wine releases under the Riverina and Ballingal Estate labels.
SUMMARY One of the large producers of the region chiefly selling wine in bulk to other producers, but the Ballingal Estate label is one to watch, particularly from the '91 vintage: the wines have won a number of show medals.

## ROBERT HAMILTON CB–B Est 1981 LR/CD $5–10 CD
ADELAIDE HILLS
Springton Wine Estate, Hamilton's Road, Springton, SA 5235
(085) 68 2264
OPEN 7 days 10–4 PRODUCTION 6000 cases
WINEMAKER Robert Hamilton
PRINCIPAL WINES Ries, Chard, Sem, Chab, Wh Burg, Shir, Cab Sauv, fortifieds.
SUMMARY A traditional range of wines sold at traditional prices; the reds are usually the best, and occasionally very good.

## ROBINSONS FAMILY DB–CB Est 1969 LR/CD/ML $8–15
CD GRANITE BELT
Curtins Road, Ballandean, Qld 4382 (076) 32 8615
OPEN 7 days 10–5 PRODUCTION 3000 cases
WINEMAKER John Robinson
PRINCIPAL WINES Chard, Gewurz, Cab Shir, Cab Sauv, sparkl.
SUMMARY One of the most fascinating vineyards, wandering in pieces through undulating bush and scrub, producing wines of at times ferocious power and intensity, which are not quite tamed in the winery; quality ranges between good and low, with bitterness and astringency often spoiling the powerful reds.

## ROBINVALE NR Est 1976 LR/CD/ML $3.50–7.90 CD
MURRAY R
Sea Lake Road, Robinvale, Vic 3549 (050) 26 3955 fax (050) 26 4399
OPEN Mon–Sat 10–6, Sun 1–6 PRODUCTION 9500 cases
WINEMAKER W. Caracatsanoudis
PRINCIPAL WINES Chard, Chen Bl, Wh Burg, Saut, Marl, Shir, Cab Sauv Fronti, fortified.
SUMMARY Producers of a fascinating range from bio-dynamic grape juice, non-alcoholic wines, flavoured, fortified, Greek, and standard table wines. Indeed, it is the only winery fully accredited with the Bio-Dynamic Agricultural Association of Australia. The wines will appeal chiefly to those for whom such matters are important.

## ROCHECOMBE NR Est 1985 LR/CD/ML $11.50–17.50 CD
PIPERS BROOK
Baxter's Road, Pipers River, Tas 7252 (003) 82 7122
OPEN 7 days 9–5 PRODUCTION Ravaged by '92 frosts
WINEMAKERS Bridget & Bernard Roche
PRINCIPAL WINES Chenin, Ries, Sauv Bl, Chard, Pinot, Cab Sauv Franc.
SUMMARY A Swiss/Australian joint venture with considerable ambition; 13 hectares of (by Australian standards) immaculate, close-

planted vineyard, with a further 20 hectares due to be planted by 1995, and a high-tech winery to boot. Malolactic Rhine Riesling is idiosyncratic, Chardonnay very restrained and pungent, herbal Sauvignon Blanc the best white in '90 and '91.

**ROCHFORD**  BA–B Est 1987 LR/ML  $9–16 CD  MACEDON
Romsey Park, Rochford, Vic 3442  (054) 29 1428
**OPEN** Not  **PRODUCTION** 1600 cases
**WINEMAKER** Bruce Dowding
**PRINCIPAL WINES** Ries, Cab Sauv, Pinot.
**SUMMARY** Construction engineer-cum-restaurateur-cum-grape grower and winemaker Bruce Dowding (and partner Sheila Hawkins) have hit the headlines with their '90 and '91 Pinot Noirs, both wines showing tremendous varietal character, the '91 having the plummy richness of a great Macedon year.

**ROCKFORD**  B–B Est 1984 LR/CD/ML/UK (AH Wines)
$7.90–15.90 CD  BAROSSA V
Krondorf Road, Tanunda, SA 5352  (085) 63 2720
**OPEN** 7 days 11–5  **PRODUCTION** 12 000 cases
**WINEMAKER** Robert O'Callaghan
**PRINCIPAL WINES** Eden Valley Ries, Botrytis Ries, Basket Press Shir, Black Shir Sparkl.
**BEST VINTAGES** W '84, '89, '90, '91  R '84, '86, '90, '91
**SUMMARY** The wines are sold through Adelaide retailers only (and cellar door), and are unknown to most eastern states wine drinkers, which is a great pity, for these are some of the most individual, spectacularly flavoured wines made in the Barossa today, with an emphasis on old low-yielding dry-land vineyards.

**ROMAVILLA**  DA–DA Est 1863 CD/ML $5–24 CD  WEST QLD
Northern Road, Roma, Qld 4455  (074) 22 1822
**OPEN** Mon–Fri 8–5, Sat 9–12  **PRODUCTION** 1300 cases
**WINEMAKER** David Wall
**PRINCIPAL WINES** 14 varietal and generic table wines, and 13 fortified wine styles including Madeira and Tawny Port are on sale at the winery.
**SUMMARY** An amazing, historic relic, seemingly untouched since its nineteenth century heyday, producing eminently forgettable table wines but still providing some extraordinary fortifieds, including a truly stylish Madeira, made from Riesling and Syrian (the latter variety originating in Persia).

**ROSEMOUNT ESTATE**  BA–A Est 1975 NR/CD/ML/UK
(Rosemount UK) $9.50–36 R  UPPER HUNTER V
Rosemount Road, Denman, NSW 2328  (065) 47 2467  fax (065) 47 2742
**OPEN** Mon–Sat 10–4, Sun 12–4  **PRODUCTION** NFP
**WINEMAKER** Philip Shaw
**PRINCIPAL WINES** Tram Ries, Chab, Wh Burg, Sem, Ries, Chard, Fumé, Shir, Cab Shir, Cab Sauv, Pinot, sparkl. Roxburgh is top of many labels including Giants Creek, Whites Creek, Kirri Billi, Show Reserve and Diamond Label.
**BEST VINTAGES** W '84, '86, '87, '91  R '80, '86, '87, '90, '91
**SUMMARY** Roxburgh Chardonnay is arguably Australia's most famous, and is certainly a flagbearer for this large and successful winery, which has been one of the export leaders, setting an exemplary path of consistency and value for money wherever it sells. 1989 Semillon, '90 Show Reserve Chardonnay and '91 Sauvignon Blanc all show Rosemount at its best.

**ROSENBERG CELLARS**  CB–BA Est 1985 LR/CD $8–10
CD  CLARE V

Main North Road, Watervale, SA 5452   (088) 43 0131
**OPEN** W'ends 10–5   **PRODUCTION** NFP
**WINEMAKER** Terry Blanden
**PRINCIPAL WINES** Chenin, Cottage White, Sparkl, Rosé, Shir.
**SUMMARY** The wines, basically white and usually with residual sugar, are made under contract at Eaglehawk and Sevenhill; not surprisingly, quality is good, particularly at the price.

**ROSEWHITE**   CB–B Est 1986 CD/ML $11.95–14.95 CD   NE VIC
Happy Valley Road, Happy Valley via Myrtleford, Vic 3737   (057) 52 1077
**OPEN** Fri 10–9, Sat–Mon 10–5   **PRODUCTION** 1000 cases
**WINEMAKER** Ron Mullett
**PRINCIPAL WINES** Chard, Pinot, Cab Sauv.
**SUMMARY** A 1988 Pinot indicated the area had real potential for this variety, but I am uncertain of progress since that time.

**ROSSETTO**   DB–B Est 1930 LR/CD/ML $2.80–12 R   MIA
Farm 576, Beelbangera, NSW 2686   (069) 63 5214
**OPEN** Mon–Sat 8.30–5.30   **PRODUCTION** NFP
**WINEMAKER** Ralph Graham
**PRINCIPAL WINES** Every generic table, fortified and flavoured wine imaginable with the premium table wines under the Mt Bingar label.
**SUMMARY** Bombora, 'a 21% alcohol Jamaican rum and coconut-flavoured sensation, delicious on the rocks, with milk, or with fruit-juice', was a featured release in 1991; Mount Bingar also offers less exotic satisfaction, with particularly good Chardonnay and Semillon.

**ROTHBURY ESTATE**   BA–A Est 1968 NFR/CD/ML/UK
(Geoffrey Roberts) $12.75–19.50 R   HUNTER V
Broke Road, Pokolbin, NSW 2321   (049) 98 7555   fax (049) 987 553
**OPEN** 7 days 9.30–4.30   **PRODUCTION** 180 000 cases
**WINEMAKER** Peter Hall
**PRINCIPAL WINES** Chard, Sem, Sauv Bl, Ries, Pinot, Herm, Shir Cab, under a range of labels and brands.
**BEST VINTAGES** **W** '86, '87, '90, '91 **R** '84, '85, '87, '91
**SUMMARY** Increasingly concentrating its efforts on Chardonnay at the top end and a range of merchant labels (including Scribbly Bark) and Denman Estate at the value end of the market. Obstinately, I continue to buy and cellar its Semillon, but do admire its voluptuous, barrel-fermented Reserve Chardonnays from both Cowra and the Hunter Valley, and no less the spectacular, fruity/oaky Shiraz from 1989 and 1990 under both the Standard and Reserve labels.

**ROTHERHYTHE**   NR Est 1969 LR/CD/ML $18 R   TAMAR V
Hendersons Lane, Gravelly Beach, Exeter, Tas 7251   (003) 34 0188
**OPEN** 7 days 10–4 at Delamere   **PRODUCTION** 1200 cases
**WINEMAKER** Dr Steve Hyde
**PRINCIPAL WINES** Chard, Pinot, Cab Sauv.
**SUMMARY** The Pinot Noir and Cabernet Sauvignon sometimes appear to have been made by Dr Jekyll; if they avoid astringency, these are great wines, particularly the Pinot. Recent vintages have unfortunately succumbed.

**ROUGE HOMME**   B–B Est 1953 NR/CD/UK (Averys)
$9.20–12.30 R COONAWARRA
Main Penola-Naracoorte Road, Coonawarra, SA 5263   (087) 36 3205
fax (087) 36 3250
**OPEN** 7 days 10–4   **PRODUCTION** NFP
**WINEMAKER** Greg Clayfield
**PRINCIPAL WINES** Chard, Pinot, Claret, Cab Sauv.
**BEST VINTAGES W & R** '86, '88, '90, '91

**SUMMARY** A reliable producer of well-priced wines, which has recently shown special flair with its Pinot Noir and in particular its sympathetic usage of oak with that variety.

**ROV ESTATE** NR Est 1919 NR/CD/ML $2.95–6.90 CD
BAROSSA V
Sturt Highway, Rowland Flat, SA 5352 (085) 24 4537 fax (085) 24 4066
**OPEN** Mon–Fri 9–4.30, w'ends 10.30–4.30
**PRODUCTION** 4500 tonnes (290 000 case equivalent)
**WINEMAKER** Christopher Schmidt
**PRINCIPAL WINES** Chiefly generic bulk fortified and table wines; top of the range (at $6.90) are Dragonfly Rhine Riesling and Cabernet Shiraz.
**SUMMARY** An old and very basic winemaking facility which, after a long period of instability, has been purchased by Miranda Wines (of the MIA).

**RUMBALARA** NR Est 1974 LR/CD/ML $6.50–12 CD
GRANITE BELT
Fletcher Road, Fletcher, Qld 4381 (076) 84 1206 fax (076) 84 1299
**OPEN** 7 days 9–5 **PRODUCTION** 2400 cases
**WINEMAKER** Chris Gray
**PRINCIPAL WINES** Ries, Ries Sylv, Sem, Shir, Pinot, Cab Sauv.
**BEST VINTAGES W** '84, '85, '86, '91 **R** '86, '87, '88
**SUMMARY** Over the years has produced some of the Granite Belt's finest, honeyed Semillon and silky, red berry Cabernet Sauvignon, but quality does vary, and has recently disappointed, though the peachy '91 Semillon shows some character.

**RYECROFT** NR Est 1888 NFR/CD/ML $7.45–11.50 R
STHN VALES
Ingoldby Road, McLaren Flat, SA 5171 (08) 383 0001
**OPEN** Mon–Sat 10–5, Sun 12–4 **PRODUCTION** NFP
**WINEMAKER** Not known at time of publication
**PRINCIPAL WINES** Marketed in two ranges, Ryecroft Traditional and Ryecroft Contemporary.
**SUMMARY** Acquired by Rosemount Estate in late 1991, and while it will continue to sell wines under the Ryecroft labels, it is reasonable to assume the somewhat modest quality of the wines will now improve with better oak handling.

**RYMILL RIDDOCH RUN** NR Est 1973 NFR $14–27 R
COONAWARRA
Old Penola Estate, Penola, SA 5277 (087) 36 5001 fax (087) 36 5001
**OPEN** Not **PRODUCTION** 18 000 cases
**WINEMAKER** John Innes
**PRINCIPAL WINES** Chard, Sauv Bl, Shir, Cab Sauv.
**SUMMARY** The Rymills are descendants of John Riddoch, and have long owned some of the finest Coonawarra soil upon which they have grown grapes since 1973. Peter Rymill has made a small amount of Cabernet Sauvignon since 1987, and has now plunged headlong into commercial production, producing an array of full-flavoured and rich red wines from the '89, '90 and '91 vintages. The white wines have been slightly less consistent.

**SADDLERS CREEK** nr Est 1990 LR/CD/ML $11.50–15 CD
HUNTER V
Marrowbone Road, Pokolbin, NSW 2321 (049) 91 1770 fax (049) 91 1778
**OPEN** 7 days 8–5 **PRODUCTION** 4000 cases
**WINEMAKER** Craig Brown-Thomas
**PRINCIPAL WINES** Vosges Chard, Sem/Chard, Fumé Bl, Cab Merl, Bluegrass Cab Sauv.

**SUMMARY** An impressive newcomer to the district producing consistently full flavoured and rich wines, with the 1990 red wines showing lovely fresh, sweet fruit and the 1991 whites having the softness and concentration one expects from this vintage.

## SALISBURY ESTATE B–A Est 1977 LR/UK (Not known at publication) $7–11 R MURRAY R

Nangiloc Road, Nangiloc, Vic 3494 (050) 29 1744 fax (050) 29 1691
**OPEN** Not **PRODUCTION** 7 million litres
**WINEMAKER** David Martin
**PRINCIPAL WINES** Chard, Chard Sem, Sauv Bl Sem, Ries, Cab Sauv; Reserve Chard is top of the range.
**SUMMARY** Salisbury Estate is the tip of the iceberg of the Alambie Wine Company, which typically processes around 4 million litres of wine a year, selling all but a fraction of the very best in bulk to other wineries. Not surprisingly, the quality of these modestly priced wines has been of medal winning standard, while the fragrant, stylish barrel-fermented '91 Reserve Chardonnay rises well above its modest price and station.

## SALTRAM B–B Est 1859 NR/CD/ML/UK (Oddbins) $7.50–35 R BAROSSA V

Angaston Road, Angaston, SA 5353 (085) 64 2200 fax (085) 64 2876
**OPEN** Mon–Fri 9–5, w'ends 10–5 **PRODUCTION** 190 000 cases
**WINEMAKER** David Norman
**PRINCIPAL WINES** A full range of varietal wines under the Estate, Classic, Mamre Brook Private Reserve and Pinnacle labels; Mr Pickwick Port is the top Tawny Port.
**BEST VINTAGES W** '82, '86, '88, '90 **R** '84, '86, '88, '90
**SUMMARY** For whatever reason, Saltram seems quite unable to market itself effectively, and the quality (and value) of its wines across the range is simply not recognised in the market place. It has done particularly well with its Sauvignon Blanc over recent vintages, while the Chardonnay seldom disappoints.

## SAMPHIRE NR Est 1982 CD $7 CD ADELAIDE HILLS

Watts Gully Road, Kersbrook, SA 5231 (08) 389 3183
**OPEN** 7 days 9–5 by appointment **PRODUCTION** 90 cases
**WINEMAKER** Tom Miller
**PRINCIPAL WINES** Riesling (from the .4 hectare vineyard).
**SUMMARY** Next after Scarp Valley, the smallest winery in Australia offering wine for sale; pottery also helps.

## SANDALFORD CB–C Est 1970 NR/CD/UK (Deinhard & Co) $11–19.40 R SWAN V AND MARGARET R

West Swan Road, Caversham, WA 6055 (09) 274 5922 fax (09) 274 2154
**OPEN** 7 days 11–4 **PRODUCTION** 40 000 cases
**WINEMAKER** Christian Morlaes
**PRINCIPAL WINES** Sem Chard, Verd, Sem Sauv Bl, Ries, Rosé, Cab Sauv, Shir, Port.
**SUMMARY** A 1990 Reserve Verdelho from Margaret River showed Sandalford can produce good wine, a proposition not evident from the remaining adequate but unexciting table wines in its portfolio.

## SANDHILLS NR Est 1920 CD/ML $5.30–10.90 CD CENTRAL WEST NSW

Sandhills Road, Forbes, NSW 2871 (068) 52 1437
**OPEN** Thur–Mon 9–5.30 **PRODUCTION** 500 cases
**WINEMAKER** John Saleh
**PRINCIPAL WINES** Chab, Dry Wh, Mos, Spat Ries, Chard, Wh Burg, Cab Shir, fortifieds.

**SUMMARY** Long owned by Jacques Genet, and now by the Saleh family, who know much about the appreciation of fine wine but are still learning how to make it.

## SANDSTONE B–B Est 1988 LR $18 R MARGARET R
Lot 5 Caves Road, Willyabrup via Cowaramup, WA 6284
(097) 55 6271 fax (097) 55 6292
**OPEN** Not **PRODUCTION** 1000 cases
**WINEMAKER** Mike Davies
**PRINCIPAL WINES** Sem, Cab.
**SUMMARY** The family operation of consultant winemakers Mike and Jan Davies, who also operate very successful mobile bottling plants. The Semillon, while in varying style, can be truly excellent, the Cabernet good.

## SCARBOROUGH A–B Est 1985 LR/CD/ML $18.50–20 R HUNTER V
Gillards Road, Pokolbin, NSW 2321 (049) 98 7563 fax (049) 98 7786
**OPEN** W'ends 10–5 or by appointment **PRODUCTION** 5000 cases
**WINEMAKER** Ian Scarborough
**PRINCIPAL WINES** Chard, Pinot.
**BEST VINTAGES W** '87, '88, '89, '91 **R** '87
**SUMMARY** Ian Scarborough put his white winemaking skills beyond doubt during his years as a consultant, and his exceptionally complex and stylish Chardonnay is no disappointment, the rich, peachy '88 drinking superbly in 1992.

## SCARPANTONI ESTATES NR Est 1979 NR/CD/ML $8–14 CD STHN VALES
Scarpantoni Drive, McLaren Flat, SA 5171 (08) 383 0186
fax (08) 383 0490
**OPEN** 7 days 10–5 **PRODUCTION** 10 000 cases
**WINEMAKERS** Michael & Filippo Scarpantoni
**PRINCIPAL WINES** Ries, Chard, Botrytis Ries, Cab Sauv, Cab Merl.
**SUMMARY** A large number of wines recently tasted in various shows have consistently disappointed all the judges, myself included, but every now and then Scarpantoni comes up with a top wine.

## SCARP VALLEY NR Est 1983 ML $15 ML PERTH HILLS
6 Robertson Road, Gooseberry Hill, WA 6076 (09) 454 5748
**OPEN** Not **PRODUCTION** 25 cases
**WINEMAKER** Peter Fimmel (Contract)
**PRINCIPAL WINES** Hermitage.
**SUMMARY** Surely the smallest producer in Australia, with its single cask each year. The '87 was a nice wine, with light but pleasant minty/leafy flavours: something went astray with the '88 and '89 vintages, the last showing strange, unpleasant taints outside my previous experience. I have not tasted the '90 or '91 vintages.

## SCHMIDTS TARCHALICE C–C Est 1984 LR/CD/ML $5–20 CD BAROSSA V
Research Road, Vine Vale via Tanunda, SA 5352 (085) 63 3005
**OPEN** 7 days 11–5 **PRODUCTION** 1000 cases
**WINEMAKER** Christopher Schmidt
**PRINCIPAL WINES** Ries, Chard, Sem, Gewurz, Pinot, Cab Sauv, Port.
**SUMMARY** Vanillan oak-flavoured Semillon and Chardonnay are among the better wines, but develop very quickly.

## SCOTCHMANS HILL B–B Est 1982 LR/ML $13.95–16.95 R GEELONG
Scotchman's Road, Drysdale, Vic 3222 (052) 51 3176 fax (052) 53 1743

'OPEN Not  PRODUCTION 10 000 cases
WINEMAKER Peter Cumming
PRINCIPAL WINES Chard, Pinot, Cab Franc.
SUMMARY In fact situated on the Bellarine Peninsula, south-east of
Geelong, with a very well equipped winery and first-class vineyards. The
wines have enjoyed spectacular sales, but are idiosyncratic; if you like very
ripe styles, these are the wines for you. Whatever else, they are most
certainly not short on flavour and body.

SEAVIEW B–A Est 1850 NR/CD/UK (Penfolds Wine Group)
$6.60–20 R  STHN VALES
Chaffeys Road, McLaren Vale, SA 5171   (08) 323 8250  fax (08) 323 9308
OPEN Mon–Fri 9–4, w'ends 11–4  PRODUCTION NFP
WINEMAKER Ed Carr
PRINCIPAL WINES Chab, Ries, Tram Ries, Wh Burg, Chard, Cab
Shir, Cab Sauv, sparkl under Seaview and Edmond Mazure labels.
BEST VINTAGES W '85, '87, '90, '91  R '86, '88, '90, '91
SUMMARY A maker of sturdy, reliable white wines, red wines which
are frequently absurdly underpriced and perhaps suffer in consequence
and, of course, of some of the country's best known sparkling wines,
which have gone from strength to strength over recent years.

SELDOM SEEN NR Est 1987 LR/CD/ML $8–12 CD  MUDGEE
Craigmoor Road, Mudgee, NSW 2850   (063) 72 4482
OPEN 7 days 9.30–5  PRODUCTION 4000 cases
WINEMAKER Barry J. Platt
PRINCIPAL WINES Sem, Chard, Tram Ries, Cab Sauv Shir.
SUMMARY A major grape grower which reserves a proportion of its crop
for making and release under its own label. Quality has been inconsistent.

SEPPELT GREAT WESTERN A–A Est 1866 NR/CD/UK
(Water Siegel) $7–25 R  GRT WESTERN
Moyston Road, Great Western, Vic 3377   (053) 56 2202  fax (053) 56 2300
OPEN Mon–Sat 9–5  PRODUCTION NFP
WINEMAKER Ian McKenzie (chief)
PRINCIPAL WINES Meth Champ comprising (from the bottom up)
Brut Reserve, Imperial Reserve, Rosé Brut, Fleur de Lys, Vintage Brut
and Salinger; also various varietal and regional sparkling wines of high
quality; also premium regional Chard, Ries, Herm; finally various brands
including much-diminished Chalambar and Moyston.
SUMMARY Australia's foremost producer of sparkling wine, always
immaculate in its given price range, but also producing excellent Great
Western-sourced table wines, especially long-lived Hermitage.

SEPPELT A–A Est 1850 NR/CD/UK (Walter Siegel) $4–2000 R
BAROSSA V
Seppeltsfield via Tanunda, SA 5352   (085) 63 2626  fax (085) 62 8333
OPEN Mon–Fri 8.30–5, w'ends 11–4  PRODUCTION NFP
WINEMAKERS J. Godfrey, N. Dolan
PRINCIPAL WINES Seppelt has had the habit of spawning brands with
gay abandon; the most humble is Glen Osmond Claret, followed by the
Queen Adelaide range, Moyston and Chalambar, the Gold Label range, the
Black Label range and the Premium range, including what one suspects to
be transients such as Harpers Range, Clover Ridge, Ironbark and so forth.
Regional based wines including Dorrien, Drumborg and Partalunga.
BEST VINTAGES W & R '86, '88, '90, '91
SUMMARY A multi-million dollar expansion and renovation program
has seen the historic Seppeltsfield winery become the production centre
for the Seppelt wines, adding another dimension to what was already the
most historic and beautiful major winery in Australia. Seppeltsfield has

always been the centre for fortified wine production, including the annual release of century-old Para Liqueur Ports with a price of around $2000 a bottle. Many magnificent tawny and liqueur ports and sherries (all Australia's finest) are available at far more normal prices. Likewise, there are high quality table wines such as Dorrien Cabernet Sauvignon, and the numerous premium wines incorporating Padthaway material. The '89 Show Shiraz is a multi-trophy winning classic.

### SERENELLA ESTATE CB–B Est 1981 LR/CD/ML $6–16 CD UPPER HUNTER V

Mudgee Road, Baerami via Denman, NSW 2333   (065) 47 5168 fax (065) 47 5164

**OPEN** Mon–Sat 10–4, Sun 12–4   **PRODUCTION** 9000 cases
**WINEMAKER** Letitia Cecchini
**PRINCIPAL WINES** Chard, Sem, Wh Burg, Cab Sauv, Herm, Shir.
**SUMMARY** Produces full-flavoured white wines in consistent style, with marked vanillan-lemon oak flavour (presumably American) and which develop quickly; these are better than the reds.

### SETTLEMENT WINE COMPANY NR Est 1976 LR/ML $10–15 ML STHN VALES

c/- Torresan Wine Estates, Martins Road, McLaren Vale, SA 5171 (08) 386 3644

**OPEN** Not   **PRODUCTION** 500 cases
**WINEMAKER** Dr David Mitchell
**PRINCIPAL WINES** Cab Sauv, Port.
**SUMMARY** A shadow of its former self, but still selling (for example) Dr David's Plasma Port, packaged in a genuine glass drip bottle.

### SETTLERS CREEK CB–B Est 1971 CD/ML $9.95–12.95 CD MUDGEE

c/- Augustine, George Campbell Drive, Mudgee, NSW 2850 (063) 72 3880

**OPEN** 7 days 10–4   **PRODUCTION** 2500 cases
**WINEMAKER** Jon Reynolds (Contract)
**PRINCIPAL WINES** Chard, Pinot.
**SUMMARY** Has had a somewhat unsettled existence, but with Jon Reynolds now making the wine under contract, good things can be expected.

### SEVENHILL CELLARS B–BA Est 1851 LR/CD/ML $5–14 CD CLARE V

College Road, Sevenhill via Clare, SA 5453   (088) 43 4222 fax (088) 43 4382

**OPEN** Mon–Sat 9–4   **PRODUCTION** 12 000 cases
**WINEMAKER** John Monten
**PRINCIPAL WINES** Wh Burg, Ries, Cab Sauv, Cab Sauv Malb, Merl Cab Franc, Shir, Port.
**BEST VINTAGES** **W** '87, '88, '89, '90 **R** '82, '85, '87, '89, '91
**SUMMARY** John Monten makes the wine under the friendly eye of Brother John May; the team is a potent one. The White Burgundy is consistently excellent despite its humble origins and label, the Riesling generous and accessible early in its life, the red wines can be of tremendous colour, flavour and depth — although the '90 reds show over-ripe fruit characters.

### SEVILLE ESTATE A–A Est 1972 NFR/ML $10–17.50 ML YARRA V

Linwood Road, Seville, Vic 3139   (059) 64 4556   fax (059) 64 3585
**OPEN** Not   **PRODUCTION** 1500 cases
**WINEMAKER** Dr Peter McMahon

**PRINCIPAL WINES** Chard, Ries, Beeren, Shir, Pinot, Cab Sauv.
**BEST VINTAGES** **W** '82, '86, '88, '90 **R** '86, '88, '90, '91
**SUMMARY** To be perfectly honest, there is an element of inconsistency in the quality of the Seville wines which the A–A rating does not indicate; on the other hand, the great majority are beyond criticism. The heavily botrytised Riesling, released usually as a Beerenauslese but sometimes Trockenbeerenauslese is a tour-de-force, made in minuscule quantities but of the highest possible quality. The Cabernet can be equal to the best, as it most certainly was in 1984, the Chardonnay (such as 1990) and Pinot Noir likewise. And then there is that glorious peppery Shiraz . . .

**SHANTELL** B–B Est 1981 LR/CD/ML $11–16 CD  YARRA V
Melba Highway, Dixons Creek, Vic 3775   (059) 65 2264
**OPEN** W'ends/hols 10–5  **PRODUCTION** 1400 cases
**WINEMAKERS** N. & T. Shanmugam
**PRINCIPAL WINES** Sem, Chard, Pinot, Cab Sauv.
**BEST VINTAGES** **W** '88, '89, '90, '91 **R** '88, '89, '90, '91
**SUMMARY** With consultancy help from Kathleen Quealy, produces consistently good examples of all four varieties, full of flavour and varietal character, reflecting the now fully mature, low-yielding vineyards. The trophy and gold medal winning '90 Chardonnay was followed by an equally impressive '91.

**SHARMANS GLEN BOTHY** NR EST 1986 ML
$9.50–12.50 ML TAS
RSD 282 Glenwood Road, Rilbia, Tas 7258
**OPEN** Not **PRODUCTION** 50 cases
**WINEMAKER** Greg O'Keefe (Contract)
**PRINCIPAL WINES** Ries, Chard, Pinot, Cab Sauv.
**SUMMARY** A light but exceptionally stylish sappy/cherry flavoured 1991 Pinot Noir won the trophy at the 1992 Tasmanian Regional Wine Show. Unfortunately, the 1992 vintage at this isolated vineyard on the North Esk River, south of Launceston, was destroyed by frost.

**SHAW AND SMITH** A–A Est 1990 NFR/UK
(Winecellars) $15–20 R  STHN VALES
Flaxman Valley Road, Adelaide, SA 5152   (08) 370 9725
**OPEN** Not **PRODUCTION** 6400 cases
**WINEMAKER** Martin Shaw
**PRINCIPAL WINES** Chard, Sauv Bl.
**SUMMARY** The partnership of Michael Hill Smith, Australia's first Master of Wine, and Martin Shaw, premier 'Flying Winemaker', has predictably produced faultless wines in 1990 and 1991, with the certainty of more to come.

**SHOTTESBROOKE** B–B Est 1984 LR/CD/ML $13–17 R
STHN VALES
Ryecroft Vineyard, Ingoldby Road, McLaren Flat, SA 5171   (08) 383 0001
**OPEN** Mon–Fri 10–5, w'ends 12–5 **PRODUCTION** 5000 cases
**WINEMAKER** Nick Holmes
**PRINCIPAL WINES** Sauv Bl, Cab Merl.
**SUMMARY** The label of former Ryecroft winemaker Nick Holmes, made from grapes grown on his vineyard at Myoponga, invariably showing clear berry fruit, subtle oak and a touch of elegance.

**SILOS, THE** NR Est 1985 CD/ML $8.50–14 CD  SOUTH COAST
Princes Highway, Jaspers Brush, NSW 2535   (044) 48 6082
**OPEN** 7 days 10–5 **PRODUCTION** 1400 cases
**WINEMAKER** Alan Bamfield

**PRINCIPAL WINES** Chard, Sem, Sauv Bl, Shir, Mal, Port.
**SUMMARY** Aimed purely at the tourist trade; wine quality has left much to be desired, but a delightful, light, pepper-spice 1990 Shiraz redresses the balance.

## SIMON HACKETT NR Est 1986 NFR/UK
(Australian Wineries UK) $11–14 R STHN VALES
off McMurtrie, McLaren Vale, SA 5171 (08) 331 7348
**OPEN** Not **PRODUCTION** 3000 cases
**WINEMAKER** Simon Hackett
**PRINCIPAL WINES** Sem, Sem Chard/Chard, Herm, Cab Sauv.
**SUMMARY** Simon Hackett makes his wines at various wineries, before maturing and packaging them at his own maturation establishment. Wine quality has varied somewhat over the years, but hit a high spot with the '91s, and in particular the tangy, lively and zesty '91 Semillon.

## SIMONS NR Est 1978 CD/ML $8–10 CD CANBERRA
Badgery Road, Burra Creek, Queanbeyan, NSW 2620
(06) 236 3216
**OPEN** W'ends 9–5 **PRODUCTION** 100 cases
**WINEMAKER** Lloyd Simons
**PRINCIPAL WINES** Chard, Tram Ries, Merl.
**SUMMARY** The tiny production is sold to the tourist trade which accepts the rustic quality of the wine.

## SKILLOGALEE B–B Est 1970 LR/CD/ML $11.85–15.40 R
CLARE V
Off Hughes Park Road, Sevenhill via Clare, SA 5453 (088) 43 4274 or (088) 43 4311
**OPEN** 7 days 9–5 **PRODUCTION** 4500 cases
**WINEMAKER** Stephen John (Contract)
**PRINCIPAL WINES** Ries, Shir, Cabernets, Vintage Port.
**SUMMARY** David and Diana Palmer purchased Skillogalee from the George family several years ago, and have capitalised to the full on the exceptional fruit quality of the Skillogalee vineyards: powerful Riesling, intense cassis berry Shiraz and potent Cabernets (a Bordeaux blend) are the result. The winery also has a well-patronised lunchtime restaurant.

## SNOWY RIVER WINERY NR Est 1989 CD/ML $10–20
ML STHN HIGHLANDS
Berriedale, NSW 2628 (064) 56 5041 fax (064) 56 5005
**OPEN** 7 days 10–5 **PRODUCTION** 2000 cases
**WINEMAKER** Geoff Carter
**PRINCIPAL WINES** Chard, Chab, Ries, Muller Thurgau, Siegerrebe, Noble Ries, Eiswein Ries, Snowy Red, Cab Sauv, fortifieds.
**SUMMARY** Claims the only Eiswein to have been made in Australia, picked on 8 June 1990 after a frost of -8° Celsius. Two Rieslings tasted, dry and sweet, have been clean, but rather simple and light.

## SORRENBERG NR Est 1985 LR/CD/ML $10.50–14.50 CD
NE VIC
Alma Road, Beechworth, Vic 3747 (057) 282 278
**OPEN** Sat, hols 10–5, Sun 1–5 **PRODUCTION** 750 cases
**WINEMAKER** Barry Morey
**PRINCIPAL WINES** Chard, Sauv Bl/Sem, Ries, Gamay, Cabernets.
**SUMMARY** Barry and Jan Morey made their first wines in 1989 from the 2.5 hectare vineyard situated on the outskirts of Beechworth. They are still learning the winemaking craft.

## SPRING VALE NR Est 1986 CD/ML $15 CD EAST COAST, TAS
Spring Vale, Swansea, Tas 7190 (002) 578 208

**OPEN** By appointment **PRODUCTION** 250 cases
**WINEMAKER** Geoff Bull (Contract)
**PRINCIPAL WINES** Pinot Noir.
**SUMMARY** Rodney Lyne has established Spring Vale on Tasmania's east coast, not far from Geoff Ball's Freycinet vineyard. An extremely lush, plummy and highly flavoured 1990 Pinot was a most auspicious start; a suspicion of lactic character does not materially detract from the impact and appeal of the wine.

## STAFFORD RIDGE A–BA Est 1980 LR/CD/ML/UK
(Oddbins) $12–19 ML ADELAIDE HILLS
2 Gilpin Lane, Mitcham, SA 5062 (residence only) (08) 272 2105
**OPEN** Sun 11–4 c/- Mount Lofty House **PRODUCTION** 3500 cases
**WINEMAKER** Geoff Weaver
**PRINCIPAL WINES** Ries, Chard, Sauv Bl, Cab Merl.
**BEST VINTAGES** W '88, '90, '91 R '88, '90, '91
**SUMMARY** Superb Riesling, Sauvignon Blanc (1991 magnificent) and Chardonnay (none better than the '90) are crafted by Thomas Hardy chief winemaker Geoff Weaver from grapes grown on his Lenswood vineyard; the wines combine elegance and intensity of flavour, with pristine varietal character.

## STANTON & KILLEEN B–B Est 1875 LR/CD/ML
$11.50–16.60 R NE VIC
Murray Valley Highway, Rutherglen, Vic 3685 (060) 32 9457
**OPEN** Mon–Sat 9–5, Sun 11–4 **PRODUCTION** Over 10 000 cases
**WINEMAKER** Chris Killeen
**PRINCIPAL WINES** Moodemere Cab Shir, Durif; numerous Ports, Muscats and Tokay.
**SUMMARY** A traditional maker of smooth, rich reds, some very good vintage ports, and attractive, fruity Muscats and Tokays.

## STAUGHTON VALE NR Est 1986 LR/CD/ML $14–15 CD
GEELONG
20 Staughton Vale Road, Anakie, Vic 3221 (052) 84 1477
**OPEN** W'ends and hols 10–5 **PRODUCTION** 3000 cases
**WINEMAKER** Paul Chambers
**PRINCIPAL WINES** Dulcinear and Bowen Hill Chard (from Ballarat), Leopold Chard (Geelong), Sauv Bl, Shir, Cab Sauv, with Ballarat Cabernets due for release 1993.
**SUMMARY** Some very promising Chardonnay ex-barrel did not make it safely to bottle, but the 1989 Shiraz and 1991 Ballarat Cabernets (the latter not bottled at the time of tasting) show what can be achieved.

## STEINS DC–CB Est 1976 LR/CD/ML $7.50–10 CD MUDGEE
Sandal Park Estate, Pipeclay Lane, Mudgee, NSW 2850 (063) 73 3991
**OPEN** 7 days 10–4 **PRODUCTION** 3000 cases
**WINEMAKER** Robert S. Stein
**PRINCIPAL WINES** Sem, Chard, Shiraz, Chab, Port.
**SUMMARY** The sweeping panorama from the winery is its own reward. Despite Bob Stein's undoubted commitment, wine quality has disappointed, although the '90 Chardonnay has some appeal.

## ST FRANCIS B–A Est 1869 NR/ML $5.50–13 CD STHN VALES
Bridge Street, Old Reynella, SA 5161 (08) 381 1925 fax (08) 322 0921
**OPEN** 7 days 9.30–4.30 **PRODUCTION** 15 000 cases
**WINEMAKERS** J. Irvine and R. Dundon
**PRINCIPAL WINES** Sparkl, Chab, Chard, Sem, Fumé, Ries, Front, Cab Merl, Cab Sauv.
**SUMMARY** A full blown tourist facility and convention centre with a

thriving cellar-door sales facility offering wines purchased in bulk from other makers (usually bottled or cleanskins). Thanks to the skill and contacts of consultants Jim Irvine and Rob Dundon, the average quality is very good, especially at the price.

**ST GREGORY'S**  NR Est 1984 CD/ML $10.50 CD  WEST VIC
Bringalbert South Road, Bringalbert Sth via Apsley, Vic 3319
(055) 86 5225
OPEN By appointment only  PRODUCTION 200 cases
WINEMAKER Gregory Flynn
PRINCIPAL WINES Port (in various styles).
SUMMARY A strictly weekend hobby of port enthusiast Greg Flynn.

**ST HALLETT**  BA–BA Est 1944 NFR/CD/ML/UK
(Australian Wine Centre) $10–17 R  BAROSSA V
St Hallett's Road, Tanunda, SA 5352  (085) 63 2319  fax (085) 63 2901
OPEN 7 days  PRODUCTION 15 000 cases
WINEMAKER Stuart Blackwell
PRINCIPAL WINES Sem, Chard, Sauv Bl, Cab Merl, Old Block Shir.
BEST VINTAGES W '89, '90, '91 R '84, '86, '88, '89, '90
SUMMARY Old Block Shiraz is a great Australian red wine, a blend of very old vines and modern winemaking, with the '89 adding a dimension of new American oak; all of the St Hallett wines are particularly well-crafted, clean and flavoursome.

**ST HUBERTS**  BA–A Est 1966 NFR/CD/ML $9.90–25 R
YARRA V
Maroondah Highway, Coldstream, Vic 3770  (03) 739 1421
fax (03) 739 1070
OPEN Mon–Fri 9–5, w'ends 10.30–5.30  PRODUCTION 15 000 cases
WINEMAKER Brian Fletcher
PRINCIPAL WINES Chard, Classic Dry White, Pinot, Cab Merl, Cab Sauv; Rowan is the second label.
BEST VINTAGES W '84, '88, '90, '91 R '82, '88, '90, '91
SUMMARY Much revived under new ownership (Baileys and hence Goodman-Fielder-Wattie) and with Brian Fletcher as winemaker. Great full blown peachy Chardonnay and rich, berryish Cabernet Sauvignon (both from 1988) are outstanding. The Rowan label offers good wines at ultra-competitive prices.

**ST LEONARDS**  B–B Est 1860 CD/ML $8.90–25 CD  NE VIC
Wahgunyah, Vic 3687  (060) 33 1004  fax (060) 33 3636
OPEN Mon–Sat 9–5, Sun 10–4  PRODUCTION 8000 cases
WINEMAKER R. Kaval
PRINCIPAL WINES Sem, Chard, Sauv Bl, Chenin, Rosé, Pinot, Cab Franc Merl, Cab Sauv.
BEST VINTAGES W '85, '87, '88, '89 R '82, '86, '88, '90
SUMMARY An old favourite, producing always-interesting wines cleverly marketed through an active mailing list and singularly attractive cellar door at the historic winery on the banks of the Murray.

**ST MATTHIAS**  B–B Est 1982 LR/CD/ML $12–18 CD
TAMAR V
Rosevears Drive, Rosevears, Tas 7251  (003) 30 1700
OPEN 7 days 10–5  PRODUCTION 3800 cases
WINEMAKER Heemskerk (Contract)
PRINCIPAL WINES Ries, Chard, Pinot, Cab Merl.
BEST VINTAGES W '86, '88, '90, '91 R '87, '88, '90, '91
SUMMARY The gloriously situated vineyard overlooking the Tamar River, with its newly built stone cellar door deliberately evoking the

feelings of a Church, is a compulsory stopping point for the wine tourist. St Matthias also sells other Tasmanian wines which are not available at their producer's cellar door during the week. A 1992 proposed sale fell through, and at the time of writing St Matthias was on the market.

**ST NEOT'S ESTATE** NR Est 1981 LR/ML $15–19 R
MORNINGTON P
63 Red Hill-Shoreham Road, Red Hill South, Vic 3937  (059) 89 2023
**OPEN** Not  **PRODUCTION** 500 cases
**WINEMAKER** Contract
**PRINCIPAL WINES** Ries, Sem, Chard, Pinot, Cab Sauv.
**SUMMARY** The last St Neot's wines tasted in 1990 showed the typical clear varietal fruit flavours one comes to expect from the district.

**ST PATRICKS WINES** NR Est 1983 LR/CD/ML $12–21 R
STHN TAS
Fleurtys Lane, Flowerpot, Tas 7054  (002) 674 604
**OPEN** 7 days at Woodbridge Hotel, Woodbridge 7162
**PRODUCTION** 300 cases
**WINEMAKER** Leigh Gawith
**PRINCIPAL WINES** Muller, Sem blend, Pinot, Cab blend.
**SUMMARY** Leigh Gawith established St Patricks at Pipers Brook in 1983, but sold the vineyard to Pipers Brook Winery in 1990 and has now relocated in the south of Tasmania at Flowerpot. The wines presently being sold are a mixture from his previous location and his new venture.

**STEVENS CAMBRAI** CA–CB Est 1975 LR/CD/ML
$4.50–12.50 CD  STHN VALES
Hamiltons Road, McLaren Flat, SA 5171  (08) 383 0251
**OPEN** 7 days 9–5  **PRODUCTION** 6000 cases
**WINEMAKER** Graham Stevens
**PRINCIPAL WINES** Chab, Gewurz, Front, Shir, Zinfandel, Cab Sauv, Vintage Port.
**BEST VINTAGES W** '86, '87, '90, '91 **R** '84, '86, '88, '90
**SUMMARY** Graham Stevens knows both his own mind and the district very well; a challenging mixture of the exotic and the run-of-the-mill, the good and the not so good, has typified the table wines, but the Vintage Ports have been of consistently high quality.

**STONE RIDGE** B–B Est 1981 LR/CD/ML $9–15 CD
GRANITE BELT
Limberlost Road, Glen Aplin, Qld 4381  (076) 83 4211
**OPEN** 7 days 10–5  **PRODUCTION** 1400 cases
**WINEMAKERS** Jim Lawrie and Anne Kennedy
**PRINCIPAL WINES** Chard, Shir, Mt Sterling Dry Red (second label).
**SUMMARY** Spicy Shiraz is the specialty, with most attractive wines appearing each vintage since 1987.

**STONEY DOMAINE A** NR Est 1973 LR/ML $9–25 ML
STHN TAS
Campania, Tas 7202  (002) 62 4174
**OPEN** By appointment only  **PRODUCTION** 300 cases
**WINEMAKER** Peter Althaus
**PRINCIPAL WINES** Ries, Sylvaner, Pinot, Cab Sauv.
**SUMMARY** The striking new black label, dominated by the single, multicoloured 'A', signifies the change of ownership from George Park to Swiss businessman Peter Althaus. The vineyard, to be much expanded, is of undoubted quality, a harbinger of the great potential of the Coal River region.

**STONIERS MERRICKS**  A–A Est 1978 NFR/CD/ML/UK
(Waterloo Wine Co) $15–20 R   MORNINGTON P
62 Thompsons Lane, Merricks, Vic 3916  (059) 699 8922
**OPEN** 7 days 11–5  **PRODUCTION** 5000 cases
**WINEMAKER** Tod Dexter
**PRINCIPAL WINES** Chard, Cab blend, Pinot, Cab Sauv; Winery
Selection range is second label.
**BEST VINTAGES** **W** '86, '88, '89, '90 **R** '84, '86, '88, '90, '91
**SUMMARY** Has now overtaken Dromana Estate as Mornington's largest
producer (of Mornington-sourced grapes) and set to become known throughout
Australia. The Winery Selection range (blended from owner Brian Stonier's own
vineyard grapes and from winemaker Tod Dexter's vineyard) offer very good
value; the Stoniers Merricks label is for the top wines, and the '90 and '91 vintage
wines (the '90 Chardonnay in particular) have had great success in all forums.

**SUMMERFIELD**  BA–A Est 1980 CD/ML $8–16 CD  PYRENEES
Moonambel-Stawell Road, Moonambel, Vic 3478  (054) 67 2264
**OPEN** 7 days 9–6  **PRODUCTION** 2500 cases
**WINEMAKER** Ian Summerfield
**PRINCIPAL WINES** Herm, Cab Sauv, Meth Champ.
**BEST VINTAGES** **R** '80, '83, '89, '90, '91
**SUMMARY** Produces superbly rich, sweet textured red wines, with
Shiraz a specialty, but the Cabernet Sauvignon is very good too. Great
1990 wines may be surpassed by even better 1991s if they safely make the
transition to bottle.

**SUNNYCLIFF WINES**  C–B Est 1980 NR $6–8 R NW VIC
Nangiloc Road, Iraak, Vic 3496 (050) 29 1426  fax (050) 24 3316
**OPEN** Not  **PRODUCTION** 8500 tonnes (500 000 case equivalent)
**WINEMAKER** David Thompson
**PRINCIPAL WINES** Chab, Chard, Colombard/Chard, Ries, Sauv Bl,
Cab Sauv.
**SUMMARY** Part of the Rentiers-Katnook group, producing grape juice,
grape concentrate and bulk wine, with a small proportion of the crush
released under the Sunnycliff label, and providing wines of pleasant quality
and modest price.

**SUTHERLAND**  B–B Est 1979 LR/CD/ML $12–14 CD
HUNTER V
Deasey's Road, Pokolbin, NSW 2321  (049) 98 7650  fax (049) 98 7603
**OPEN** 7 days 10–5  **PRODUCTION** 6000 cases
**WINEMAKER** Neil Sutherland
**PRINCIPAL WINES** Chard, Sem, Chen Bl, Sem Chard, Shir.
**BEST VINTAGES** **W** '85, '87, '90, '91 **R** '88, '89, '90, '91
**SUMMARY** Consistently good white wines in 1990 headed by super-
rich, botrytis-touched Chardonnay, and brawny, regional reds from 1989,
have done much to restore Sutherland to an even keel; the '91s should by
rights be better still.

**TALIJANCICH**  CA–B Est 1932 LR/CD $12.90–68 CD  SWAN V
121 Hyem Road, Herne Hill, WA 6056  (09) 296 4289  fax (09) 296 4289
**OPEN** Sun–Fri 11–5  **PRODUCTION** 2500 cases
**WINEMAKER** James Talijancich
**PRINCIPAL WINES** Sem, Grenache Rosé, Verd, Shir, Port, Muscat, Tokay.
**SUMMARY** A fortified-wine specialist which now produces a small range of
table wines, the latter with consultancy advice from 1989, which happily
transformed their quality. The 1961 Muscat remains supreme at $68 a bottle.

**TALLARA**  B–B Est 1970 LR/CD $12 CD  MUDGEE
'Tallara' Cassilis Road, Mudgee, NSW 2850  (063) 72 2408

**OPEN** W'ends 9–5 **PRODUCTION** 300 cases
**WINEMAKER** Phillip Shaw
**PRINCIPAL WINES** Chard, Cab Sauv.
**SUMMARY** Leading Sydney chartered accountant Rick Turner's weekend hobby, with smooth, full-flavoured Chardonnay made by Phillip Shaw at Rosemount.

**TALTARNI** BA–A Est 1972 NFR/CD/ML/UK (Taltarni UK) $8.50–28.50 R PYRENEES
Taltarni Road, Moonambel, Vic 3478 (054) 67 2218 fax (054) 67 2306
**OPEN** 7 days 10–5 **PRODUCTION** 41 000 cases
**WINEMAKERS** D. Portet, G. Gallagher
**PRINCIPAL WINES** Ries, Fumé, Shir, Cab Sauv, Merl Cab Franc, sparkl.
**BEST VINTAGES** R '84, '88, '89, '90, '91
**SUMMARY** The red wines are uncompromising in style; tannin usually teeters on the edge of acceptability, and sometimes the second label Reserve de Pyrenees can out-perform its betters simply because it is softer. These are, above all else, wines for the long haul, although the '89 Cabernet Sauvignon is (relatively speaking) soft and elegant.

**TAMBURLAINE** CB–CB Est 1966 LR/CD/ML $10–16 CD HUNTER V
McDonalds Road, Pokolbin, NSW 2321 (049) 98 7570
**OPEN** 7 days 9.30–5 **PRODUCTION** 10 000 cases
**WINEMAKERS** G. Silkman, M. Davidson
**PRINCIPAL WINES** Chard, Sem, Cab Shir, Cab Sauv, Cab Merl.
**BEST VINTAGES** W '86, '87, '89, '91 R '86, '87, '88, '89, '91
**SUMMARY** Burnt, medical aromas have marred the most recent white wines ('90 and '91) but the red wines have continued to show good depth of flavour.

**TANAMI RED** NR Est 1987 CD $7–10 CD STHN VALES
McMurtie Road, McLaren Vale, SA 5171 (08) 383 0351
**OPEN** Most w'ends/hols 11–5 **PRODUCTION** 350 cases
**WINEMAKER** Les Payne
**PRINCIPAL WINES** Bin 2, Spinetax and Mulga Shiraz.
**SUMMARY** No rating, simply because I have not tasted the wines.

**TANGLEWOOD DOWNS** NR Est 1986 LR/CD/ML $13–16.90 R MORNINGTON P
Bulldog Creek Road, Mornington Rural, Vic 3931 (059) 74 3325
**OPEN** First Sat of the month/Sun/hols **PRODUCTION** 800 cases
**WINEMAKER** Kevin McCarthy
**PRINCIPAL WINES** Chard, Tram, Ries, Pinot, Merl, Cabernet.
**SUMMARY** After a modest start in 1990, Tanglewood made lovely wines in 1991, with a peachy, passionfruit Chardonnay and a big, rich, plummy Pinot Noir leading the charge. A winery on the way up.

**TARCOOLA** NR Est 1971 CD/ML $8–10 CD GEELONG
Spillers Road, Lethbridge, Vic 3332 (052) 81 9245 fax (052) 819 311
**OPEN** 7 days 10–5 **PRODUCTION** 4000 cases
**WINEMAKER** Keith Wood
**PRINCIPAL WINES** Ries, Muller, Hilltop Shir, River Flat Shir, Cab Sauv.
**SUMMARY** After a period of slow decline, Tarcoola was purchased in 1990 by Keith Wood, who is determined to breathe new life into the vineyard and winery. Old, sub-standard stock has been disposed of, and new labels introduced, emphasising those wines made from estate-grown grapes. Some raw, aggressive oak held the 1990 wines in check, other than the massive, extractive 1990 Hilltop Shiraz.

**TARRAHILL ESTATE**  CB–B Est 1985 LR/ML $15–17 ML
YARRA V
Old Healesville Road, Yarra Glen, Vic 3775  (03) 439 7425
fax (03) 435 9138
OPEN  Not  PRODUCTION  750 cases
WINEMAKER  Ian Hanson
PRINCIPAL WINES  Cab Sauv, Cab Franc.
SUMMARY  An immensely concentrated and deep-coloured 1990
Cabernet Sauvignon seemed to have been bottled rather precipitantly but
underlines the potential.

**TARRAWARRA**  A–BA Est 1983 NFR/ML/UK (Lawlers)
$10–25 R  YARRA V
Healesville Road, Yarra Glen, Vic 3775  (059) 6 3311  fax (059) 623 887
OPEN  Not  PRODUCTION  6000 cases
WINEMAKER  David Wollan
PRINCIPAL WINES  Chard, Pinot; second label is Tunnel Hill, third is
Ryrie.
BEST VINTAGES  W '87, '88, '89, '90  R '88, '89, '90
SUMMARY  Slowly evolving Chardonnay of great structure and
complexity is the winery specialty; robust Pinot Noir also needs time and
evolves impressively if given it. The second label Tunnel Hill wines are
more accessible when young, and better value for those who do not wish to
wait for the TarraWarra wines to evolve.

**TARWIN RIDGE**  NR Est 1983 LR/ML  $11–14.50 ML
GIPPSLAND
Whittles Road, Leongatha South, Vic (vineyard only); postal:
PO Box 498, Leongatha, Vic 3953  (056) 643 211
OPEN  Not  PRODUCTION  500 cases
WINEMAKER  Brian Anstee
PRINCIPAL WINES  Fumé, Pinot, Cab Merl; Cherry Tree Creek is
second label.
SUMMARY  For the time being Brian Anstee is making his wines at
Nicholson River under the gaze of fellow social worker Ken Eckersley; the
initial realeases of '90 Fumé Blanc and '89 Cabernet Merlot showed
promise, particularly the light but fragrant and clean Cabernet Merlot.

**TAYLORS**  CB–A Est 1972 NR/CD $5.94–10.95 R  CLARE V
Mintaro Road, Auburn, SA 5451 (088) 49 2008  fax (088) 49 2240
OPEN  Mon–Fri 9–5, Sat/pub hols 10–5, Sun 10–4.
PRODUCTION  160 000 cases
WINEMAKER  Andrew Tolley
PRINCIPAL WINES  Chard, Ries, Wh Burg, Pinot, Cab Sauv, Herm.
BEST VINTAGES  W '84, '87, '89, '91  R '86, '89, '90, '91
SUMMARY  The Chardonnay and Cabernet Sauvignon are both major
brands, each selling in excess of 50 000 cases a year, and selling out; what
is more, not a bottle is exported. The Chardonnay is light-bodied and
subtle, developing in bottle for five years or more; the Cabernet Sauvignon
is deliberately made in a similarly light style, fully ready when released
with four years age. The wines sell in such large volumes simply because
they are so well priced.

**TEMPLE BRUER**  CB–B Est 1981 LR/CD/ML $7–17.50 CD
LANGHORNE CREEK
Milang Road, Strathalbyn, SA 5255  (085) 37 0203
OPEN  7 days 10.30–4.30  PRODUCTION  NFP
WINEMAKER  David Bruer
PRINCIPAL WINES  Chab, Ries, Sparkl Burg, Cab Merl, Rosé, Shir Malb.
SUMMARY  Unusual, sappy rather vegetal Cabernet Merlot (the '88 a

gold medal winner in 1991), some excellent Eden Valley-sourced Riesling, a velvety Sparkling Burgundy and good botrytis Riesling are among the eclectic range of wines on offer.

**TERRACE VALE**  CA–B Est 1971 LR/CD/ML $11–14 CD HUNTER V

Deasey's Lane, Pokolbin, NSW 2321   (049) 98 7517  fax (049) 98 7814
**OPEN** 7 days 10–4  **PRODUCTION** 7000 cases
**WINEMAKER** Alain Le Prince
**PRINCIPAL WINES** Sem, Chard, Gewurz, sparkl, Shir, Pinot, Cab Sauv, Herm, Port.
**BEST VINTAGES W** '84, '87, '89, '91 **R** '81, '83, '85, '89, '91
**SUMMARY** Every now and then Terrace Vale bobs up with a lovely wine such as the 1989 Cabernet Sauvignon Bin 7; normally, the white wines are better, solid and slow-developing (witness the 1989 Bin 2 Chardonnay) as befits the region.

**T'GALLANT**  B–B Est 1990 LR/CD $13–14 R  MORNINGTON P
237 Myers Road, Bittern, Vic 3918   (059) 83 1058  fax (059) 77 7093
**OPEN** Summer w'ends by appointment 10–5
**PRODUCTION** 3000 cases
**WINEMAKERS** K. Quealy, K. McCarthy
**PRINCIPAL WINES** Chard, Holystone.
**SUMMARY** Consultant winemakers Kathleen Quealy and Kevin McCarthy have specialised in unwooded Chardonnay for their own label sourced from low-yielding, relatively mature vineyards, adding Holystone, a unique, unwooded Pinot Noir-Chardonnay table wine blend in 1991.

**THALGARA ESTATE**  NR Est 1985 CD/ML $12.50–15 CD HUNTER V
DeBeyers Road, Pokolbin, NSW 2321   phone and fax (049) 98 7717
**OPEN** 7 days 10–5  **PRODUCTION** 1500 cases
**WINEMAKER** Steve Lamb
**PRINCIPAL WINES** Chard, Sem Chard, Shir, Shir Cab.
**SUMMARY** No wines tasted recently; the 1988 red wines were rather oaky, but had plenty of flavour.

**THISTLE HILL**  CB–B Est 1976 LR/CD/M $9–13 CD  MUDGEE
McDonalds Road, Mudgee, NSW 2850   (063) 73 3546
**OPEN** 7 days 9–5  **PRODUCTION** 3300 cases
**WINEMAKERS** David Robertson and Richard Tarrant
**PRINCIPAL WINES** Ries, Chard, Pinot, Cab Sauv.
**SUMMARY** David Robertson tries hard with his Pinot, but succeeds best with Chardonnay and Cabernet Sauvignon, the latter providing lovely wines from '85 to '88 inclusive. More recent vintages have been disappointing.

**THOMAS**  NR Est 1976 CD/ML $15.95 CD  SW COASTAL
23–24 Crowd Road, Gelorup, WA 6230   (097) 95 7925
**OPEN** By appointment only  **PRODUCTION** 600 cases
**WINEMAKER** Gill Thomas
**PRINCIPAL WINES** Pinot, Cab Sauv.
**SUMMARY** I have not tasted the elegant wines of Bunbury pharmacist Gill Thomas for several years; they are only sold to a local clientele.

**THOMAS FERN HILL**  CB–CB Est 1975 LR/CD/ML $4.50–15 CD STHN VALES
Ingoldby Road, McLaren Flat, SA 5171   (08) 383 0167  fax (08) 383 0107
**OPEN** Mon–Fri 10–5, w'ends 12–5  **PRODUCTION** 6500 cases
**WINEMAKER** Wayne Thomas
**PRINCIPAL WINES** Brut, Ries, Chard, Sauv Bl, Cab Sauv, Shir, Port.

SUMMARY Some very good wines, some not so good, the latter slightly surprising given Wayne Thomas's considerable district experience. A fleshy, soft '91 Sauvignon Blanc and rather oaky '90 Shiraz show the winery to best advantage.

**THOMAS HARDY** A–A Est 1853 NR/CD/UK (Whiclar & Gordon) $6–22 R  STHN VALES
Reynella Road, Reynella, SA 5161  (08) 381 2266  fax (08) 381 1968
OPEN 7 days 10–4.30
PRODUCTION 10 000 tonnes (650 000 case equivalent)
WINEMAKERS David O'Leary & Tom Newton
PRINCIPAL WINES A large renge of brands, moving upwards from the Bird series, next the Siegersdorf series, next the Hardy Collection and finally super premium Eileen Hardy; all major varieties and generic styles covered.
BEST VINTAGES W '80, '86, '88, '90 R '82, '86, '90, '91
SUMMARY A major player in the mid to upper sector of the table wine market, with brands covering every significant price point and style. The Padthaway-based white wines are usually outstanding, while the red wines have improved out of sight over the past few years right across the range. The '89 Eileen Hardy Chardonnay deserves its trophies.

**TILBA VALLEY** D–C Est 1983 CD/ML $10.50–12.50 CD
SOUTH COAST
Glen Eden Vineyard, Corunna Lake via Tilba, NSW 2546  (044) 73 7308
OPEN 7 days 10–5  PRODUCTION 1600 cases
WINEMAKER Barry Field
PRINCIPAL WINES Chard, Tram Ries, Sem, Sem Chard, Cab Sauv, Cab Herm.
SUMMARY A strongly tourist-oriented operation, but wine quality is a worry, with oxidation spoiling all the white wines tasted.

**TIM ADAMS** A–A Est 1985 LR/CD/ML/UK (Enotira) $9.50–13 R  CLARE V
Warenda Road, Clare, SA 5453  phone and fax (088) 42 2429
OPEN 7 days 11–5  PRODUCTION 6500 cases
WINEMAKER Tim Adams
PRINCIPAL WINES Ries, Sem, Botrytis Sem, Shir.
BEST VINTAGES W '87, '88, '89, '90 R '86, '88, '89, '90, '91
SUMMARY Has made a series of superb wines in recent years, none better than the beautifully handled and oaked 1990 Semillon and its botrytised sister from the same year. His Shiraz (as in 1989) is a wine of enormous depth and power, made from very old vines growing near Wendouree, the '90 Cabernet Sauvignon very nearly as good. Their price belies their quality.

**TIM KNAPPSTEIN** BA–BA Est 1976 NFR/CD/UK (Oddbins) $11.25–19.95 R  CLARE V
2 Pioneer Avenue, Clare, SA 5453  (088) 42 2600  fax (088) 42 3831
OPEN Mon–Fri 9–5, Sat 10–5, Sun 11–4  PRODUCTION 40 000 cases
WINEMAKER Tim Knappstein
PRINCIPAL WINES Ries, Gewurz, Chard, Fumé, Sem, Cab Merl, Cab Sauv.
BEST VINTAGES W '82, '86, '89, '90 R '82, '84, '86, '89, '91
SUMMARY Long regarded as one of the foremost makers of Rhine Riesling in Australia, and as a fine exponent of Cabernet-based reds, Tim Knappstein came up with the best 1990 Chardonnay out of the Clare Valley, a wine in the class of his absolutely superb Beerenauslese Riesling, following it with a very good '91 Rhine Riesling, crammed with soft, rich fruit.

**TINGLE-WOOD** A–A Est 1976 CD/ML $10–12  LWR GRT STHN

Glenrowan Road, Denmark, WA 6333 (098) 40 9218
**OPEN** 7 days 9–5 **PRODUCTION** 950 cases
**WINEMAKER** John Wade (Contract)
**PRINCIPAL WINES** Ries, Shir Cab Sauv.
**SUMMARY** This remote, forest-encircled vineyard has produced some quite
lovely wines for owner Bob Wood, with a fine, steely citrus-tinged 1990
Rhine Riesling, followed by the equally fine, lime and toast 1991 Riesling,
winner of the trophy for Best Riesling at the 1991 Mount Barker Show.

**TINLINS** NR Est 1978 CD/ML $2–4 CD **STHN VALES**
Kangarilla Road, McLaren Flat, SA 5171 (08) 323 8649
**OPEN** 7 days 8–5 **PRODUCTION** 32 000 cases
**WINEMAKER** Don Tinlin
**PRINCIPAL WINES** Generic table, fortified and flavoured wines sold in
bottle, in flagons, 6 L casks and 25 L kegs for as little as $1 a litre.
**SUMMARY** A staggeringly large direct sale operation relying on strong
cellar and sales driven by prices which disappeared elsewhere 20 years ago.

**TISDALL** CB–B Est 1979 NR/CD/ML/UK (Mt Helen Pty Ltd)
$9.20–10.50 R **NTH GOULBURN R**
Cornelia Creek Road, Echuca, Vic 3564 (054) 82 1911 fax (054) 82 2516
**OPEN** Mon–Fri 9–5, w'ends 10–5 **PRODUCTION** 90 000 cases
**WINEMAKER** Jeff Clarke
**PRINCIPAL WINES** Chard, Sauv Bl Sem, Ries, Chenin, Gewurz, Cab
Sauv, Cab Merl.
**SUMMARY** In recent times the red wines have been rather better than
the rather chalky, slightly smelly whites, particularly in the Tisdall range;
the 1990 Cabernet Merlot continues the long line of success with its fresh,
red berry fruit.

**TIZZANA** NR Est 1985 CD $5.50–16.50 CD **SYDNEY DISTRICT**
Tizzana Road, Sackville Reach, NSW 2756 (045) 79 1150
**OPEN** W'ends/hols 12–6 **PRODUCTION** 300 cases
**WINEMAKER** Peter Auld
**PRINCIPAL WINES** Estate grown and made Shir, Cab Sauv; 'cleanskin'
wines under Tizzana Selection label.
**SUMMARY** The only estate wines tasted (several years ago) were not good,
but the historic stone winery is most certainly worth a visit, and a wide
selection of Tizzana Selection wines from other makers gives a broad choice.

**TOLLANA** BA–BA Est 1888 NR/UK (Penfolds UK) $4.60–12.60
R **BAROSSA V**
Tanunda Road, Nuriootpa, SA 5355 (085) 62 0389 fax (085) 62 1669
**OPEN** Mon–Sat 10–5, Sun 12–4 **PRODUCTION** NFP
**WINEMAKER** John Duval
**PRINCIPAL WINES** Ries, Botrytis Ries, Chard, Sauv Bl, Herm, Cab
Sauv TR222.
**BEST VINTAGES W** '82, '87, '90, '91 **R** '82, '86, '88, '90
**SUMMARY** Another pawn on the S. A. Brewing chessboard, and before
that on the Penfold chessboard; the quality of its tangy, lime-accented
Eden Valley Rhine Riesling, its elegant, tangy 1990 Chardonnay, and its
stylish Cabernet Sauvignon TR222 suggest it has deserved better under its
various corporate owners.

**TOLLEY PEDARE** B–A Est 1892 NR/CD/UK (O. W. Loeb)
$4.99–11.50 R **BAROSSA V**
30 Barracks Road, Hope Valley, SA 5090 (08) 264 2255
fax (08) 263 7485
**OPEN** Mon–Sat 9–5 **PRODUCTION** 160 000 cases
**WINEMAKER** Christopher Tolley

**PRINCIPAL WINES** Chard, Champ, Sauv Bl, Colomb Sem, Ries, Gewurz, Cab Sauv, Pinot; Cellar Reserve is the cheaper, Pedare Range the premium line.
**BEST VINTAGES W** '82, '85, '87, '90, '91 **R** '83, '86, '87, '90
**SUMMARY** The quality never falters, the style no less consistent: vibrant, spicy-lychee Gewurztraminer (one of the two best in the country), lemony, oaky Semillon which needs (and is given) at least four years bottle-age, and solid, dark berry flavoured Cabernet Sauvignon are usually the pick of an undervalued bunch. The '91 Pedare Gewurztraminer and '89 Cellar Reserve Cabernet Shiraz stood out in 1992.

## TORRESAN'S HAPPY VALLEY NR Est 1972 CD $6–13 CD STHN VALES

Manning Road, Flagstaff Hill, SA 5159 (082) 70 2500
**OPEN** Mon–Sat 8–5 **PRODUCTION** 13 000 cases
**WINEMAKER** Michael Torresan
**PRINCIPAL WINES** Ries, Sem, Cab Shir, Cab Sauv, fortified.
**SUMMARY** A substantial cellar door trade and local clientele accounts for most sales of mature but uninspiring wines.

## TRENTHAM ESTATE B–BA Est 1986 LR/CD/ML $7.50–11 CD MURRAY R

Sturt Highway, Trentham Cliffs, NSW 2738 (050) 24 8747
fax (050) 24 8800
**OPEN** 7 days 9–5 **PRODUCTION** 10 000 cases
**WINEMAKER** Anthony Murphy
**PRINCIPAL WINES** Chard, Sauv Bl Fumé, Colomb Chard, Chab, Ries, Pinot, Cab Sauv.
**BEST VINTAGES W** '87, '89, '90, '91 **R** '86, '87, '88, '89, '91
**SUMMARY** Remarkably consistent tasting notes across all wine styles from all vintages since 1989 attest to the expertise of ex-Mildara winemaker Tony Murphy, now making the Trentham wines from his family vineyards, with a soft, buttery '90 Chardonnay and a flavoursome soft '91 Riesling offering early drinking. The winery restaurant is also recommended.

## TUERONG ESTATE NR Est 1984 CD $25 CD MORNINGTON P

Mornington-Flinders Road, Red Hill, Vic 3937 (059) 89 2129
**OPEN** W'ends 12–5 **PRODUCTION** 180 cases
**WINEMAKER** Peter Cumming
**PRINCIPAL WINES** Chard, Meth Champ 'Morning Star'.
**SUMMARY** A most unusual operation, which is in reality a family Italian style restaurant at which the wine is principally sold and served, and which offers something totally different on the Mornington Peninsula.

## TULLOCH CB–B Est 1893 NR/CD $9.50–14.30 R HUNTER V

De Beyers Road, Pokolbin, NSW 2321 (049) 98 7503 fax (049) 98 7862
**OPEN** Mon–Fri 9–4.30, w'ends 10–4.30 **PRODUCTION** 32 000 cases
**WINEMAKER** Patrick Auld
**PRINCIPAL WINES** Ranging upwards from J. Y. Chab, Sem, Chard, Verd, Herm to Hector of Glen Hermitage as premium release; however brand structure under review and likely to change.
**BEST VINTAGES W** '74, '76, '86, '91 **R** '65, '75, '86, '91
**SUMMARY** A once-great name and reputation which suffered enormously under multiple ownership changes, with a complete loss of identity and direction. A solid, rich, rather oaky '90 Chardonnay commands attention, but the future direction of Tulloch is still unclear.

**TYRRELLS** A–A Est 1853 NR/CD/ML/UK (Avery's) $6–25 R
HUNTER V
Broke Road, Pokolbin, NSW 2321  (049) 98 7509  fax (049) 98 7723
**OPEN** 7 Days 9–5  **PRODUCTION** 450 000 cases
**WINEMAKER** Murray Tyrrell
**PRINCIPAL WINES** A very large range starting at the bottom with Long
Flat Red and White, then the commercial Old Winery series (Chard, Sem,
Sauv Bl, Herm, Cab Merl) and thence to the premium vat wines (notably
Vat 1 Sem, Vat 47 Chard and vats 5, 7, 8, 9, 10 and 11 all Herm).
**BEST VINTAGES W** '76, '79, '86, '91 **R** '65, '75, '83, '91
**SUMMARY** A quite extraordinary family winery which has grown up
from an insignificant base in 1960 to become one of the most influential
mid-sized companies, successfully competing with wines running all the
way from cheap, volume-driven Long Flat White up to the super-premium
Vat 47 Chardonnay, which challenges Roxburgh for the title of Australia's
best. There is a similar range of price and style with the red wines, but in
recent years Tyrrell has barely faltered within the parameters of price and
style, with the '91 Old Winery Chardonnay and '89 Old Winery Cabernet
Merlot quite outstanding.

**VASSE FELIX** BA–BA Est 1967 NFR/CD/ML/UK
(Alex Findlater) $15.80–23.80 R MARGARET R
Cnr Caves Road and Harmans Road South, Cowaramup, WA 6284
(097) 55 5242  fax (097) 55 5425
**OPEN** 7 days 10–4.30  **PRODUCTION** 20 000 cases
**WINEMAKER** D. Gregg, C. Otto
**PRINCIPAL WINES** Chard, Verd, Classic Dry White, Shir, Classic Dry
Red, Cab Sauv.
**BEST VINTAGES W** '82, '84, '89, '90 **R** '82, '85, '86, '89, '91
**SUMMARY** Long regarded as one of the foremost wineries in the region,
producing elegant, fine Cabernet Sauvignon; in 1988 and again in 1990, it
came up with an equally elegant Hermitage, and subsequently with a quite
superb botrytised Riesling. The Classic White and Red (the latter a bizarre
blend of Cabernet Franc and Pinot Noir) are not in the same class.

**VERITAS** CA–BA Est 1951 LR/CD/ML/UK (Lay & Wheeler)
$7–10 CD BAROSSA V
94 Langmeil Road, Tanunda, SA 5352  (085) 63 2330
**OPEN** Mon–Fri 9–5, w'ends 11–5  **PRODUCTION** 8000 cases
**WINEMAKER** Rolf Binder
**PRINCIPAL WINES** Ries, Sem Sauv Bl, Tramino, Leanyka, Cab Franc
Merl, Cab Sauv, Shir Cab, Bikaver Bull's Blood, Heysen Vineyard Shir,
fortifieds.
**BEST VINTAGES W** '84, '86, '88, '90 **R** '84, '85, '88, '90
**SUMMARY** The Hungarian influence is obvious in the naming of some
of the wines, but Australian technology is paramount in shaping the
generally very good quality. The red wines can be superb, with fresh fruit
and excellent oak handling, exemplified by the 1989 Heysen Vineyard
Shiraz, with echoes of the Rhone Valley in its gamey/spicy complexity.

**VICARYS** CB–A Est 1923 CD/ML $1.25–16 CD SYDNEY
DISTRICT
Northern Road, Luddenham, NSW 2745  (047) 73 4161
**OPEN** Tues–Fri 9–6, w'ends 11.30–5.30
**PRODUCTION** 3500 cases
**WINEMAKER** C. Niccol
**PRINCIPAL WINES** Chard, Sem, Ries, Gewurz, Cab Sauv, sparkl,
fortifieds.
**BEST VINTAGES W** '84, '86, '88, '91 **R** '83, '85, '89, '91

SUMMARY Takes its grapes from a variety of regions — principally the Hunter Valley — and has made some very good wines from these, particularly Chardonnay and Semillon. $1.25 for the generic table wines (Riesling, Rosé, Moselle etc) is the lowest-priced wine I am aware of in Australia today — and there is a discount of 10% by the case!

## VINTINA ESTATE C–C Est 1985 CD $14 CD MORNINGTON P
1282 Nepean Highway, Mt Eliza, Vic 3930   (03) 787 8166
OPEN 7 days 9–5   PRODUCTION 500 cases
WINEMAKER K. McCarthy
PRINCIPAL WINES Chard, Sem, Cab Sauv, Pinot.
SUMMARY The initial releases of Vintina (the only wines tasted to date), were mediocre. With competent contract winemaking, improvement can be expected.

## VIRGIN HILLS A–A Est 1968 LR/ML $27 R MACEDON
Salisbury Road, Lauriston West via Kyneton, Vic 3444   (054) 23 9169
OPEN By appointment only   PRODUCTION 3000 cases
WINEMAKER Mark Sheppard
PRINCIPAL WINES A single Cab Sauv Shir Merl blend called Virgin Hills.
BEST VINTAGES R '82, '85, '88, '90, '91
SUMMARY The Macedon region is not normally a kind host to the Cabernet Sauvignon family nor Shiraz, but in the warmer vintages in particular, Virgin Hills produces one of Australia's great red wines. The '88 was great, the '90 vibrantly spicy and, while most enjoyable, somewhat atypical; watch for the '91.

## WA DE LOCK VINEYARDS NR Est 1987 LR/CD/ML EAST GIPPSLAND
Stratford Road, Maffra, Vic (051) 47 3244  fax (051) 43 1421
OPEN By appointment   PRODUCTION 1300 cases
WINEMAKER Graeme Little
PRINCIPAL WINES Chard, Sauv Bl, Pinot, Cab Sauv.
SUMMARY A range of wines from the 1991 vintage showed fairly light fruit characters, perhaps indicative of young vineyards. The light, delicate, whole-bunch pressed Rhine Riesling was the best.

## WALKERSHIRE NR Est 1984 CD/ML $11.50–13.50 CD GOULBURN V
Rushworth Road, Bailieston, Vic 3608   (057) 94 9257
OPEN 7 days 10–6   PRODUCTION NFP
WINEMAKER John Walker
PRINCIPAL WINES Shir Cab, Port.
SUMMARY Bearded Yorkshireman John Walker fills his tiny tasting room with his presence, and does likewise in far grander venues. His wines match his personality: they are monumental, indeed fearsome. The best are very good, but more recent tastings have disappointed; because it is some years since my last encounter, I feel it unfair to give a rating.

## WANDIN VALLEY ESTATE NR Est 1973 CD/ML $9.50–12.50 CD HUNTER V
Talga Road, Allandale, NSW 2321   (049) 30 7317
OPEN Wed–Mon 10–5   PRODUCTION 3500 cases
WINEMAKER Geoff Broadfield
PRINCIPAL WINES Meth Champ, Chard, Sauv Bl, Ruby Cab, Cab Sauv, Shir, Pinot.
SUMMARY The former Millstone vineyard now owned by the producer of 'A Country Practice' who has acquired the services of Allanmere

winemaker Geoff Broadfield. A curiously tropical 1991 Sauvignon Blanc has Hunter Valley Benchmark status, but I prefer the fleshy berry, if rather ripe, flavours of the 1990 Ruby Cabernet.

## WANINGA B–B Est 1989 CD/ML $9–11 CD CLARE V

Hughes Park Road, Sevenhill via Clare, SA 5453 (088) 42 2555
OPEN W'ends, hols 10–5 PRODUCTION 2000 cases
WINEMAKER Tim Adams, J. Grosset
PRINCIPAL WINES Ries, Chenin, Chard, Shir, Cab Sauv.
SUMMARY The large vineyards owned by Waninga were established in 1974, but it was not until 1989 that a portion of the grapes were withheld from sale and vinified for the owners. A glorious '89 Shiraz handsomely justified the decision, bursting with red berry and spice fruit and was followed by a passionfruit-tinged '91 Riesling of considerable quality. The Chardonnay and Cabernet have not been in the same class.

## WANTIRNA ESTATE NR Est 1963 LR/ML $18 ML

YARRA V
Bushy Park Lane, Wantirna South, Vic 3152 (03) 801 2367
fax (03) 887 0225
OPEN Not PRODUCTION 1000 cases
WINEMAKER Reg Egan
PRINCIPAL WINES Chard, Pinot, Cab, Merl.
SUMMARY Limited tastings in recent years preclude judgement.

## WARDS GATEWAY CELLARS C–B Est 1979 CD/ML

$7–12 CD BAROSSA V
Barossa Valley Highway, Lyndoch, SA 5351 (085) 24 4138
OPEN 7 days 9–5.30 PRODUCTION 3000 cases
WINEMAKER Ray Ward
PRINCIPAL WINES Ries, Colomb, Wh Burg, Chablis, Fronti, Shir, Shir Cab, Cab Sauv, Port.
SUMMARY The very old vines surrounding the winery produce the best wines, which are made without frills or new oak and sold without ostentation.

## WARRABILLA NR Est 1986 LR/ML $14.85–18 ML NE VIC

Indigo Valley, Rutherglen (Vineyard); postal PO Box 41, Rutherlgen, Vic 3685 (0603) 351 233
OPEN Not PRODUCTION 1000 cases
WINEMAKER Andrew Sutherland-Smith
PRINCIPAL WINES Shir, Cab Merl, Pinot, Touriga Vintage Port.
SUMMARY All Saints winemaker Andrew Sutherland-Smith has leased a small winery at Corowa to make the Warrabilla wines from a vineyard developed by himself and Carol Smith in the Indigo Valley.

## WARRAMATE CB–CB Est 1970 LR/CD/ML $13–18 CD

YARRA V
4 Maddens Lane, Gruyere, Vic 3770 (059) 64 9219
OPEN Sat/hols 9–6, Sun 10–6 PRODUCTION 800 cases
WINEMAKER Jack Church
PRINCIPAL WINES Ries, Shir, Cab Sauv.
SUMMARY Excellent red wines made in 1988 (with consultancy advice from Kathleen Quealy) showed what this high quality, mature, non-irrigated vineyard can produce; the light, spicy/cherry '90 Shiraz was a pleasant follow-on, although the Riesling is less convincing.

## WARRENMANG CB–B Est 1974 LR/CD $5–17 CD PYRENEES

Mountain Creek Road, Moonambel, Vic 3478 (054) 67 2233
OPEN 7 days 9–5 PRODUCTION 1500 cases
WINEMAKER Luigi Bazzani

**PRINCIPAL WINES** Chard, Tram Ries, Cab Sauv, Shir, Grand Pyrenees.
**SUMMARY** Warrenmang is now the focus of a superb accommodation and
restaurant complex created by former restaurateur Luigi Bazzani and wife
Athalie, which is in much demand as a conference centre as well as for
weekend tourism. The wines are, to put it mildly, robust, but the '87 Grand
Pyrenees has attractive red berry and mint fruit, and is not over-extracted.

## WATER WHEEL NR Est 1972 NFR/CD/ML $8–17 R
BENDIGO .

Bridgewater-on-Loddon, Bridgewater, Vic 3516   (054) 37 3060
fax (054) 37 3082
**OPEN** Mon–Sat 9–5, Sun 12–5   **PRODUCTION** 10 000 cases
**WINEMAKER** Peter Cumming
**PRINCIPAL WINES** Chard, Ries, Chablis, Pinot, Herm, Cab Sauv;
grapes from other districts under premium Wing Fields label.
**SUMMARY** Peter Cumming gained great respect as a winemaker during
his four-year stint with Hickinbotham winemakers, and his 1989 purchase
of Water Wheel was greeted with enthusiasm by followers of his wines.
The '90 Water Wheel Shiraz and '90 Cabernet have abundant weight and
sweet fruit, and are the most impressive of the releases to date.

## WEIN VALLEY ESTATES NR Est 1985 LR/CD/ML
$2.95–7.95 CD   RIVERLAND

Nixon Road, Monash, SA 5342   (085) 83 5255
**OPEN** Mon–Fri 9–4.30, Sat 11–3
**PRODUCTION** 7000 tonnes (450,000 case equivalent)
**WINEMAKER** Otto Konig
**PRINCIPAL WINES** The usual array of generic table, fortified and
flavoured wines, with premium varietals under the Langhill Estate label.
**SUMMARY** A major producer of bulk and packaged wine; much is sold
to other makers for blending or repackaging. The quality basically reflects
the price.

## WELLINGTON WINES NR Est 1990 LR/ML $14–17.95
R TAS

34 Cornwall Street, Rose Bay, Tas 7015 (002) 43 7320  fax (002) 62 4390
**OPEN** Not  **PRODUCTION** 1800 cases
**WINEMAKER** Andrew Hood
**PRINCIPAL WINES** Chard, Pinot, Easy Cab.
**SUMMARY** Consultant winemaker Andrew Hood (ex-Charles Sturt
University) and wife Jenny purchase grapes from various vineyards and
vinify these at Stoney Domaine A winery. The aim is to produce wines for
early to medium term consumption, showing distinctive varietal and
regional fruit flavours, with minimal oak interference. The early releases
have achieved that aim; the 1991 Chardonnay in particular showing
attractive, tangy/grapefruit cool-climate flavours.

## WENDOUREE CELLARS A–A Est 1895 LR/CD/ML
$12–15 CD   CLARE V

Wendouree Road, Clare, SA 5453   (088) 42 2896
**OPEN** Mon–Sat 10–4.30  **PRODUCTION** 2100 cases
**WINEMAKER** Tony Brady
**PRINCIPAL WINES** Shir Malb, Shir, Cab Malb, Cab Sauv.
**BEST VINTAGES** R '83, '86, '89, '90
**SUMMARY** The iron fist in a velvet glove best describes these
extraordinary wines. They are fashioned with passion and yet precision
from the very old vineyard with its unique *terroir* by Tony and Lita Brady,
who see themselves as custodians of a priceless treasure. The '90 red wines
are monuments, destined to live for 30 years or more.

**WEST END** CA–BA Est 1945 CD/ML $4.50–9.50 CD MIA
1283 Brayne Road, Griffith, NSW 2680 (069) 62 2868
**OPEN** Mon–Sat 8.30–6, Sun 10–5 **PRODUCTION** 65 000 cases
**WINEMAKER** W. Calabria
**PRINCIPAL WINES** Chard, Chab, Tram Ries, Ries, Herm, Cab Sauv.
**SUMMARY** The '82, '84 and '89 Cabernet Sauvignons have each won a
gold medal at national wine shows, the '89 at Canberra (in 1990), which is
a remarkable achievement in itself for a little-known Riverina winery.

**WESTERING** B–B Est 1980 LR/ML $8–12 ML CANBERRA
Federal Highway, Collector, NSW 2581 (06) 295 8075
**OPEN** Not **PRODUCTION** 300 cases
**WINEMAKER** Captain G. P. Hood
**PRINCIPAL WINES** Ries, Chard, Shir, Cab Sauv.
**SUMMARY** Has made some lovely Chardonnay; the wines are snapped
up by a loyal local clientele.

**WESTFIELD** B–B Est 1922 LR/CD/ML $9.80–15 CD SWAN V
Cnr Memorial Avenue & Great Northern Highway, Millendon, WA 6056
(09) 296 4356
**OPEN** Mon–Sat 8.30–5.30, Sun 10.30–4 **PRODUCTION** 3000 cases
**WINEMAKER** J. Kosovich
**PRINCIPAL WINES** Verd, Chard, Chenin, Sem, Ries, Wh Burg, Merl,
Cab Sauv, Shir.
**SUMMARY** Consistent producer of a surprisingly elegant and complex
Chardonnay; the other wines are more variable, but from time to time has
made attractive Verdelho and excellent Cabernet Sauvignon.

**WICKHAM HILL** C–B NR $4.35 R MIA
Griffith, NSW 2680 (069) 62 2605 fax (069) 62 7121
**OPEN** Not **PRODUCTION** NFP
**WINEMAKER** David Morris
**PRINCIPAL WINES** Colombard/Sem, Ries, Spat Lexia, Shir.
**SUMMARY** A brand of Orlando with its grape sources and winery based
in the Murrumbidgee Irrigation Area. The wines are basically of cask quality
sold in bottles, but do use the Orlando discipline and production skills.

**WIGNALLS** A–A Est 1982 LR/CD/ML/UK (Whittakers Wines)
$11.60–18.70 CD LWR GRT STHN
Chester Pass Road (Highway 1), Albany, WA 6330
phone and fax (098) 41 2848
**OPEN** Mon–Sat 10–4, Sun 12–4 **PRODUCTION** 3500 cases
**WINEMAKER** John Wade
**PRINCIPAL WINES** Chard, Sauv Bl, Fronti, Pinot, Port.
**BEST VINTAGES** W '85, '88, '89, '90 R '85, '86, '88, '90
**SUMMARY** One of the rare outposts of high quality Pinot Noir production:
the Pinots show excellent varietal definition and are very well made, adding
complexity to the gently sappy, plummy fruit. The Chardonnay is usually
just as good, smoky and citrusy, the Sauvignon Blanc often so.

**WILDWOOD** NR Est 1983 LR/CD/ML $15 CD MACEDON
St John's Lane, Wildwood, Bulla, Vic 3428 (03) 307 1118
**OPEN** By appointment only **PRODUCTION** 1200 cases
**WINEMAKER** Dr Wayne Stott
**PRINCIPAL WINES** Chard, Sem, Pinot, Cabs, Shir.
**SUMMARY** Wine quality continues to disappoint.

**WILLESPIE** A–BA Est 1976 LR/CD/ML $11–17.50 CD
MARGARET R
Harmans Mill Road, Willyabrup via Cowaramup, WA 6284 (097) 55 6210

**OPEN** 7 days 10–4.30 **PRODUCTION** 4000 cases
**WINEMAKERS** Kevin Squance and Michael Lemmes
**PRINCIPAL WINES** Ries, Sem, Verd, Cab Sauv, Port.
**BEST VINTAGES W** '85, '87, '90, '91 **R** '85, '87, '88, '89
**SUMMARY** A string of very impressive '90 and even better '91 white wines in mainstream Margaret River style, herbaceous and tangy, has lifted the already good reputation of Willespie; the pick of the '91 wines are the high-toned Germanic Riesling and positive, herbaceous-gooseberry Sauvignon Blanc.

**WILLOW BEND** NR Est 1990 LR $12.50 R BAROSSA V
Lyndoch Valley Road, Lyndoch, SA 5351 (085) 244 169; postal PO Box 107, Lyndoch, SA 5351
**OPEN** Not **PRODUCTION** 500 cases
**WINEMAKER** Wayne Dutschke
**PRINCIPAL WINES** Chard, Shir/Merl/Cab Sauv/Cab Fr.
**SUMMARY** Wayne Dutschke has had ten years of winemaking experience with major wine companies in South Australia, Victoria and New South Wales, but has returned to South Australia to join his uncle Ken Semmler, a leading grape grower in the Barossa Valley and now in the Adelaide Hills. The sparingly distributed wines have received much praise, and are certainly full of fruit flavour.

**WILLOWS, THE** CB–B Est 1987 LR/CD/ML $7.50–13 CD
BAROSSA V
Light Pass Road, Light Pass, Barossa Valley, SA 5355 (085) 62 1080
**OPEN** 7 days 10.30–4.30 **PRODUCTION** 2800 cases
**WINEMAKERS** Peter and Michael Scholz
**PRINCIPAL WINES** Ries, Sem, Pinot, Shir, Cab Sauv.
**SUMMARY** The Scholz family have been grape growers for generations. Current generation winemakers Peter and Michael Scholz could not resist the temptation to make smooth, well-balanced and flavoursome wines under their own label, led by the vanillan-oaked but flavoursome '90 Semillon.

**WILSON VINEYARD** CA–B Est 1974 LR/CD/ML/UK
(Boxford Wine Co) $9–14 CD CLARE V
Polish Hill River, Sevenhill via Clare, SA 5453 (088) 43 4310
**OPEN** Mon–Fri 12–4.30, w'ends 10–4.30 **PRODUCTION** 3500 cases
**WINEMAKER** John Wilson
**PRINCIPAL WINES** Ries, Chard, Zinfan, Cab Sauv, Shir Cab, Pinot.
**BEST VINTAGES W** '85, '86, '88, '90, '91 **R** '84, '86, '88, '89
**SUMMARY** Dr John Wilson is a tireless ambassador for the Clare Valley and for wine (and its beneficial effect on health) in general. His wines are made using techniques and philosophies garnered early in his wine career, and are often idiosyncratic: some succeed brilliantly (both the '90 and '91 Riesling), some don't.

**WILTON ESTATE** CA–B Est 1976 NR $6.99–18.30 R MIA
Whotton Stock Route, Yenda, NSW 2681 (069) 68 1303 fax (069) 68 1328
**OPEN** Not **PRODUCTION** 2000 tonnes (128 000 case equivalent)
**WINEMAKERS** Lincoln Sauer and John Ellis
**PRINCIPAL WINES** Sem/Sauv Bl, Chard, Marsanne, Botrytis Sem, Cab Merl, Cab Sauv; Hidden Valley is the second label.
**SUMMARY** The former St Peters distillery has been transformed into a table wine producer, drawing grapes and wine from various parts of Southern Australia and New South Wales for its dry table wines, but having outstanding success with its botrytis Semillon from locally grown fruit.

**WINCHELSEA ESTATE** CB–CB Est 1984 LR $13–19 R
GEELONG

Winchelsea, Vic 3241 (vineyard only)
**OPEN** Not **PRODUCTION** NFP
**WINEMAKER** Bailey Carrodus (Contract)
**PRINCIPAL WINES** Ries, Chard, Shir.
**SUMMARY** Owned by Melbourne retailer Nick Chlebnikowski, and the
wines are sold only through the Nick's chain of stores. Vibrantly peppery
Shiraz has been the best of the wines by far.

**WINEWOOD** NR Est 1985 CD $9–14 CD GRANITE BELT
Sundown Road, Ballandean, Qld 4382 (076) 84 1187
**OPEN** W'ends 9–5 **PRODUCTION** 400 cases
**WINEMAKER** Ian Davis
**PRINCIPAL WINES** Sem, Chard, Cab Mer Franc, Shir, Shir Mars.
**SUMMARY** A weekend and holiday activity for schoolteacher Ian
Davis and town planning wife Jeanette; the tiny winery is a model
of neatness and precision planning. The Rhone-style Shiraz
Marsanne blend shows that Ian Davis has high aspirations.
(Viognier is on the way, too.)

**WIRRA WIRRA** B–B Est 1969 NFR/CD/UK
(Boxford Wine Co) $13.90–19.90 R STHN VALES
McMurtrie Road, McLaren Vale, SA 5171 (08) 323 8414 fax (08) 323 8596
**OPEN** Mon–Sat 10–5, Sun 11–5 **PRODUCTION** 25 000 cases
**WINEMAKER** Benjamin Riggs
**PRINCIPAL WINES** Sparkl, Ries, Sauv Bl, Chard, Sem Sauv Bl, Cab
Sauv, Port.
**BEST VINTAGES W** '82, '84, '86, '89, '90 **R** '86, '89, '90
**SUMMARY** A consistent producer of finely tuned and balanced white
wines which age with particular grace; the red wines have been a little
pedestrian, but the rich, dark berry/cassis Angelus Cabernet Sauvignon
confirms the promise of the 1989 vintage.

**WOLF BLASS** BA–B Est 1973 NFR/CD/ML/UK
(George Morton Co) $9.20–19 R BAROSSA V
Bilyara Vineyards, Sturt Hwy, Nuriootpa, SA 5355 (08) 236 0888
fax (085) 62 2156
**OPEN** Mon–Fri 9–4.30, w'ends 12–4.30 **PRODUCTION** 500 000 cases
**WINEMAKER** J. Glaetzer
**PRINCIPAL WINES** White wines under White, Yellow, Green and
Gold labels, with emphasis on Ries and blended Classic Dry White; red
wines under Red, Yellow, Brown, Grey and Black labels with emphasis on
Cab Sauv, Shir and blends of these. Also sparkling and fortified wines.
**BEST VINTAGES W** '80, '82, '88, '90 **R** '80, '83, '84, '90
**SUMMARY** Now merged with Mildara, but the brands will undoubtedly
be kept separate. The belief is the merger will hasten the style changes
already in the pipeline at Wolf Blass, and in particular a scaling-back on
the extreme reliance on massive usage of American oak in the wood-
matured whites and all of the red wines. Recent lift in emphasis on
Chardonnay, with some good results.

**WOODLANDS** C–C Est 1973 LR/ML $18–19.50 R
MARGARET R
Cnr Caves and Metricup Road, Willyabrup via Cowaramup, WA 6284
(09) 294 6155
**OPEN** By appointment only **PRODUCTION** 450 cases
**WINEMAKER** David Watson
**PRINCIPAL WINES** Chard, Pinot, Cab Sauv.
**SUMMARY** Burst on the scene with some superlative Cabernet
Sauvignons early on, but has not managed to maintain the momentum; the
difficulties of weekend winemaking from a Perth base have not helped. A

Pinot in a Rosé style is the most recent addition to the line.

**WOODONGA HILL** NR Est 1986 LR/CD/ML $8–14 CD
HILLTOPS
Cowra Road, Young, NSW 2594 (063) 82 2972
**OPEN** 7 days 9–5 **PRODUCTION** 2400 cases
**WINEMAKER** Jill Lindsay
**PRINCIPAL WINES** Ries, Hock, Chard, Gewurz, Shir, Cab Sauv.
**SUMMARY** Oxidation, possibly at bottling, has been and continues to be
a major problem, which Jill Lindsay is trying to overcome.

**WOODSTOCK** BA–B Est 1973 NFR/CD/ML/UK (Barwell &
Jones) $6.50–14 CD STHN VALES
Douglas Gully Road, McLaren Flat, SA 5171 (08) 383 0156
fax (08) 383 0437
**OPEN** Mon–Fri 9–5, w'ends 12–5 **PRODUCTION** 15 000 cases
**WINEMAKER** Scott Collett
**PRINCIPAL WINES** Ries, Sem, Chard, Sauv Bl, Botrytis, Shir, Cab
Sauv, Tawny Port.
**BEST VINTAGES W** '85, '87, '90, '91 **R** '82, '84, '88, '89
**SUMMARY** Some of the best Cabernet Sauvignon to come from McLaren
Vale has been made by Scott Collett, but in years such as 1989 he proves
his mastery of Shiraz as well, producing a wonderfully textured, soft but
rich dark berry wine which will live for a decade. Just to prove his
versatility he also makes some superb botrytis whites made from a diverse
range of grapes but sharing exceptional intensity of flavour and style.

**WOODY NOOK** NR Est 1987 CD/ML $10.50–18 CD
MARGARET R
Metricup Road, Busselton, WA 6280 (097) 55 7547 fax (097) 55 5464
**OPEN** 7 days 10–4.30 **PRODUCTION** 1900 cases
**WINEMAKER** Neil Gallagher
**PRINCIPAL WINES** Sem, Sauv Bl, Sem/Sauv Bl, Chenin, Cab Sauv.
**SUMMARY** The Gallaghers — with help from consultant John Smith —
are learning winemaking the hard way: by experience. Much of the wine is
sold through the on-site restaurant in the pretty, forested property which
inspired the somewhat twee name. The astringent but powerful 1990
Cabernet Sauvignon won the trophy for best West Australian wine in
classes 14–18 in the 1991 Perth Royal Show.

**WRIGHTS** NR Est 1973 LR/CD/ML/UK (Peter Diplock) $11–16
CD MARGARET R
Harmans South Road, Cowaramup, WA 6284 (097) 55 5314
fax (097) 55 5459
**OPEN** 7 days 10–4.30 **PRODUCTION** 2500 cases
**WINEMAKER** Henry Wright
**PRINCIPAL WINES** Sauv Bl, Sem, Chard, Herm, Cab Sauv, Port.
**SUMMARY** The red wines of 1988 were the best for some years, but the
'89s slipped back again. I have not tasted the 1990 or 1991 vintage wines.

**WYANGA PARK** NR Est 1972 CD/ML $9–15 CD
GIPPSLAND
Baades Road, Lakes Entrance, Vic 3909 (051) 55 1508
**OPEN** 7 days 9–5 **PRODUCTION** 3200 cases
**WINEMAKER** Andrew Smith
**PRINCIPAL WINES** Trioblanc, Sauv Bl Sem, Boobialla, Shir, Cab Sauv,
fortified, flavoured.
**SUMMARY** A leafy, herbaceous cool-climate 1990 Cabernet Sauvignon
from local grapes is the best wine in a collection overall directed at the
tourist trade and of diverse provenance.

**WYNDHAM ESTATE** B–B Est 1970 NR/CD/ML/UK
$7.95–13.95 R  HUNTER V
Dalwood Road, Branxton, NSW 2335   (049) 38 3444 fax (049) 1840
**OPEN** 7 days 9–5  **PRODUCTION** 1.1 million cases
**WINEMAKER** Brian J. McGuigan
**PRINCIPAL WINES** A full range of premium varietal wines, released
under various Bin No. or descriptive labels, but all emphasising the
Wyndham name.
**BEST VINTAGES  W** '81, '85, '87, '89, '91  **R** '81, '85, '87, '88, '91
**SUMMARY** An absolutely reliable producer of keenly priced mid-range
table wines which are smoothly and precisely aimed at those who enjoy
wine but don't wish to become over-involved in its mystery and intrigue.
Hit the jackpot with two outstanding wines from the 1991 vintage: Oak
Cask Chardonnay and Bin 222 Semillon Chardonnay, showing fragrant,
tangy, stylish, barrel-ferment characters.

**WYNNS** A–A Est 1891 NR/CD/UK (Hatch Mansfield) $6–27 R
COONAWARRA
Memorial Drive, Coonawarra, SA 5263   (087) 36 3266 fas (087) 36 3202
**OPEN** 7 days 10–4  **PRODUCTION** NFP
**WINEMAKER** Peter Douglas
**PRINCIPAL WINES** Ries, Chard, Herm, Cab Herm, Pinot, Cab Sauv
and John Riddoch Cab Sauv.
**BEST VINTAGES  R** '55, '62, '66, '76, '80, '82, '84, '86, '87, '88, '90, '91
**SUMMARY** The immense production has in no way prevented Wynns
from producing excellent wines covering the full price spectrum from the
bargain basement Riesling and Hermitage through to the deluxe John
Riddoch Cabernet Sauvignon. The reduction in prices over 1991 put all
the wines other than John Riddoch under $10 a bottle in discount houses,
a price position without rhyme or reason given the quality of the wines.

**YALUMBA** BA–BA Est 1863 NR/CD/UK (Geoffrey Roberts)
$7–15.40 R  BAROSSA V
Eden Valley Road, Angaston, SA 5353   (085) 64 2423 fax (085) 64 2549
**OPEN** Mon–Sat 8.30–5, Sun 12–4  **PRODUCTION** 800 000 cases
**WINEMAKER** Brian Walsh
**PRINCIPAL WINES** Under the Yalumba label (in ascending order)
Oxford Landing range, Galway Herm and Christobels Dry White, Family
Selection range and Signature Collection. Separate brand identities for Hill
Smith Estate, Pewsey Vale, and Heggies, with strong emphasis on key
varietals Ries, Chard, Sem and Cab Sauv. Angas Brut is a leader in the
sparkling wine market.
**BEST VINTAGES  W** '82, '87, '88, '90, '91  **R** '76, '84, '86, '88, '90, '91
**SUMMARY** Family-owned and run by Robert Hill-Smith; much of its
prosperity in recent years has turned on the great success of Angas Brut in
export markets, but the company has always had a commitment to quality
and shown great vision in its selection of vineyard sites and brands. Very
recently Oxford Landing has been a major success, with Chardonnay
representing great value for money and perceived as such in the United
States, but the Riesling also appeals.

**YARRA BURN** NR Est 1976 LR/CD/ML/UK (Lay & Wheeler)
$13–23 R  YARRA V
Settlement Road, Yarra Junction, Vic 3797   (059) 67 1428
fax (059) 67 1146
**OPEN** 7 days 10–6  **PRODUCTION** 6000 cases
**WINEMAKER** David Fyffe
**PRINCIPAL WINES** Sem, Chard, Sparkl Pinot, Pinot, Cab Sauv.
**BEST VINTAGES  W** '83, '86, '88, '90  **R** '84, '86, '88, '90

SUMMARY Excelled itself (and a difficult vintage) with its '89 Pinot Noir and '89 Cabernet Sauvignon, auguring well for the '90 vintage red wines, a foretaste of which came with its mouth-filling '90 Sauvignon Blanc Semillon. However, at the time of writing Yarra Burn was facing a bitter struggle to beat the effects of the recession and the earlier failure of its Sydney distributor.

**YARRA EDGE** NR Est 1984 LR/ML/CD $13.50 CD YARRA V
Lot 3 Edward Road, Lillydale, Vic 3140 (03) 735 3473
fax (03) 735 4853; postal PO Box 711, Lillydale, Vic 3140
OPEN By appointment PRODUCTION 1200 cases
WINEMAKER Michael Zitzlaff (Contract)
PRINCIPAL WINES Chard, Cabernets.
SUMMARY The Bingerman family has made an auspicious entry, releasing two quite beautiful wines from the 1990 vintage: a clean, soft, berry/plum Cabernet with a touch of vanillan oak, and an outstanding Chardonnay, with smooth, melon/peach fruit, subtle oak and length. The 1991 Chardonnay, tasted from barrel, is every bit as good.

**YARRA RIDGE** BA–A Est 1983 NFR/ML $13.95–14.95 R YARRA V
Glenview Road, Yarra Glen, Vic 3755 (03) 730 1613 fax (03) 629 8488
OPEN W'ends, hols 10–5.30 PRODUCTION 30 000 cases
WINEMAKER Louis Bialkower
PRINCIPAL WINES Chard, Sauv Bl, Botrytis Sem, Pinot, Cab Sauv.
BEST VINTAGES W '88, '89, '91 R '88, '90, '91
SUMMARY Has risen from obscurity to prominence through a mixture of good winemaking, keen pricing and aggressive marketing. The Sauvignon Blanc has become something of a cult wine since its debut in 1989 (when outstanding) but in truth the other wines in the portfolio are every bit as good.

**YARRA VALE** NR Est 1983 LR/CD/ML $8.95–18 CD YARRA V
Lot 7 Maroondah Highway, Coldstream, Vic 3770 (059) 62 5266
OPEN 7 days 10–6 PRODUCTION 5000 cases
WINEMAKER Domenic Bucci plus contract
PRINCIPAL WINES Chard, Ries, Tram, Sauv Bl, Cab, Pinot, Shir.
SUMMARY Some excellent wines made in 1990 and 1991 which, if safely bottled, will do much for the reputation of the winery. It was, however, being offered for sale in 1992.

**YARRA YERING** A–A Est 1969 LR/CD/ML/UK (Nicks Wines Intern'l) $15–35 R YARRA V
Briary Road, Coldstream, Vic 3770 (059) 64 9267
OPEN W'ends while stocks available PRODUCTION 5100 cases
WINEMAKER Bailey Carrodus
PRINCIPAL WINES Dry White No. 1 (Sauv Sem), Chard, Pinot, Dry Red No. 1 (Bordeaux-blend), Dry Red No. 2 (Rhone blend).
BEST VINTAGES R '80, '81, '86, '89, '90, '91
SUMMARY After a distinct and uncharacteristic wobble in 1988, returned to top form with the 1989 vintage reds, which belie the difficult year, even if they are on the elegant side. Quite lovely wines, especially the spicy No. 2 Dry Red, while the 1990s are better again. All in all, one of the jewels of the valley.

**YELLOWGLEN** B–B Est 1975 NR/CD/UK (Lawlers) $14–21 R BENDIGO
White's Road, Smythesdale, Vic 3551 (054) 42 8617
OPEN Mon–Sat 10–5, Sun 12–5 PRODUCTION NFP

**WINEMAKER** Jeffrey Wilkinson
**PRINCIPAL WINES** Brut non-vintage, Brut Cremant, Brut Rosé, Cuvee Victoria vintage; also recently introduced Lassetter range.
**SUMMARY** Generally reckoned to be the most profitable sparkling wine maker in Australia (wholly owned by Mildara) producing wines which clearly please the public palate, though not always mine. Over the last three years, however, quality has improved significantly, the improvement accelerating with wines such as its 1990 Chardonnay Pinot Noir Brut.

**YERINGBERG** A–A Est 1862 LR/ML/UK (Nicks Wines Intern'l) $14–20 CD YARRA V
Maroondah Highway, Coldstream, Vic 3770 (03) 739 1453
**OPEN** Not **PRODUCTION** 14 200 cases
**WINEMAKER** Guill De Pury
**PRINCIPAL WINES** Chard, Marsanne, Roussane, Pinot, Yeringberg (a Bordeaux-blend).
**BEST VINTAGES W** '85, '88, '90, '91 **R** '81, '86, '88, '91
**SUMMARY** Makes wines for the next millennium from the low yielding vines re-established on the heart of what was one of the most famous (and infinitely larger) vineyards of the nineteenth century. The red wines have a velvety generosity of flavour which is rarely encountered, yet never lose varietal character, while the Marsanne takes students of history back to Yeringberg's fame in the nineteenth century, and Roussane is a unique offering. The '90 Chardonnay is a particularly attractive wine, its delicate melon/grapefruit flavours showing the Yarra Valley at its best.

**ZEMA ESTATE** BA–BA Est 1982 LR/CD/ML $9–14 CD COONAWARRA
Main Penola-Naracoorte Road, Coonawarra, SA 5263 (087) 36 3219
**OPEN** 7 days 9–5 **PRODUCTION** 5000 cases
**WINEMAKER** Ken Ward
**PRINCIPAL WINES** Ries, Shir, Cab Sauv.
**BEST VINTAGES R** '82, '84, '86, '88, '90
**SUMMARY** Spotlessly clean, full-bodied, smooth red wines from 1988 and 1990 add to the reputation of Zema Estate, with hand pruning and hand picking (extremely rare in Coonawarra) no doubt playing a role.

**ZUBER ESTATE** CB–CB Est 1971 LR/CD $10 CD BENDIGO
Northern Highway, Heathcote, Vic 3523 (054) 33 2142
**OPEN** 7 days 10–6 **PRODUCTION** NFP
**WINEMAKER** Lew Knight (Contract)
**PRINCIPAL WINES** Shir.
**SUMMARY** A somewhat erratic winery which is capable of producing the style of Shiraz for which Bendigo is famous but does not always do so.

# NZ WINERIES

**ABEL & CO** NR Est 1970 LR/CD/ML $NA KUMEU
Pomona Road, RD 1, Kumeu (09) 412 8622
**OPEN** Mon–Sat 9–5
**PRINCIPAL WINES** Mer, Franc, Cab Sauv.
**SUMMARY** After a period of dormancy, purchased by the Hunter family in 1991; winemaking was due to recommence in 1992. The cellar door sales area also offers wines from other producers, as does the on-site restaurant.

**AKARANGI** NR Est 1981 CD/ML $9.90–15 CD HAWKE'S BAY
River Road, Havelock North (068) 877 8228
**OPEN** Sat/pub hols 10–5, **PRODUCTION** 650 cases
**WINEMAKER** Morton Osborne
**PRINCIPAL WINES** Sauv Bl, Chen Bl, Rosé, Cab Sauv.
**SUMMARY** Former contract grapegrowers now making and selling tiny quantities cellar door.

**ALAN SCOTT WINES AND ESTATES** NR Est 1990
NR/CD/ML/UK (TBA) $8.75–17 CD MARLBOROUGH
Jacksons Road, RD 3, Blenheim (03) 572 9054 fax (03) 572 9053
**OPEN** **PRODUCTION** 4400 cases
**WINEMAKER** Alan Scott
**PRINCIPAL WINES** Ries, Autumn Ries, Sauv Bl, Chard.
**SUMMARY** Highly regarded wines have emanated since the first release, no surprise given Alan Scott's career as Corban's chief viticulturist for many years, not to mention his involvement in the establishment of Cloudy Bay.

**AMBERLEY ESTATE** CB–CB Est 1979 LR/CD/ML $8–16
CD CANTERBURY
Reserve Road, RD 1, Amberley (0331) 48409 fax (0331) 48562
**OPEN** 7 days 11–5 **PRODUCTION** 1000 cases
**WINEMAKER** Jeremy Prater
**PRINCIPAL WINES** Muller, Gewurz, Ries, Chard, Sauv Bl, Pinot.
**BEST VINTAGES W** '86, '87, '91 **R** '89, '90, '91
**SUMMARY** Jeremy Prater learnt winemaking in France, Germany and Switzerland, and obtained a diploma in viticulture and oenology in the latter country — relevant training for the cool Canterbury region. The Pinot Noir (Kinross and Special Reserve) shows promise in an essency, strawberry-accented style, and a '91 Chardonnay tremendous flavour early in its life.

**ASPEN RIDGE ESTATE** NR Est 1968 CD $8–9.50 CD
WAIKATO
Waerenga Road, Te Kauwhata (0817) 63 595
**OPEN** Mon–Sat 9–6 **PRODUCTION** 4000 cases
**WINEMAKER** Alastair McKissock
**PRINCIPAL WINES** Sauv Bl, Ries, Rosé, Cab/Merl.
**SUMMARY** A specialist in unfermented, non-alcoholic sparkling grape juice, a strange niche for a former head of the Te Kauwhata Research Station with a master's degree in oenology from UCLA Davis to boot.

**ATA RANGI** A–A Est 1980 LR/CD/ML $18–22 CD
MARTINBOROUGH
Puruatanga Road, Martinborough (0553) 69 570
**OPEN** W'ends from Nov till sold out **PRODUCTION** 2500 cases
**WINEMAKER** Clive Paton
**PRINCIPAL WINES** Chard, Gewurz, Celebre (Cab Merl Shir), Pinot.
**BEST VINTAGES W** '88, '89, '91 **R** '86, '88, '89, '90, '91
**SUMMARY** Absolutely superb wines from 1989 and 1990 lifted Ata

Rangi into the highest category. 1989 Celebre is one of the all-time great New Zealand red wines, with 1989 and 1990 Pinot Noir and Chardonnay in much the same class.

## BABICH  B–B Est 1916 NR/CD/ML/UK (Deinhard & Co) $7.25–19 CD  HENDERSON

Babich Road, Henderson    (09) 833 7859  fax (09) 833 9929
**OPEN** Mon–Sat 9–5.30  **PRODUCTION** Approximately 65 000 cases
**WINEMAKER** Joe Babich
**PRINCIPAL WINES** Muller, Ries Sylv, Chab, Gewurz, Chard, Pinot, Cab Sauv.
**BEST VINTAGES W** '84, '86, '89, '91 **R** '83, '85, '86, '89, '91
**SUMMARY** Has moved with the times and maintained the reputation it gained in the 60s, albeit for new wine styles headed by the oaky, complex Irongate Chardonnay (Hawke's Bay) and the crisp and tangy Sauvignon Blanc and Fumé Vert. The 1991 Marlborough Sauvignon Blanc shows pungant, rich herbal/gooseberry fruit with plenty of substance and power.

## BENFIELD AND DELAMERE  NR Est 1987 LR/ML $26 R MARTINBOROUGH

Cambridge Road, Martinborough    (04) 38 48894
**OPEN** By appointment  **PRODUCTION** 200 cases
**WINEMAKER** Bill Benfield
**PRINCIPAL WINES** A single Cab Sauv/Merl/Cab Franc blend.
**SUMMARY** The partnership of Bill Benfield and Sue Delamere has lofty ambitions; Bill Benfield is convinced that the Martinborough region will produce a great Bordeaux-style red, and takes strong exception to those who suggest it is particularly or necessarily suited to Pinot Noir. The 1990 Benfield and Delamere release shows strong pyrazine characters, very much in a leafy, cool-climate mould. However, the success of Ata Rangi with later ripening varieties suggests Benfield's aspirations are not without reason.

## BLOOMFIELD VINEYARDS  NR Est 1981 LR/ML $18–32 R MARTINBOROUGH

119 Solway Crescent, Masterton    (06) 377 5505
**OPEN** Not  **PRODUCTION** 2200 cases
**WINEMAKER** David Bloomfield
**PRINCIPAL WINES** Sauv Bl, Pinot, Cab Sauv/Merl/Cab Franc.
**SUMMARY** Tiny quantities of the wines sold to date have been eagerly snapped up by the local clientele, but wines are now being distributed (sparingly) through Kitchener Wines.

## BROOKFIELDS  B–B Est 1937 LR/CD/ML $12.95–24.95 CD HAWKE'S BAY

Brookfields Road, Meeanee, Napier    (06) 834 4615  fax (06) 834 4622
**OPEN** Mon–Sat 9–5, Sun 12–4  **PRODUCTION** 6000 cases
**WINEMAKER** Peter Robertson
**PRINCIPAL WINES** Chard, Gewurz, Sauv Bl Fumé, Pinot Gris, Cab.
**BEST VINTAGES W** '86, '87, '89, '90 **R** '83, '87, '89, '90
**SUMMARY** Peter Robertson has worked hard since acquiring Brookfields in 1977, producing grassy Sauvignon Blanc, lightly oaked, understated Chardonnay and — best of all — Cabernet Merlot with distinct overtones of St Emilion, and blackcurrant-flavoured Reserve Cabernet Sauvignon.

## CELLIER LE BRUN  B–B Est 1985 NFR/CD/ML/UK (Hedley, Wright & Co) $18–42.95 R  MARLBOROUGH

Terrace Road, Renwick    (03) 572 8859  fax (03) 572 8814
**OPEN** 7 days 9–5  **PRODUCTION** 15 000 cases
**WINEMAKER** Daniel Le Brun
**PRINCIPAL WINES** Meth Champ, Rosé.

**BEST VINTAGES** W '86, '88
**SUMMARY** French-born and trained (in Champagne) Daniel le Brun has only ever sought to make one wine style: Méthode Champenoise. After a few early problems, he is doing better than anyone else in New Zealand (if you put Montana Deutz into a category of its own). I particularly enjoyed his soft, creamy Blanc de Blancs made from 100% Chardonnay.

## CHARD FARM  NR Est 1986 LR/CD/ML $14.80–16.50 CD CENTRAL OTAGO

Gibbston, RD 2, Queenstown   (03) 442 6110
**OPEN** 7 days 11–5   **PRODUCTION** 2500 cases
**WINEMAKER** Rob Hay
**PRINCIPAL WINES** Sauv Bl, Ries, Gewurz, Chard, Pinot.
**SUMMARY** Perched precariously between sheer cliffs and the fast-flowing waters of the Kawarau River, Chard Farm is a tribute to the vision and courage of Rob and Gregory Hay. At a latitude of 45°S, viticulture will never be easy, but a stylish, full-flavoured 1990 Chardonnay was followed by three well-made 1991 white wines: a scintillating Sauvignon Blanc with complex gooseberry/asparagus flavours, a delicate, spicy Gewurztraminer and a citrus/lime Rhine Riesling with pronounced acidity. A winery of real quality.

## CHIFNEY  NR Est 1983 CD/ML $10–25 CD  MARTINBOROUGH

Huangarua Road, Martinborough   (06) 306 9495
**OPEN**   **PRODUCTION** 1150 cases
**WINEMAKER** Stan Chifney
**PRINCIPAL WINES** Chard, Chenin, Gewurz, Cab Sauv; Garden of Eden white and red are second label wines.
**BEST VINTAGES** R '85, '86, '88, '90
**SUMMARY** A retirement hobby which became rather more than that when the 1986 Cabernet Sauvignon won a gold medal at the 1988 Auckland Easter Show; I have tasted that wine, but none more recently and hence do not give a rating.

## C. J. PASK  NR Est 1986 LR/CD/ML/UK (Lay & Wheeler) $7–19 CD  HAWKE'S BAY

Omahu Road, Hastings   (06) 879 7906  fax (06) 879 6428
**OPEN** Mon–Sat 8–5   **PRODUCTION** 9500 cases
**WINEMAKER** Kate Marris
**PRINCIPAL WINES** Chard, Ries, Sauv Bl, Pinot, Cab Sauv, Cab Merl.
**BEST VINTAGES** W '86, '87, '89, '90 R '85, '86, '89, '90
**SUMMARY** Ex-cropduster pilot C. J. Pask became one of the most highly regarded grapegrowers in Hawke's Bay; his coup in securing former Vidal winemaker Kate Marris should see wines of world class emerge.

## CLOUDY BAY  A–A Est 1985 NFR/CD/ML $A15–21 R MARLBOROUGH

Jacksons Road, Blenheim   (057) 28914  fax (057) 28065
**OPEN** Mon–Sat 10–4.30   **PRODUCTION** 50 000 cases
**WINEMAKER** Kevin Judd
**PRINCIPAL WINES** Sauv Bl, Chard, Cab Merl.
**BEST VINTAGES** W '85, '89, '90, '91 R '86, '88, '89
**SUMMARY** The other arm of Cape Mentelle, masterminded by David Hohnen and realised by Kevin Judd, his trusted lieutenant from day one. A marketing tour de force, it became a world recognised brand in only a few years, but the wine quality and style should not be underestimated: quite simply Hohnen and Judd took New Zealand Sauvignon Blanc from curiosity to respectability. Each year the Sauvignon Blanc becomes more complex (and more international) in style; the '91 is a far cry from the '85. The '90 Chardonnay is also an exceptionally fine wine.

**COLLARDS** A–A Est 1910 NR/CD/ML/UK (Bibendum) $7.85–25.10 CD HENDERSON

303 Lincoln Road, Henderson, Auckland 8 (09) 838 8341

**OPEN** Mon–Sat 9–5.30 **PRODUCTION** 14 000 cases

**WINEMAKER** Bruce Collard

**PRINCIPAL WINES** Chard (Rothesay, Hawke's Bay & Marlborough), Chenin, Sauv Bl (Rothesay and Martinborough), Ries, Wh Burg, Gewurtz, Claret, Cab Merl.

**BEST VINTAGES** **W** '86, '87, '89, '90 **R** '83, '85, '86, '89

**SUMMARY** A model of overall consistency which has, however, excelled itself in recent years with its Chardonnays. Although made from diverse grape sources, these particular wines show a restraint and purity of flavour which point the future direction of this variety in New Zealand, and are unhesitatingly recommended.

**COOKS** A–A Est 1969 LR/CD/UK (Caxton Tower Wines Ltd) $7.60–20.78 R HENDERSON

Great North Road, Henderson (09) 837 3390 fax (09) 836 0005

**OPEN** Mon–Sat 9–5 **PRODUCTION** 7000 tonnes (450 000 case equivalent)

**WINEMAKER** Kerry Hitchcock

**PRINCIPAL WINES** Top of the range is Winemakers Res Chard, Sauv Bl, Cab Sauv, LH Sauv/Sem; Longridge Chard, Fumé Bl, Gewurtz, Cab Merl; Discovery Collection Chard, Sauv Bl, Cab Sauv.

**BEST VINTAGES** **W** '83, '86, '89, '91 **R** '83, '86, '89, '91

**SUMMARY** The quality of Cooks Wines in general, and Chardonnay in particular, has never been in dispute; but wines such as the 1989 Winemakers Reserve Chardonnay are not only international in style but of world class, this wine having almost explosive, very pure citric varietal flavour, great length and complexity, and sensitively handled oak.

**COOPER'S CREEK** BA–BA Est 1980 NFR/CD/ML/UK (Ehrmanns Wine Shippers) $9–23.50 CD HUAPAI

State Highway 16, Huapai (09) 412 8560 fax (09) 547 558

**OPEN** Mon–Sat 9.30–5.30 **PRODUCTION** 25 000 cases

**WINEMAKER** Kim Crawford

**PRINCIPAL WINES** Ries, Gewurz, Sauv Bl, Coopers Dry, Fumé, Chard, Cab Sauv, Cab Merl; Swamp Road Chard is prestige wine.

**BEST VINTAGES** **W** '86, '89, '90, '91 **R** '83, '86, '89, '91

**SUMMARY** Stylish makers of very good white wines and adequate, if unexciting, reds. Cooper's Dry (a blend of Semillon Chardonnay and Chenin Blanc) is a low priced special, while Swamp Road Chardonnay can be excellent (the most recent releases being less convincing than one would hope), and in years such as 1991 the standard Chardonnay having an almost essence-like concentration of fruit flavour.

**CORBANS** CA–BA Est 1902 NR/CD/ML/UK (Caxton Tower Wines Ltd) $3.26–20.78 R HENDERSON

Great North Road, Henderson (09) 837 3390 fax (09) 836 0005

**OPEN** Mon–Sat 9–6 **PRODUCTION** 750 000 cases plus 3 million casks

**WINEMAKER** Kerry Hitchcock

**PRINCIPAL WINES** Stoneleigh Chard, Ries, Sauv Bl, Cab Sauv (premium range); Gewurz, Chard, Fumé, Cab Merl (Private Bin range); others under generic or varietal names.

**BEST VINTAGES** **W** '86, '89, '90, '91 **R** '85, '86, '89, '91

**SUMMARY** New Zealand's second largest wine group (it also owns Cooks and Robard and Butler) making a complete range of wines under a plethora of brand names (St Arnaud, Montel, Velluto, Liebestraum, Seven Oaks) from vineyards in all parts of New Zealand. Private Bin Cabernet

Merlot and Sauvignon Blanc are excellent wines, as is the punchy, lime-juice 1991 Stoneleigh Rhine Riesling, reminiscent of a good German Riesling from the Mosel.

**CRAB FARM** NR Est 1989 NR/CD/ML $10–17 CD
HAWKE'S BAY
125 Main Road, Bay View, Hawke's Bay (06) 836 6678
**OPEN** Mon–Sat 10–5 **PRODUCTION** 2000 cases
**WINEMAKER** Hamish Jardine
**PRINCIPAL WINES** Tram Ries, Fumé, Petane (Cab Pinot) blend, Pinot, Cab Sauv.
**SUMMARY** Hamish Jardine has worked at both Chateau Reynella and Matawhero; the family vineyards were planted in 1980 and are now mature, so given the equable Hawke's Bay climate there is no reason why the wines should not succeed. A spicily-oaked barrel sample of 1991 Chardonnay looked promising.

**DANIEL SCHUSTER OMIHI HILLS** NR Est 1984
NFR/CD/ML/UK (Windrush Wines) $15–26 CANTERBURY
Reeces Road, Omihi, North Canterbury (vineyard); postal 5 Paulus Terrace, Christchurch 2 (03) 337 1763 fax (03) 79 8638
**OPEN** Not **PRODUCTION** 1900 cases
**WINEMAKER** Danny Schuster
**PRINCIPAL WINES** Chard, Pinot Blanc, Pinot.
**SUMMARY** After a tentative start, the high expectations held for this vineyard were fulfilled with the 1990 Pinot Noir, an extremely stylish wine with spicy, strawberry-accented fruit and a lively finish.

**DELEGAT'S** CA–B Est 1947 NR/CD/ML/UK (Geoffrey Roberts)
$10.95–19.95 CD HENDERSON
Hepburn Road, Henderson (09) 836 0129 fax (09) 836 3282
**OPEN** Mon–Fri 9–5, Sat 9–6 **PRODUCTION** 120 000 cases
**WINEMAKER** Brent Marris
**PRINCIPAL WINES** Winery Estate label of Chard, Sauv Bl and Cab Merl; top-of-the-range Proprietors Reserve label of Chard, Fumé Bl, Cab Sauv and Merl. Also vineyard-designated Chard from Hawke's Bay.
**BEST VINTAGES** **W** '84, '87, '89, '90 **R** '86, '87, '89, '90
**SUMMARY** Delegat's now sources almost all its grapes from Hawke's Bay, utilising its own vineyards there and contract growers. The Proprietors Reserve Chardonnays from both 1990 and 1991 are of the highest class, with pronounced but well handled charred/spicy oak and high-toned, zesty fruit, while the '90 Vicarage Road Chardonnay is a lighter but elegant wine in a more simple mould.

**DE REDCLIFFE ESTATES** CB–B Est 1976 NR/CD/ML
$10–21 R WAIKATO
Lyons Road, Mangatawhiri, near Pokeno (09) 302 3325
**OPEN** 7 days 9–5 **PRODUCTION** 12 000 cases
**WINEMAKER** Mark Compton
**PRINCIPAL WINES** Chard, Ries, Fumé, Sem Chard, White Lady, Coral Reef, Pinot, Cab Merl Franc.
**BEST VINTAGES** **W** '87, '89, '90, '91 **R** '86, '87, '89, '91
**SUMMARY** The Waikato's answer to the Napa Valley, with the $7 million Hotel du Vin, luxury restaurant, wine tours, lectures, the lot; briefly listed on the Stock Exchange, but now Japanese-owned. The white wines are by far the best, with honest Chardonnays in both 1989 and 1990 and a fine, clean and intense '91 Rhine Riesling.

**DRY RIVER** BA–BA Est 1979 LR/ML $16–31 ML
MARTINBOROUGH

Puruatanga Road, Martinborough  phone and fax (06) 306 9388
**OPEN** Not **PRODUCTION** 2200 cases
**WINEMAKER** Neil McCallum
**PRINCIPAL WINES** Chard, Gewurz, Ries, Sauv Bl, Fumé, Pinot Gris, Pinot.
**BEST VINTAGES** **W** '84, '87, '89, '90 **R** '89, '90, '91
**SUMMARY** Another of the brightly shining stars of Martinborough
/Wairarapa adding Pinot Gris and Gewurztraminer to the repertoire of the
district. Neil McCallum has also produced some world class botrytis wines
from Riesling, Traminer and Chardonnay. Any wine bearing the label can
be purchased with confidence if you are quick enough — each year sells
out rapidly.

**ESK VALLEY ESTATE** A–BA Est 1933 NFR/CD/UK
(Whittaker Wines) $9.75–15.40 CD  HAWKE'S BAY
Main Road, Bay View, Napier  (09) 275 6119  fax (09) 275 6618
**OPEN** Sum 9.45–6, Win 9.45–5 **PRODUCTION** 20 000 cases
**WINEMAKER** Grant Edmonds
**PRINCIPAL WINES** Chard, Ries, Sauv Bl, Muller, Cab Sauv, Cab Merl.
**BEST VINTAGES** **W** '89, '90 **R** '87, '89, '90, '91
**SUMMARY** The little brother in the Villa Maria-Vidal family and, in
typical brash small boy fashion, has on a number of occasions recently
upstaged the others. The '91 Chardonnays are disappointing, lacking fruit
intensity and varietal character, but the '90 Reserve Merlot, while not
quite in the class of the '89, has abundant lifted sweet fruit with piercing
leafy/minty overtones.

**FORREST ESTATE** NR EST 1989 LR/CD/ML $12–22 CD
MARLBOROUGH
Blicks Road, Renwick, Marlborough  (03) 572 9084  fax (03) 572 8915
**OPEN** Mon–Sat 12–5 **PRODUCTION** 1900 cases
**WINEMAKER** John Forrest
**PRINCIPAL WINES** Chard, Sem, LH Sauv Bl, Cab Rosé, Claret, Merl.
**SUMMARY** Former bio-chemist and genetic engineer John Forrest has had
considerable success since his first vintage in 1990, relying initially on
purchased grapes but with a 4 hectare vineyard now planted. His 1990
Cabernet Rosé won the trophy for Champion Rosé/Blush style at the Air
New Zealand Wine Show of that year, and was followed up by an
attractive 1991 wine, with high flavoured cherry-fruit and a touch of
residual sugar, pointing it perfectly at the commercial market.

**FRENCH FARM VINEYARDS** NR Est 1991 LR/CD/ML
CANTERBURY
French Farm Valley Road, Akaroa  (03) 304 5784  fax (03) 304 5785
**OPEN** 7 days 9–6 **PRODUCTION** 3000 cases
**WINEMAKER** Tony Bish
**PRINCIPAL WINES** Fumé Bl, Sauv Bl, Cab Sauv/Cab Franc, Rosé.
**SUMMARY** The name of the enterprise drives from the fact that French
immigrants planted vines at Akaroa (one hour's drive south of
Christchurch) as early as 1840, and owner/winemaker Tony Bish believes
the climate is ideally suited to Pinot Noir and Chardonnay. For the time
being, grapes are being purchased to supplement the recently planted 3-
hectare estate vineyard.

**GIBBSTON VALLEY** CB–CB Est 1981 LR/CD/ML $12–25
CD  CENTRAL OTAGO
Gibbston RD2, Queenstown  (03) 442 6910  fax (03) 442 6909
**OPEN** Mon–Sat 10–6, Sun 12–6 **PRODUCTION** 4500 cases
**WINEMAKER** Rob Hay
**PRINCIPAL WINES** Sauv Bl, Ries, Gewurz, Pinot Gris, Pinot all estate
grown; Southern Selection is cheaper range of non-estate wines purchased

or blended.

**BEST VINTAGES** **W** '87, '90 **R** '89, '90

**SUMMARY** A highly professional and attractive winery, restaurant and cellar door sales facility situated near Queenstown which has been an outstanding success since the day it opened. Viticulture poses special problems, and both varietal selection, choice and style will inevitably take time. Pinot Gris and Pinot Noir have particular promise, the latter bursting into flower with a dark purple, intensely rich and soft prune, plum and spice-flavoured '90 Pinot Noir.

## GIESEN CA–B Est 1981 NR/CD/ML/UK (Friarwood Ltd) $10–19 CD CANTERBURY

Burnham School Road, RD5, Christchurch  (03) 25 6729  fax (03) 66 6815
**OPEN** Mon–Sat 10–5  **PRODUCTION** 25 600 cases
**WINEMAKER** Marcel Giesen
**PRINCIPAL WINES** Ries, Chard, Sauv Bl, Chab, Muller, Ehrenfelser, Gewurz, Botrytis Rics, Cab Sauv. Top wines under Reserve label.
**BEST VINTAGES** **W** '86, '89, '90 **R** '86, '89, '91
**SUMMARY** Determination, skill and marketing flair have seen Giesen grow from obscurity to one of the largest family-owned and run wineries in New Zealand. Given the Giesen's Rhine Valley origins it is not surprising they have concentrated on aromatic, non-wooded white wines, nor that they swept all before them at the 1991 Auckland Easter Show with their 1990 Botrytised Riesling, winning the Trophy for Champion Wine of the Show.

## GLADSTONE NR Est 1985 LR/CD/ML $15–17 CD MARTINBOROUGH

Gladstone Road, Gladstone, Waipara  phone and fax (06) 379 8563
**OPEN** Mon–Sat 11–6 by appointment  **PRODUCTION** 1200 cases
**WINEMAKER** Dennis Roberts
**PRINCIPAL WINES** Ries, Sauv Bl, Cab Sauv.
**SUMMARY** Dennis Roberts has taken early retirement from a professional career to concentrate on his childhood love of vineyards and wines. A handsome winery presides over an immaculate vineyard situated roughly halfway between Martinborough and Masterton on alluvial soils laid down by the nearby Ruamahanga River. The label design, incidentally, is a model of elegance and simplicity.

## GLENMARK CB–CB Est 1981 LR/CD/ML $8.90–15.80 CD CANTERBURY

State Highway 1, Waipara  (0504) 31 46828
**OPEN** Sat 11–5 or by appointment  **PRODUCTION** 1200 cases
**WINEMAKER** Heiko Tutt
**PRINCIPAL WINES** Ries, Gewurz, Muller, Waipara White, Waipara Red, Port.
**BEST VINTAGES** **W** '87, '89, '90 **R** '86, '88, '89, '90
**SUMMARY** A consistent bronze medal winner at New Zealand wine shows, with Riesling and a light-bodied, early maturing Waipara Red (predominantly Cabernet Sauvignon) its most successful wines.

## GLOVER'S VINEYARD NR Est 1984 LR/CD/ML NELSON

Gardner Valley Road, Upper Moutere  (03) 543 2698
**OPEN** Mon–Sat 10–4  **PRODUCTION** 800 cases
**WINEMAKER** Dave Glover
**PRINCIPAL WINES** Sauv Bl, Pinot, Cab Sauv.
**SUMMARY** David Glover studied winemaking and viticulture at Charles Sturt University in southern New South Wales during a 17-year stay in Australia. He returned with wife Penny to establish their own vineyard in 1984, struggling with birds and other predators before producing their first wines in 1989.

**GOLDWATER ESTATE** NR Est 1978 LR/CD/ML/UK
(Hallgarten Wines Ltd) $17–35 CD  WAIHEKE ISLAND
Causeway Road, Putiki Bay  (09) 372 7493 fax (09) 372 6827
**OPEN** Mon–Sat 10–4  **PRODUCTION** 6400 cases
**WINEMAKER** Kim Goldwater
**PRINCIPAL WINES** Chard, Sauv Bl, Cab Merl Franc.
**BEST VINTAGES  W** '87, '89, '90 **R** '85, '87, '89, '90, '91
**SUMMARY** A vertical tasting of the '88, '89 and '90 wines in late 1990
was a disappointment; only the '90 appeared to have the concentration of
flavour normally attributed to Goldwater. It is fair to say others have been
far more impressed with the wines, and in particular with the '89. The
arrival of the '91 Chardonnay has vastly increased production, doubtless
adding to the already high profile which Goldwater deservedly enjoys.

**GRAPE REPUBLIC** NR Est 1984 LR/CD/ML $14–26 R
WELLINGTON
State Highway One, Te Horo  phone and fax (06) 364 3284
**OPEN** 7 days 10–5  **PRODUCTION** 1900 cases
**WINEMAKER** Alastair Pain
**PRINCIPAL WINES** Chard, Sauv Bl, Ries, Rosé, Gewurtz, Cab Sauv,
selection of fruit wines.
**SUMMARY** A marketing and promotion tour-de-force using direct mail
and wine club techniques, with a vast array of flavoured wines and smaller
quantities of more expensive table wines which are distinctly austere. Alastair
Pain says this is the European style he is aiming for. I am not so sure.

**GROVE MILL** BA–B Est 1988 LR/CD/ML/UK (Boxford)
$12.95–23.50 R  MARLBOROUGH
1 Dodson Street, Blenheim  phone and fax (03) 578 9190
**OPEN** Mon–Sat 9–5  **PRODUCTION** 6000 cases
**WINEMAKER** David Pearce
**PRINCIPAL WINES** Ries, Gewurz, Chard, Cab Pinotage, Cab Merl
Pinotage, Rosé; Blackbirch is top-of-the-range red, Lansdowne Chardonnay
the top white wine.
**BEST VINTAGES  W** '88, '89, '90 **R** '89, '90
**SUMMARY** Burst on the scene with a superb '89 Chardonnay, but other
wines since suggest this was no fluke, even if they are not quite in the same
league. The winery also runs a restaurant, adding to the attraction of the
130-year-old cellar-door sales building.

**HIGHFIELD ESTATE** NR Est 1990 NFR/CD/ML
$10.50–17.50 CD MARLBOROUGH
RD2 Brookby Road, Blenheim  phone and fax (03) 572 8592
**OPEN** Mon–Sat 10–5  **PRODUCTION** 7500 cases
**WINEMAKER** Tony Hooper
**PRINCIPAL WINES** Ries, Chard, Sauv Bl, Merl.
**SUMMARY** Highfield Estate has been growing (and selling) grapes for
17 years before establishing its own brand, with New Zealand born ex-
Yarra Burn (Yarra Valley, Vic) winemaker Tony Hooper presiding over the
first on-site vintage.

**HUNTER'S** A–A Est 1983 NFR/CD/ML $12.95–21.95 CD/UK
(AH Wines Ltd)  MARLBOROUGH
Rapaura Road, Blenheim  (057) 28 489
**OPEN** Mon–Sat 9–5  **PRODUCTION** 27 000 cases
**WINEMAKER** Gary Duke
**PRINCIPAL WINES** Sauv Bl, Chard, Cab Sauv, Pinot.
**BEST VINTAGES  W** '88, '89, '91 **R** '87, '88, '89, '91
**SUMMARY** Without question, one of New Zealand's finest producers of
white wines, aided by some skilled consultancy advice from Australia.

Wonderfully pure Sauvignon Blanc, glorious in 1991 (in two versions, oaked and unoaked), and Chardonnay (cunningly barrel-fermented) are invariably outstanding, while the strongly structured, full-flavoured '89 Cabernet Sauvignon was a milestone achievement compared to its earlier red wines. Has a particularly strong market in England.

## JACKSON ESTATE NR Est 1991 NFR/ML MARLBOROUGH

Jacksons Road, Blenheim  (05) 69 6547
**OPEN** Not fixed at time of writing  **PRODUCTION**  5000 cases
**WINEMAKER** Warwick Stichbury
**PRINCIPAL WINES** Sauv Bl, Chard, Ries, Pinot.
**SUMMARY** Long term major grape growers John and Warwick Stichbury, with leading viticulturist Richard Bowling in charge, own substantial vineyards in the Marlborough area, and have now established their own winery and brand to vinify part of the production, the balance still being sold to others. The initial release of the 1991 Sauvignon Blanc was rated top wine in *Cuisine* magazine's tasting of 86 wines from this variety. Clearly a winery to watch.

## KUMEU RIVER B–B Est 1944 NFR/CD/ML/UK (Boxford Wine Co) $12–31 R  KUMEU

2 Highway 16, Kumeu   (09) 412 8415  fax (09) 412 7627
**OPEN** Mon–Sat 9–5.30  **PRODUCTION**  18 000 cases
**WINEMAKER** Michael Brajkovich
**PRINCIPAL WINES** Chard, Sauv Bl, Merl Cab, Cab Franc, Pinot, under three labels: Kumeu River (top), Brajovich (next) and San Marino (cheapest).
**BEST VINTAGES  W** '86, '87, '89, '90 **R** '85, '87, '89, '90, '91
**SUMMARY** The wines of Michael Brajkovich defy conventional classification, simply because the highly trained, highly skilled and highly intelligent Brajkovich does not observe convention in crafting them, preferring instead to follow his own French-influenced instincts and preferences. Not altogether surprisingly, the wines have won high praise overseas.

## LANDFALL-REVINGTON CB–B Est 1987 LR/CD/ML $7–23 CD  GISBORNE

State Highway 2, Manutuke, Gisborne   (06) 862 8577
**OPEN** 7 days 9–6  **PRODUCTION**  5000 cases
**WINEMAKER** John Thorpe
**PRINCIPAL WINES** Revington Chard, Gewurz; Landfall Muller, Chard, Blush and Gisborne Red.
**SUMMARY** A fairly complicated joint venture (the brainchild of lawyer/partner Ross Revington) and name changes have kept Australian wine writers on their toes. The Revington label wines come from the 4 hectare Revington vineyard, the Landfall label wines come partly from its own 4 hectare vineyard, partly from Revington vineyard and partly from local growers. Landfall wines were previously called Whitecliffs. The '91 Revington wines are pleasant, but not great, the Gewurztraminer showing either botrytis or skin contact (or both).

## LARCOMB BA–BA Est 1985 CD/ML $8–16 CD  CANTERBURY

Larcombs Road, 5RD, Christchurch   (03) 347 8909
**OPEN** Nov–Feb, Tues–Sun 9–5  **PRODUCTION**  2000 cases
**WINEMAKER** John Thom
**PRINCIPAL WINES** Ries, Gewurz, Pinot Gris, Pinot.
**SUMMARY** Highly regarded maker of fine, elegant citrus Rhine Riesling, fleshy, gently-oaked Pinot Gris and generous Pinot Noir; the winery restaurant (open from November to February) is extremely popular and contributes substantially to sales.

## LIMEBURNERS BAY CA–CB Est 1978 CD/ML $7–19.75 CD  KUMEU

112 Hobsonville Road, Hobsonville   (09) 416 8844
**OPEN** Mon–Sat 9–6   **PRODUCTION** 3500 cases
**WINEMAKER** Alan Laurenson
**PRINCIPAL WINES** Muller, Sem Chard, Sauv Bl, Chard, Cab Merl, Cab Sauv.
**BEST VINTAGES** **W** '87, '89, '90, '91 **R** '84, '85, '87, '89
**SUMMARY** Has rapidly established a reputation for itself as a producer of high class Cabernet Sauvignon, doing especially well with its '84, '87 and '89 wines.

**LINCOLN** C–CB Est 1937 NR/CD/ML/UK (Neville Cox)
$6.95–15.75 CD   HENDERSON
130 Lincoln Road, Henderson   (09) 838 6944  fax (09) 838 6984
**OPEN** Mon–Sat 9–6   **PRODUCTION** 38 000 cases
**WINEMAKER** Nick Chan
**PRINCIPAL WINES** Chard (East Coast and Parklands), Sauv Bl, Ries, Chenin, Muller, Gewurz, Dry Red, Cab, Merl, fortified, sparkl.
**BEST VINTAGES** **W** '86, '87, '89, '90 **R** '83, '85, '86, '89, '91
**SUMMARY** A former fortified wine specialist which has moved towards table wine production with the aid of a Roséworthy-graduate winemaker and avant-garde labels. A complex though idiosyncratic Sauvignon Blanc and soft Chardonnay are the best so far tasted; the '90 Cabernet Merlot did not impress.

**LINTZ ESTATE** NR Est 1989 LR/CD/ML $12–19.50 CD
MARTINBOROUGH
Kitchener St, Martinborough   (06) 306 9174;  postal PO Box 177 Martinborough
**OPEN** While stocks last   **PRODUCTION** 1000 cases
**WINEMAKER** Chris Lintz
**PRINCIPAL WINES** Tram, Sauv Bl, Dry White, Pinot, Cab Sauv, sparkl.
**SUMMARY** New Zealand born Chris Lintz comes from a German winemaking family, and graduated from Geisenheim. The first stage of the Lintz winery, drawing grapes from the 9 hectare vineyard, was completed in 1991, and production is eventually planned to increase to around 13,000 cases.

**LOMBARDI** NR Est 1948 LR/CD/ML $9.25–14.50 R
HAWKE'S BAY
Te Mata Road, Havelock North   (06) 877 7985
**OPEN** 7 days 9–5   **PRODUCTION** 32 000 cases
**WINEMAKER** Hamish Binns
**PRINCIPAL WINES** Hock, Ries Sylv, Sauternes, Pinotage, Sherry, Vermouth, Marsala, and flavoured fortifieds.
**SUMMARY** The Australian Riverland transported to the unlikely environment of Hawke's Bay, with a half-Italian, half-English family concentrating on a kaleidoscopic array of Vermouths and sweet, flavoured fortified wines.

**MARTINBOROUGH** A–A Est 1980 NFR/CD/ML/UK
(Lay & Wheeler, Haughton) $9.50–25.50 CD   MARTINBOROUGH
Princess Street, Martinborough   (06) 306 9955  fax (06) 306 9217
**OPEN** Mon–Sat 11–5   **PRODUCTION** 8000 cases
**WINEMAKER** Larry McKenna
**PRINCIPAL WINES** Chard, Sauv Bl, Ries, Gewurz, Muller, Pinot.
**BEST VINTAGES** **W & R** '86, '88, '89, '90, '91
**SUMMARY** Australian born and trained Larry McKenna has produced the best Pinot Noir to come from New Zealand together with several brilliant Chardonnays. The Pinot Noir goes from strength to strength; after a hugely powerful '89, the elegance, finesse and length of the '90 put

the world class quality of this winery's Pinot Noir beyond question.

## MATAWHERO  DA–CA Est 1975 LR/CD/ML $11–24.50 CD
GISBORNE

Riverpoint Road, Matawhero   (06) 868 8366  fax (06) 867 9856

**OPEN** Mon–Sat 9–5   **PRODUCTION** 10 000 cases

**WINEMAKER** Hatsch Kalberer

**PRINCIPAL WINES** Gewurz, Chard, Sauv Bl, Chenin, Pinot, Cab Merl.

**BEST VINTAGES** W & R '78, '82, '83, '87, '89

**SUMMARY** The wines have always been cast in the mould of Matawhero's unpredictable founder and owner Denis Irwin: at their best, in the guise of the Gewurztraminer from a good vintage, they are quite superb, racy and powerful; at their worst, they are poor and exhibit marked fermentation problems.

## MATUA VALLEY  B–BA Est 1974 NFR/CD/ML/UK
(OW Loeb, Domaine Drouhin Assoc) $6.95–17.40 CD   WAIMAUKU

Waikoukou Road, Waimauku   (09) 411 8301  fax (09) 411 7982

**OPEN** Mon–Sat 9–5   **PRODUCTION** 100 000 cases

**WINEMAKER** Spence/Robertson

**PRINCIPAL WINES** Chab, Muller, Chenin, Chard (Judd Estate and Shingle Beach), Sem, Gewurz, Pinot Gris, Cab Sauv.

**BEST VINTAGES** W '81, '84, '89, '91  R '85, '86, '89, '91

**SUMMARY** Has been so successful because of the consistency of its wines and the astute marketing of Ross Spence. Overall, the Cabernet Sauvignon impresses most, with a particular, slightly gamey, house style, but the intense grapefruit/melon '91 Shingle Beach Chardonnay and the '90 and '91 Judd Estate Chardonnay are good wines, even if the oak used in the Judd Estate is a touch hard and plain.

## MCDONALD WINERY, THE  NR Est 1897 NR/CD/ML
$NA  HAWKE'S BAY

200 Church Road, Taradale   (070) 44 2053

**OPEN** Mon–Sat 9–5   **PRODUCTION** NFP

**WINEMAKER** Tony Prichard

**PRINCIPAL WINES** Chard, Cab Sauv.

**SUMMARY** Montana's acquisition of the historic McDonald winery in 1989 and its investment of $2 million on refurbishment followed by the announcement of the Cordier joint venture, together with the acquisition of premium Hawke's Bay vineyards, signalled Montana's determination to enter the top end of the market with high quality Chardonnay and Cabernet Sauvignon. After a quiet start with the 1990 Chardonnay, the Winery has released a thoroughly convincing 1991 Church Road Chardonnay with fine, melon/peach fruit and an even better 1990 Church Road Cabernet Sauvignon, with ripe plum/cassis fruit vaguely reminiscent of Malbec, and well-handled oak.

## MERLEN  B–B Est 1987 CD/ML/UK (Western Wines, Bridgworth)
$12.50–17.50 CD  MARLBOROUGH

Rapaura Road, Renwick  phone and fax (057) 29 151

**OPEN** 7 days 9–6   **PRODUCTION** 5000 cases

**WINEMAKER** Almuth Lorenz

**PRINCIPAL WINES** Rh Ries, Gewurz, Sauv Bl, Fumé, Chard, Muller.

**BEST VINTAGES** W '87, '89, '90

**SUMMARY** Almuth Lorenz has a strong, indeed overwhelming, personality and makes appropriately strong, rich, vivid white wines, with the Chardonnays (high in alcohol, with strong barrel ferment and malolactic characters) leading the way, along with a superb, intense lime juice 1991 Rhine Riesling, free from any distracting botrytis or phenolic overtones.

**MILLS REEF** NR Est 1989 NR/CD/ML/UK (Fine Wines of NZ) $13.95–21.80 R BAY OF PLENTY
RD 1 Belk Road, Tauranga   (07) 543 0926   fax (07) 543 0728
**OPEN** Mon–Fri 9–4.30   **PRODUCTION**   6000 cases
**WINEMAKER**   Paddy Preston
**PRINCIPAL WINES**   Chard, Sauv Bl, Rh Ries, Gewurz.
**SUMMARY**   Mills Reef might only have one neighbour, but it is a powerful one: Morton Estate. Like Morton Estate, all of the grapes are in fact grown in Hawke's Bay and shipped to the winery. The initial releases were of very high quality, very clean and with abundant varietal flavour and deservedly won a gold medal at the 1991 International Winemakers Competition in Sydney.

**MILLTON** CA–B Est 1984 LR/CD/ML/UK (Bottle Green) $10.85–24.25 CD  GISBORNE
Papatu Road, Manutuke, Gisborne   (06) 862 8680   fax (06) 862 8869
**OPEN**  Mon–Sat 10–6, by appointment June–Oct
**PRODUCTION**  9600 cases
**WINEMAKER**  James Millton
**PRINCIPAL WINES**  Chard, Chenin, Sauv Bl Sem, Muller, Ries, Cab Sauv, Merl, usually from separately designated vineyards.
**BEST VINTAGES**  **W** '86, '89, '90 **R** '86, '89, '91
**SUMMARY**  The only registered organic vineyards in New Zealand using bio-dynamic methods and banning insecticides and herbicides; winemaking methods are conventional, but seek to limit the use of chemical additives wherever possible. The white wines, particularly botrytised, can be of the highest quality; a germanic, lime-flavoured Opou Vineyard Riesling also appealed to me.

**MISSION** CB–CB Est 1851 NR/CD/ML $6.95–12.50 CD HAWKE'S BAY
Church Road, Taradale   (06) 844 2259   fax (06) 844 6023
**OPEN**  Mon–Sat 8–5   **PRODUCTION**  40 000 cases
**WINEMAKER**  Paul Mooney
**PRINCIPAL WINES**  Chard, Fumé, Gewurz, Muller, Sauv Bl, Sem, Pinot Gris, Cab Sauv.
**BEST VINTAGES**  **W** '83, '87, '89, '91 **R** '83, '87, '89, '91
**SUMMARY**  New Zealand's oldest winemaker, owned by the Society of Mary, making honest, basically unpretentious wines at suitably modest prices; the softly rich (if oaky) '89 Cabernet Sauvignon emphasised that one should not dismiss the wines out of hand.

**MONTANA** A–A Est 1977 NR/CD/ML/UK (House of Seagram) $10.95–15.20 R  AUCKLAND, GISBORNE AND MARLBOROUGH
171 Pilkington Road, Glen Innes, Auckland   (09) 570 5549
fax (09) 527 1113
**OPEN**  7 days 9.30–5.30   **PRODUCTION**  26 000 tonnes
(1.65 million case equivalent)
**WINEMAKER**  John Simes
**PRINCIPAL WINES**  Sauv Bl, Chard, Ries, Meth Champ, Cab Sauv; brand names include Blenheimer and Wohnsiedler; premium wines include Private Bin and Brancott Estate.
**BEST VINTAGES**  **W** & **R** '80, '82, '83, '87, '89, '91
**SUMMARY**  Has a far more dominant position than does S. A. Brewing through Seppelts-Penfolds-Lindemans in Australia, as it produces 50% of New Zealand's wine. Having parted company with Seagrams many years ago, it is now seeking equity partners, and has formed joint ventures with Deutz for sparkling wine making and Cordier with its McDonald winery offshoot. As one might expect the wines are invariably well crafted right across the range, even if most attention falls on its consistently award-

winning Marlborough Sauvignon Blanc (as good as ever in 1991), which is a showcase for pristine Sauvignon Blanc varietal character, and a superb 1990 Hawke's Bay Chardonnay, high toned and stylish, which seemed to me to outshine the McDonald Winery contribution of the same year though not that of 1991.

## MORTON ESTATE  BA–B Est 1982 NR/CD/ML/UK
(Berkmann's) $11–23 R  WAIKATO
State Highway 2, Kati Kati    (07) 552 0795  fax (07) 552 0651
**OPEN** 7 days 10.30–5  **PRODUCTION** 50 000 cases
**WINEMAKER** Steve Bird
**PRINCIPAL WINES** Chard, Gewurz, Sauv Bl, Pinot Blush, Cab Sauv.
**BEST VINTAGES** **W** '83, '86, '89, '91 **R** '86, '89, '90, '91
**SUMMARY** I was for long out of step with the market and the majority of the commentators and judges, finding most of the Chardonnays and Sauvignon Blancs from this highly rated winery far too heavy and lacking clear varietal character. Whether I have mellowed or the wine styles have changed I do not know, but I much like and admire the '89 Winemakers Selection Chardonnay with its tangy grapefruit and charred oak aroma and flavour, and the alliance of spicy oak and ripe, sweet gooseberry fruit in the '89 winery Reserve Fumé Blanc. The '90 vintage wines, it must be said, seemed more in the mould of earlier vintages, with botrytis phenols to the fore although there was a return to form with the 1991 Reserve Fumé Blanc.

## NAUTILUS  BA–BA Est 1986 NR/UK (Geoffrey Roberts) $15–19
R AUCKLAND
130–138 St Georges Bay Road, Parnell, Auckland (office only)
(09) 366 1356 fax (09) 366 1357
**OPEN** Not  **PRODUCTION** 9000 cases
**WINEMAKER** Allan Hoey
**PRINCIPAL WINES** Sauv Bl, Chard, Cab Merl.
**SUMMARY** Nautilus is ultimately owned by Yalumba of Australia; the wines are made by Yalumba winemaker Alan Hoey at Matua Valley from Hawke's Bay Sauvignon Blanc and Marlborough Chardonnay. The wines have been consistently good, none better than the vibrant and intense grapefruit/melon 1991 Chardonnay, the fruit flavour of which is augmented by sensitively handled oak. A Cabernet Merlot was added to the range in 1992, and a sparkling wine is scheduled for 1993.

## NEUDORF  A–A Est 1977 LR/CD/ML/UK (Haughton Fine Wines)
$13.90–22 CD  NELSON
Neudorf Road, Upper Moutere    (03) 543 2643  fax (03) 543 2955
**OPEN** Mon–Sat 10–5, late Oct–Easter  **PRODUCTION** 2900 cases
**WINEMAKER** Tim Finn
**PRINCIPAL WINES** Chard, Sauv Bl, Ries, Gewurz, Pinot, Cab Sauv
**BEST VINTAGES** **W** '85, '87, '88, '89 **R** '83, '88, '89, '90
**SUMMARY** Any winemaker able to produce a Chardonnay of the sumptuous quality of the '89 Neudorf is entitled to rest on his laurels, but I have the strong feeling Tim Finn will resist the temptation, and his track record prior to and since that wine is impressive enough anyway.

## NGATARAWA  CA–B Est 1981 LR/CD/ML/UK
(Fine Wines of NZ) $11–25 CD HAWKE'S BAY
Ngatarawa Road, Bridge Par Hastings    (068) 79 7603
**OPEN** Mon–Sat 11–5  **PRODUCTION** 10 000 cases
**WINEMAKER** Alwyn Corban
**PRINCIPAL WINES** Chard, Sauv Bl, Ries, Botrytis Ries, Cab Merl.
**BEST VINTAGES** **W** '86, '87, '89, '90, '91 **R** '85, '86, '89, '90, '91
**SUMMARY** Alwyn Corban is a highly qualified and highly intelligent winemaker from a famous New Zealand wine family, who has elected to

grow vines organically and make wines which sometimes (but certainly not always) fall outside the mainstream. Challenging and interesting, and not to be taken lightly.

## NOBILO  CB–C Est 1943 NR/CD/ML/UK (Avery's) $8–34 R AUCKLAND

Station Road, Huapai    (09) 412 9148

**OPEN** Mon–Fri 9–5   **PRODUCTION** 200 000 cases

**WINEMAKER** Nick Nobilo Jnr

**PRINCIPAL WINES** Gewurz, Chard, Sauv Bl, Muller, Pinot, Cab Sauv variously sourced from Gisborne, Hawke's Bay and Marlborough.

**BEST VINTAGES** **W** '85, '86, '87, '89, '90 **R** '85, '86, '87, '89, '90

**SUMMARY** Unhappy handling of oak, resulting in hard, raw flavours, has run through many of the wooded white wines; the Cabernet Sauvignon can be rather better, but not always; the Marlborough Sauvignon Blanc is good, as is the high-flavoured, peachy '89 Dixon Vineyard Chardonnay.

## PACIFIC  CB–BA Est 1936 LR/CD $7.10–14 CD  HENDERSON

90 McLeod Road, Henderson   (09) 836 9578

**OPEN** Mon–Sat 9–6   **PRODUCTION** 12 000 cases

**WINEMAKER** Steve Tubic

**PRINCIPAL WINES** Chard, Sauv Bl, Gewurz, Ries, Muller, Cab Sauv, Sherry, Port, the best under the Reserve label. Also large quantities of coolers, casks (Chatenberg, Bernhoffen).

**BEST VINTAGES** **W** '86, '89, '90 **R** '86, '87, '89, '90

**SUMMARY** A very large winery with its 12 000 case production of premium wines dwarfed by its 1000 tonne crush but, nonetheless, gaining both recognition and respect in the wake of recent consistent show success.

## PALLISER ESTATE  BA–B EST 1989 LR/CD/ML/UK (Peter Diplock) $16–24 CD  MARTINBOROUGH

Kitchener Street, Martinborough    (06) 306 9109  fax (06) 306 9946

**OPEN** Mon–Sat 10–5   **PRODUCTION** 8000 cases

**WINEMAKER** Allan Johnson

**PRINCIPAL WINES** Chard, Sauv Bl, Ries, Pinot.

**SUMMARY** A fast-rising, high-profile, no expense spared winery which is bound to raise public awareness of the Martinborough region still further. Its 1989 Pinot Noir was one of a trio of gold medal winners at the 1990 Air New Zealand Wine Show, all from Martinborough and all exhibiting exceptional colour, depth, structure and flavour.

## PARKER METHODE CHAMPENOISE  NR Est 1987 LR/ML $NA GISBORNE

91 Banks Street, Gisborne   phone and fax  (06) 867 6967

**OPEN** By appointment only  **PRODUCTION** 2000 cases

**WINEMAKER** Phil Parker

**PRINCIPAL WINES** Brut Meth Champ, Light Red.

**SUMMARY** A new and highly rated Méthode Champenoise specialist which has caused much interest and comment. Has not entered the show ring and I have not tasted the wines.

## PELORUS  NR Est 1983 CD/ML $8–184.50 CD  NELSON

Patons Road, Richmond, Nelson   phone and fax (03) 542 3868

**OPEN** Dec–Mar, Mon–Sat 10–5  **PRODUCTION** 600 cases

**WINEMAKER** A. Greenhough

**PRINCIPAL WINES** Ries, Gewurz, Chard, Muller, Dry White, Pinot, Cab Sauv.

**SUMMARY** Until recently called Ranzau; the new owners Andrew Greenhough and Jennifer Wheeler plan to rationalise and expand production concentrating on premium varieties.

**PENINSULA ESTATE** NR Est 1986 LR/ML
WAIHEKE ISLAND
52A Korora Road, Oneroa, Waiheke Island   phone and fax   (09) 72 7866
**OPEN** Not   **PRODUCTION**   650 cases
**WINEMAKER**   Doug Hamilton
**PRINCIPAL WINES**   In the tradition of Waiheke Island a single
Bordeaux blend of Cab Sauv, Merl, Cab Franc and Malbec.
**SUMMARY**   The single wine comes from a 2 hectare estate vineyard
situated on a peninsula overlooking Oneroa Bay. Owners Doug and Anne
Hamilton were inspired to plant grapes by the gold waters, and have learnt
their winemaking on Waiheke Island, trading engineering skills for
winemaking expertise. The '89 red was an inspired start, redolent of high-
toned cassis berry fruit and sweet oak, followed by a firmer and less exotic
'90, well balanced and with a cellaring future.

**PIERRE ESTATE** NR Est 1969 LR/ML $13.95–19 ML
WAIKANAE
Elizabeth Street, Waikanae  (04) 293 4604;  postal  326 Lambton Quay,
Wellington
**OPEN** Not   **PRODUCTION**   NFP
**WINEMAKER**   Peter Heginbotham
**PRINCIPAL WINES**   Blanc du Noir (Pinot Noir), Cab Sauv.
**SUMMARY**   Waikanae is situated on the coast north of Wellington; the
wines are estate grown, made and produced in the 'Chateau' and
underground cellars completed in 1991. I have not tasted the wines.

**PLEASANT VALLEY** CB–BA Est 1902 LR/CD $5.95–14.95
CD HENDERSON
322 Henderson Valley Road, Henderson   (09) 836 8857
**OPEN** Mon–Sat 9–5   **PRODUCTION**   6500 cases
**WINEMAKER**   Stephan Yelas
**PRINCIPAL WINES**   Fumé, Muller, Wh Burg, Gewurz, Pinot, Cab Sauv,
Port under Pleasant Valley label; Sem, Ries, Cab Merl under premium
Yelas Estate label.
**SUMMARY**   A former moribund fortified wine maker, revitalised since
1984 and helped further by the arrival of Roseworthy graduate Peter Evans
in 1988. Table wine quality has improved in leaps and bounds, with clean
well-made wines available at low prices.

**RIPPON** A–B Est 1976 LR/CD/ML/UK (Fine Wines of NZ)
$11.50–28.50 CD CENTRAL OTAGO
Mt Aspiring Road, Wanaka   phone and fax (03) 443 8084
**OPEN** Mon–Sat 2.30–5.30 or by appointment
**PRODUCTION**   2000 cases
**WINEMAKER**   Rudolf Bauer
**PRINCIPAL WINES**   Chard, Ries, Sauv Bl, Gewurz, Dry White, Pinot,
Rosé.
**SUMMARY**   Owners Rolf and Lois Mills took the slow road between 1976
and 1989 but, buoyed by their very considerable success in 1989 and 1990, are
doubling the vineyard to 8 hectares and planning a new lakeside winery for
1993. Their confidence is fully justified, for the Rieslings and Chardonnays
made in 1989 and 1990 have abundant flavour and varietal character.

**ROBARD & BUTLER** A–A Est 1972 NFR/CD/UK
(Caxton Tower Wines Ltd) $7.22–16.84 HENDERSON
426–448 Great North Road, Henderson, Auckland   (09) 837 3390
**OPEN** Mon–Sat 9–6   **PRODUCTION**   NFP
**WINEMAKERS**   Kerry Hitchcock, Simon Waghorn
**PRINCIPAL WINES**   Chab, Gisborne Chard, Marlborough Fumé Bl,
Hawke's Bay Cab Merl, Amberly Ries, Marlborough Ries and other

intermittent releases.

**SUMMARY** Strictly a brand, owned by Corbans, from or through which it acquires its wines. However, it has always limited itself to top class wines, sourced not only from New Zealand but from Australia and even France (the house brand Champagne). The quality of the wines I have tasted under the Robard & Butler labels has been uniformly high.

**RONGOPAI** CA–B Est 1982 LR/CD/ML $8.50–16 CD WAIKATO

71 Waerenga Road, Te Kauwhata    (0817) 63 981  fax (0817) 63 462
**OPEN** Mon–Sat 8–5  **PRODUCTION** 5500 cases
**WINEMAKER** Tom Van Dam
**PRINCIPAL WINES** Muller, Gewurz, Ries, Chard, Sauv Bl, Waerenga.
**BEST VINTAGES W** '86, '87, '90 **R** '87, '91
**SUMMARY** The highly trained research scientist partners of Rongopai make an eclectic range of wines, of which the best (and most consistent) are the botrytis styles; others vary disconcertingly in terms of both style and quality.

**RUBY BAY** NR Est 1976 LR/CD/ML $10.50–15.80 CD NELSON
Korepo Road, RD 1, Upper Moutere Nelson    (03) 540 2825
**OPEN** 7 days 10–6  **PRODUCTION** 650 cases
**WINEMAKER** David Moore
**PRINCIPAL WINES** Chard, Sauv Bl, Ries, Gewurz, Pinot, Cab Sauv, Pinot Rosé.
**SUMMARY** The beautifully sited former Korepo winery, purchased by the Moore family in 1989, is well known for its restaurant; wine quality in recent times has been disconcertingly variable.

**SACRED HILL** B–B Est 1986 NR/CD/ML $15–20 CD HAWKE'S BAY

Dartmoor Road, RD 6, Napier   (06) 844 2576
**OPEN** By appointment only  **PRODUCTION** 3800 cases
**WINEMAKER** Mark Mason
**PRINCIPAL WINES** Chard, Fumé, Sauv Bl, Gewurz, Pinot Noir; released under Sacred Hill, Dartmoor and Whitecliffs labels.
**BEST VINTAGES W** '87, '89, '90, '91 **R** '87, '89, '90, '91
**SUMMARY** A relative newcomer, with an impressive list with opulent, oaky Fumé Blanc, intense, tangy Sauvignon Blanc, spicy-lime Gewurztraminer and a strikingly sweet, honeyed Chardonnay.

**ST GEORGE ESTATE** NR Est 1985 CD/ML $8.50–20 CD HAWKE'S BAY

St Georges Road South, Hastings  (06) 877 5356
**OPEN** Mon–Sat 9–5  **PRODUCTION** 2500 cases
**WINEMAKER** Michael Bennett
**PRINCIPAL WINES** Chard, Sauv Bl, Ries, Gewurz, Cheval Blanc, Rosé, Cab Merl.
**SUMMARY** When I saw Cheval Blanc I imagined there was a misprint in the cellar-door/mail list brochure. Not so; it is a blend of Rhine Riesling, Sauvignon Blanc and Muscat, which may or may not amuse the owners of Cheval Blanc in St Emilion. Such irrelevances to one side, former Te Mata Estate winemaker Michael Bennett (1980-84) produces a range of well-regarded wines which I, for some obscure reason, have not tasted. They may be purchased by the glass at the winery's restaurant.

**ST HELENA** CB–CB Est 1978 NFR/CD/ML/UK (Lay & Wheeler) $9–16 CD CANTERBURY

Coutts Island RD, Christchurch  phone and fax (03) 23 8202.
**OPEN** Mon–Sat 10–5  **PRODUCTION** 16 000 cases

**WINEMAKER** Peter Evans
**PRINCIPAL WINES** Muller, Ries, Pinot Gris, Pinot Blanc, Chard, Pinot.
**BEST VINTAGES** W '84, '86, '89, '90 R '82, '84, '85, '88, '91
**SUMMARY** Whether in its moments of success or otherwise, controversy has never been far from St Helena's door. After a spectacular debut for its Pinot Noir in 1982, there has been a roller-coaster ride, up with the 1988, and down again with the 1989, and not too much joy in between. The 1990 Pinot Blanc was a crisp, clean and well-made wine.

**ST JEROME** B–B Est 1968 LR/CD/ML $7.50–22.50 CD
HENDERSON
219 Metcalfe Road, Henderson (09) 833 6205
**OPEN** Mon–Sat 9–7 **PRODUCTION** 6500 cases
**WINEMAKER** Davorin Ozich
**PRINCIPAL WINES** Ries, Chard, Muller, Chablis, Gewurz, Cab Merl, Port.
**SUMMARY** Originally called Nova, then Ozich and now St Jerome, a record which belies the exceptional consistency (and quality) of the concentrated, complex and long-lived Cabernet Merlot, made from 1986 to 1989 inclusive. This wine is a tribute to the potential of the Auckland area, and to winemaker Davorin Ozich's practical winemaking experience gained at Chateau Margaux and Chateau Cos d'Estournel (in Bordeaux) and to his theoretical knowledge gained from a Master of Science degree from Auckland University. In 1992 St Jerome was offering to buy back its 1986 Cabernet Sauvignon for $NZ100 a bottle, an astute move reminiscent of the Antipodean marketing initiatives.

**ST NESBIT** A–A Est 1980 LR/ML/NFR/CD/ML/UK
(Lay & Wheeler) $24–28.30 CD SOUTH AUCKLAND
Hingaia Road, RD 1 Papakura (09) 298 5057 fax (09) 77 6956
**OPEN** Not **PRODUCTION** 1000 cases
**WINEMAKER** Dr A. P. Molloy QC
**PRINCIPAL WINES** Cab Sauv, Cab Franc, Merl, Malb, Petit Verdot.
**BEST VINTAGES** R '84, '87, '89, '90, '91
**SUMMARY** Tony Molloy is a leading tax lawyer with a weekend passion; his Bordeaux-blend is revered in New Zealand and very well regarded elsewhere. A vertical tasting of the 84–89 vintages in late 1990 showed wines in varying style, with the '84 and '87 the best, the '89 very ripe, perhaps too ripe.

**SAVIDGE ESTATES** NR Est 1969 LR/ML/UK
(Rawlings Voigt) $10.50–16.45 R GISBORNE
Solander Street, Gisborne (06) 867 6995 fax (06) 867 8357
**OPEN** Not **PRODUCTION** 6000 cases
**WINEMAKER** Corbans (Contract)
**PRINCIPAL WINES** Chenin, Chard, Sauv Bl, Cab Merl.
**SUMMARY** The Savidge family are large landholders in the Gisborne district, producing prime beef and lamb as well as 1000 tonnes of grapes a year from their Tolaga Bay vineyards. The grapes have been sold to Corbans for many years; now around 5% is made by Corbans for Savidge Estates (initially marketed as Venture Vineyards) and is sold both in New Zealand and the United Kingdom.

**SEIBEL WINES** NR Est 1988 LR/ML AUCKLAND
24 Kakariki Avenue, Mount Eden, Auckland (09) 688 463
**OPEN** Not **PRODUCTION** 3000 cases
**WINEMAKER** Norbert Seibel
**PRINCIPAL WINES** Chard, Sauv Bl, Gewurtz, Ries (from dry to select Noble Late Harvest), Cab Sauv, Cab Merl.
**SUMMARY** After seven years with Corbans, German-born and trained (at Geisenheim) Norbert Seibel has established his own brand, using the wineries of others to produce the wines. An unusual Blanc de Noir Blush

from 1990 showed distinct and inappropriate botrytis influences; the 1989 Chardonnay was of European style, and really not acceptable by conventional Australasian standards.

## SEIFRIED ESTATE  NR Est 1974 NR/CD/ML/UK
(Fine Wines of NZ) $10–14 R  NELSON
Sunrise Valley Road, Upper Moutere 7152, Nelson  (054) 32 795
**OPEN** Mon–Sat 9–5  **PRODUCTION** 33 000 cases
**WINEMAKER** Saralinda MacMillan
**PRINCIPAL WINES** Ries, Gewurz, Muller, Chard, Sauv Bl, Beeren, Pinot, Cab Sauv.
**SUMMARY** A fragrant, tangy gooseberry-accented and subtly oaked 1990 Sauvignon Blanc shows the winery at its best; the white wines are those to seek out, with the botrytis styles sometimes outstanding, but there is overall variation in style and quality.

## SELAKS  BA–B Est 1934 NR/CD/ML/UK (Boxford Wine Co)
$6.85–26.50 CD  KUMEU
Cnr Highway 16 and Old North Road, Kumeu  (09) 412 8609
fax (09) 412 7524
**OPEN** Mon–Sat 8.30–5.30  **PRODUCTION** 51 000 cases
**WINEMAKER** Darryl Woolley
**PRINCIPAL WINES** Muller, Sauv Bl, Sauv Bl Sem, Chard, Meth Champ, Cab Sauv.
**BEST VINTAGES** W '83, '85, '86, '89, '91 R '83, '85, '87, '89, '91
**SUMMARY** With Montana, first brought Sauvignon Blanc to the attention of overseas markets, especially Australia. Its Sauvignon Blanc and Sauvignon Semillon blends continue to be its forte, always good, sometimes outstanding; a nutmeg/spice oaked 1990 Chardonnay also appeals.

## SHERWOOD ESTATE  NR Est 1986 CD/ML CANTERBURY
Corner Weedons Ross Road/Johnson Road, West Melton, Christchurch (03) 347 9060 fax (03) 66 7069
**OPEN** Tues–Sun 11–5  **PRODUCTION** 1000 cases
**WINEMAKER** Dayne Sherwood
**PRINCIPAL WINES** Muller, Ries, Chard, Pinot.
**SUMMARY** Dayne and Jill Sherwood made their first wines in 1990, utilising a barn-style winery with a tasting room and garden bar above the vineyard. The bar offers snacks and lunches during the summer months.

## SOLJANS  CB–BA Est 1937 LR/CD/ML $6.95–12.95 CD
HENDERSON
263 Lincoln Road, Henderson  (09) 838 8365
**OPEN** Mon–Sat 9–6  **PRODUCTION** NFP
**WINEMAKER** Tony Soljan
**PRINCIPAL WINES** Muller, Chard, Gewurz, Sauv Bl, Cab Sauv, Pinotage, many fortifieds.
**BEST VINTAGES** W & R '86, '87, '89, '90
**SUMMARY** Well-made wines sold at very modest prices which deserve a wider audience.

## STONYRIDGE  A–A Est 1982 NFR/CD/ML/UK
(Fine Wines of NZ) $42 R  WAIHEKE ISLAND
Onetangi Road, Waiheke Island  phone and fax (09) 372 8822
**OPEN** Mon–Sat 3–5  **PRODUCTION** 700 cases
**WINEMAKER** Stephen White
**PRINCIPAL WINES** A single red wine under the Stonyridge label, a blend of Cab Merl Franc Malb; second label is Airfield, a similar blend.
**BEST VINTAGES** R '87, '89, '90, '91
**SUMMARY** The winery which justifies the hype about Waiheke Island;

the '87 was a quite lovely wine, balanced, fine and cedary, the '89 even better, with tremendous concentration of rich, sweet fruit, good tannins and again some of those hallmark cedary/briary aromas.

## TARAMEA C–CB Est 1987 LR/CD $10–15 CD
CENTRAL OTAGO
Speargrass Flat Road RD 1, Queenstown (03) 442 1453
OPEN Sat 1–6 Nov–March PRODUCTION 250 cases
WINEMAKER Michael Wolter
PRINCIPAL WINES Gewurz, Muller, Pinot Gris.
SUMMARY Small quantities of wines of modest quality which are free of winemaking faults and invariably sell out before the next release.

## TE KAIRANGA DC–DC Est 1984 LR/CD/ML/UK
(Fine Wines of NZ) $12–20.50 CD MARTINBOROUGH
Martins Road, Martinborough (06) 306 9122 fax (06) 306 9322
OPEN Mon–Sat 10–5 PRODUCTION 7500 cases
WINEMAKER Chris Buring
PRINCIPAL WINES Gewurz, Chard, Classic Wh, Chenin, Pinot, Durif.
SUMMARY Consistently disappointing wines which simply do not show the quality expected of the region, although I have not tasted the '91 vintage wines.

## TE MATA ESTATE A–A Est 1978 NFR/CD/ML/UK
(Michael Druitt) $10–30 CD HAWKE'S BAY
Te Mata Road, Havelock North (06) 877 4399 fax (06) 877 4397
OPEN Mon–Sat 9–5 PRODUCTION 14 000 cases
WINEMAKER Peter Cowley
PRINCIPAL WINES Elston Chard, Castle Hill and Cape Crest Sauv Bl, Awatea and Coleraine Cab Merl.
BEST VINTAGES W '83, '85, '87, '89, '91 R '82, '83, '85, '89, '91
SUMMARY The supple, elegant, fragrant '89 Awatea Cabernet Merlot and the profound, deep, dark berry '89 Coleraine Cabernet Merlot are the greatest reds since the '82, which is a wine of world class and gets better each time I taste it. One has to marvel at and applaud the $30.40 cellar-door price of the Coleraine, which is worth every cent. The '91 red wines are regarded by John Buck as his best yet: they will be something to watch for.

## TE WHARE RA CA–B Est 1979 CD/ML $11–17 CD
MARLBOROUGH
Anglesea Street, Renwick, Marlborough (03) 572 8581
OPEN 7 days 9–5 PRODUCTION 2500 cases
WINEMAKER Allen Hogan
PRINCIPAL WINES Chard, Fumé, Gewurz, Ries, Botrytis, Cab Sauv Merl.
BEST VINTAGES W '86, '87, '89, '91 R '86, '87, '88, '89, '91
SUMMARY Best known for intermittent superb releases of botrytised wines, made variously from Riesling, Muller Thurgau, Traminer and Sauvignon Blanc.

## TOTARA C–CB Est 1950 NR/CD $7–12 R
WAIKATO
Main Road, Thames (0843) 86 798 fax (0843) 88 729
OPEN Mon–Sat 9–5.30 PRODUCTION 10 000 cases
WINEMAKER Gilbert Chan
PRINCIPAL WINES Gewurz, Chard, Fumé, Chenin, Muller, Rosé, Cab Sauv; Private Bin wines are top-of-the-range; also casks and proprietary wines including Fu Gai and City of Sails.
SUMMARY A substantial operation which, however, has had its share of problems, leading to a decision to remove all its vineyards in 1986 under the Vine-Pull scheme; it now relies on local growers to provide the grapes

for its wines. The '90 Reserve Chardonnay (with potent, charred oak and high-toned, botrytis-enriched fruit) and the standard Chardonnay of the same year are both good wines.

**VAVASOUR**  A–A Est 1986 NFR/CD/ML/UK (Peter Diplock) $16.70–24.50 CD  MARLBOROUGH
Redwood Pass Road, Awatere Valley   (03) 575 7481  fax (03) 575 7240
**OPEN**  Mon–Fri 9–5, Sat 10–4   **PRODUCTION**  8500 cases
**WINEMAKER**  Glenn Thomas
**PRINCIPAL WINES**  Reserve range of Chardonnay, Sauvignon and Cab Sauv/Cab Franc; Dashwood is second label for Chard, Sauv Bl and Cab Sauv.
**BEST VINTAGES**  **W** '89, '90, '91  **R** '89, '90
**SUMMARY**  A high-profile newcomer which has quickly fulfilled the expectations held for it. The drier, slightly warmer climate of the Awatere Valley and the unique river terrace stony soils on which the vineyard is established are producing grapes of great intensity of flavour, which are in turn being skilfully handled in the winery. Both the 1990 and 1991 white wines have unusual intensity and length of flavour, while the 1990 Reserve Cabernet Sauvignon/Cabernet Franc has the quality of the very best Hawke's Bay reds, with intense colour, potent red berry/cassis fruit and good tannin structure.

**VICTORY**  NR Est 1967 LR/CD $6–8 R  NELSON
Main Road South, Stoke   (03) 547 6391
**OPEN**  7 days 9–6   **PRODUCTION**  500 cases
**WINEMAKER**  Rod Neill
**PRINCIPAL WINES**  Chasselas, Seibel, Cab Sauv, Gamay Beaujolais.
**SUMMARY**  A part-time occupation for orchardist Rod Neill.

**VIDAL**  BA–A Est 1905 NR/CD/ML/UK (Fine Wines of NZ) $9.95–25.95 R  HAWKE'S BAY
913 St Aubyns Street East, Hastings   (070) 68 105
**OPEN**  Mon–Sat 11–9   **PRODUCTION**  35 000 cases
**WINEMAKER**  Elise Montgomery
**PRINCIPAL WINES**  Chard, Fumé, Gewurz, Muller, Cab Sauv, Cab Sauv Merl, under Private Bin and Reserve Bin labels.
**BEST VINTAGES**  **W** '85, '86, '89  **R** '83, '87, '89, '90, '91
**SUMMARY**  Together with Te Mata, Villa Maria and Esk Valley, consistently produces New Zealand's finest red wines; they have ripeness, richness and balance, a far cry from the reds of bygone years. The '89 reds are superb (none better than the Reserve Cabernet Merlot) but it must be said the '90 and '91 Chardonnays are distinctly less impressive.

**VILLA MARIA**  A–A Est 1961 NR/CD/ML/UK (Fine Wines of NZ, Hatch Mansfield)) $9.95–27 R  AUCKLAND
5 Kirkbride Road, Mangere, Auckland   (09) 275 6119
**OPEN**  Mon–Sat 10.15–6   **PRODUCTION**  100 000 cases
**WINEMAKER**  Kym Milne
**PRINCIPAL WINES**  Gewurz, Sauv Bl, Chard, Cab Sauv, Cab Merl under Private Bin and Reserve Bin labels.
**BEST VINTAGES**  **W** '84, '86, '89, '90, '91  **R** '83, '87, '89, '91
**SUMMARY**  Villa Maria, Vidal and Esk Valley (all stablemates) absolutely dominated the Cabernet and Cabernet Merlot classes of the 1990 Air New Zealand National Wine Show in an awesome display of power and consistency. The style is a house style, if you wish: it just happens to be far more complete and harmonious than that of any other exhibitor (Te Mata does not enter shows). The range was extended with a quite beautiful flowery, limey 1991 Marlborough Rhine Riesling, and a quintessential 1991 Marlborough Sauvignon Blanc.

**VOSS ESTATE** NR Est 1988 CD/ML MARTINBOROUGH
Puruatanga Road, Martinborough   (04) 389 2406
**OPEN** Mon–Sat 9–9   **PRODUCTION** 500 cases
**WINEMAKER** Gary Voss
**PRINCIPAL WINES** Chard, Pinot, Cab Sauv/Cab Franc, Merl.
**SUMMARY** Voss Estate has been established by Annette Atkins and
Gary Voss; the latter spent a year studying winemaking in Australia before
working for New Zealand wineries in both Auckland and Martinborough.
Estate-grown wines will come on-stream from the 1992 vintage, in the
meantime being supplemented by Hawke's Bay grapes. Ultimate
production is planned to be 2000 cases.

**WAIPARA SPRINGS** NR Est 1990 LR/CD/ML/UK
(Waterloo Wines) $13–21CD   CANTERBURY
Waipara Springs Vineyard, RD 3, Amberley   (03) 314 6777
**OPEN** 7 days 10–7   **PRODUCTION** 5500 cases
**WINEMAKER** Mark A. Rattray
**PRINCIPAL WINES** Sauv Bl, Chard, Ries, Pinot.
**SUMMARY** The newly established venture (although the vineyards were
planted earlier) of ex-St Helena winemaker Mark Rattray.

**WAITAKERE ROAD VINEYARD** NR Est 1986
LR/CD/ML $10.50–17.50 CD KUMEU
Waitakere Road, Kumeu (09) 412 7256
**OPEN** Sat 12–6   **PRODUCTION** 3000 cases
**WINEMAKER** Tim Harris
**PRINCIPAL WINES** Uppercase Red, Harrier Rise Red.
**SUMMARY** The project of Auckland lawyer and wine writer Tim Harris,
who purchased half of the vineyard in 1986, and the balance (with 15-year-
old Cabernet Sauvignon planted) in 1988. Uppercase Red is a beaujolais-
style light-bodied wine made from a blend of Cabernet Sauvignon,
Cabernet Franc and Merlot, with high yielding vines; Harrier Rise is a
much more concentrated Cabernet from lower yielding vines, providing a
strong style contrast.

**WEST BROOK** CB–CB Est 1937 LR/CD/ML $7–12.50 CD
HENDERSON
34 Awaroa Road, Henderson   (09) 838 8746
**OPEN** Mon–Sat 9–6   **PRODUCTION** 7000 cases
**WINEMAKER** Anthony Ivicevich
**PRINCIPAL WINES** Sauv Bl, Chard, Sem, Chenin, Gewurz Ries, Cab Sauv,
Cab Merl.
**SUMMARY** Unpretentious producer of wines of reliable quality, seldom
aspiring to greatness but — with the white wines in particular — capable
of a very pleasant surprise from time to time; the Rhine Riesling and
Sauvignon Blanc have done particularly well.